WEAPONS

=== *of* ===

MASS DELUSION

WEAPONS

of

MASS DELUSION

*When the Republican
Party Lost Its Mind*

ROBERT DRAPER

PENGUIN PRESS NEW YORK 2022

PENGUIN PRESS
An imprint of Penguin Random House LLC
penguinrandomhouse.com

Photo credit © Louie Palu

LIBRARY OF CONGRESS CATALOGING-IN-PUBLICATION DATA

Names: Draper, Robert, author.
Title: Weapons of mass delusion : when the Republican
Party lost its mind / Robert Draper.
Description: New York : Penguin Press, 2022. | Includes index.
Identifiers: LCCN 2022021741 (print) | LCCN 2022021742 (ebook) |
ISBN 9780593300145 (hardcover) | ISBN 9780593300152 (ebook)
Subjects: LCSH: Trump, Donald, 1946—Influence. |
Republican Party (U.S. : 1854-) | Conspiracy theories—Political aspects—
United States. | Capitol Riot, Washington, D.C., 2021. |
United States—Politics and government—2021-
Classification: LCC JK2356 .D73 2022 (print) |
LCC JK2356 (ebook) | DDC 324.2734—dc23/eng/20220729
LC record available at https://lccn.loc.gov/2022021741
LC ebook record available at https://lccn.loc.gov/2022021742

Printed in the United States of America
1st Printing

Set in Adobe Caslon Pro

In memory of my father,
Robert E. Draper

Mass movements can rise and spread without a belief in a god, but never without a belief in a devil.

ERIC HOFFER, *THE TRUE BELIEVER*, 1951

Just say the election was corrupt and leave the rest to me and the Republican congressmen.

PRESIDENT DONALD TRUMP TO ACTING ATTORNEY GENERAL JEFFREY ROSEN, DECEMBER 27, 2020

CONTENTS

PART SIX
THE PARTY OF RETRIBUTION

AUTHOR'S NOTE

A s a journalist, I have written books and lengthy magazine stories about the Republican Party for over two decades. Though I've done my best not to shade these accounts, I must confess that they've tended to bear the telltale influence of my father, a lifelong Republican.

At his best, Bob Draper epitomized the GOP's best. He was an optimist and a man who went by the facts while following the guidance of his Christian faith. He trusted individuals while nurturing a healthy suspicion of authority figures. He was immune to cultism. He would not dream of cheating to get ahead or of blaming someone else for his shortcomings. And though I'm sure he viewed his life trajectory—marine, taxpayer, capitalist, family man, community servant—as that of an American patriot, he never once felt the need to say so, or to assert that someone who voted differently from him—as his wife of sixty-four years nearly always did—was therefore a socialist, a traitor, or human scum.

As my eighty-nine-year-old father withered away in a Houston hospital bed in November 2019, he remained doggedly cogent. Among his final thoughts was the observation that his political party had become even less recognizable than he now was. Referring to President Donald Trump, my father rasped, "All he knows how to do is lie." A week before his death, Bob Draper expressed the fervent hope to his two sons and his minister that a Democrat would defeat Trump and that the GOP would thereafter come to its senses.

A year later, only one of those wishes would come true.

This book focuses primarily on the eighteen-month period after the Trump presidency when—if my father could have had his way—the defeated

GOP would have obligingly retreated to its traditional mooring and, after due penance, sought to reclaim its valor as a party tethered to reason. Except, of course, that is not at all what happened.

What occurred instead is that the Republican Party plunged deeper into a Trumpian cult of compulsive dissembling and conspiracy mongering. It fell hostage to the party's most fevered extremists, self-described "patriots" who habitually characterized their ideological opponents on the other side of the aisle as communists, traitors, and terrorists. It became anti-civility, anti-science, anti–law and order. It ostracized the few Republicans willing to up-braid the party's descent into madness. Its leaders ceased to lead. Its longtime legislators—the "adults in the room," establishment regulars, favorites on the K Street fundraising circuit—meekly receded into their tornado shelters, as-suring themselves that the storm would pass soon. Meanwhile, its Democratic adversaries mostly abandoned the usual victor's schadenfreude, instead re-garding the Republicans with astonishment and outright fear.

In short, the Republican Party lost its mind. The mass migration from Rea-gan's "Morning in America" to Trump's "Make America Great Again" to the former president's wild-eyed "Save America" is one in which the usual partisan differences gave way to an existential call to arms. Given that America has or-ganized its entire governing system around the presumption of two healthy po-litical parties, the GOP's growing commitment to a funhouse-mirror version of reality would seem to represent a threat to the nation's democratic experiment.

The period I chronicle here constitutes a moment when the *this is not normal* fretfulness accompanying the seemingly anomalous Trump era metas-tasized into *this is dangerous and is not going away*. Evidence of this alarming development would crop up across the country and throughout the greater Republican Party, from Florida to Washington state, from GOP presidential aspirants down to local precinct chairpersons. But the tension between the party's reality-based wing and the lost-its-mind wing would most acutely re-veal itself within the 211-member Republican Conference, the minority party in the U.S. House of Representatives.

This narrative therefore focuses in particular on the key actors in the House GOP at a moment of reckoning for the party. It is a moment I viewed mostly at close range—beginning with the morning of January 6, 2021.

PART ONE

ONE DAY IN WASHINGTON

Representative Paul Gosar

Chapter One

THE DENTIST-PATRIOT

At eight thirty in the morning on January 6, 2021, a tall and wispy-haired man in a gray tweed overcoat with a red necktie stood at the Ellipse with his back to the Washington Monument—seemingly alone, except that he happened to be posing for a photograph that would soon be posted to his Twitter account beneath the phrase "Morning in America." He wore a COVID face mask decorated with the American flag, pulled well below his nose. He moved with a slightly rolling gait from a hip injury and twitched a bit from an unspecified neurological disorder but otherwise cut an indistinct figure—the kind of man who managed to draw attention only through painstaking effort.

Paul Gosar was his name. He was a dentist by trade and by disposition, the kind of fellow one could easily imagine pleasantly humming ancient melodies and cracking cornball jokes while his fingers rifled through the mouth of a captive audience.

Gosar was no one's idea of a historymaker. But history swivels, more often than not, from rogue acts committed by rogue actors who trip the wire and blow up the bridge and then are barely heard from again.

This, at least, was Paul Gosar's intention, except for the barely-heard-from-again part.

For the past decade, Gosar had been a U.S. congressman. He was a Republican whose district in Arizona was one of the most conservative in America. His ten-year span of legislative accomplishment was relatively thin: a few post office renamings, several federal land exchanges, a couple of lucrative federal works projects in his district, and most of all, four years of assisting the Trump administration in slashing environmental protections on Arizona's federally owned lands.

Until that day, Paul Gosar's reputation, to the extent that he had one, was not the kind an officeholder traditionally sought to cultivate. His fellow House Republicans found him odd and occasionally offensive. Some harbored deeper concerns about the man. As one of Gosar's office staffers was advised by a top Republican operative, "You need to get out of there. That man is *insane*."

And as another senior GOP aide would reflect, "Gosar was my nominee to be that guy who comes in with a sawed-off shotgun one day."

But Gosar was in fact ahead of his time. He had dedicated much of his political career to building a portfolio of outrageous conduct even before social media's "attention economy" was fully capable of rewarding him for it. First, as a candidate in 2010, he espoused doubts about President Obama's American citizenship. Then came Obama administration mini scandals—the tragic attack on the U.S. embassy in Benghazi, Libya; the gunrunning fiasco gone awry in Operation Fast and Furious; the appearance that the IRS was targeting conservative groups—each of which Gosar cast as Watergate-scale malfeasances.

As his congressional tenure wore on, the Arizona dentist appeared to drift increasingly further from the mainstream. In 2015, Gosar, a devout Roman Catholic, became the only legislator to refuse to attend the historic address of Pope Francis to Congress organized by Gosar's Republican leader in the House, Speaker John Boehner. The reason for his boycott, he said, was that the pope's views on climate change amounted to "socialist talking points." Two years later, Gosar speculated to an astonished journalist from *Vice* that the violent white-supremacist rally in Charlottesville was actually "created by the left" and underwritten by the Hungarian-born Jewish liberal donor George Soros, who, Gosar baselessly claimed, "turned in his own people to the Nazis." By 2019, he and a fellow Republican outlier, Louie Gohmert from Texas, were insisting to bewildered colleagues that all social media companies had conspired to design and install a kind of uber-algorithm to suppress conservative speech. In early 2020, Gosar implored Trump's secretary of education to withhold federal funding from the University of Arizona, as two of its faculty members had voiced criticisms of Israel.

But everything would change for Paul Gosar later that same year. On the evening of November 3, he was watching the election returns in a casino conference room outside of Prescott, Arizona. His own race had been called early, with Gosar's routing his Democratic opponent in the state's ultraconservative Fourth District by nearly 40 points. When the Fox News Decision Desk projected, at 9:20 P.M. local time, that Joe Biden would win Arizona, a loud gasp overtook the conference room.

Immediately, Gosar smelled a rat. Trump could not possibly have lost Arizona. Gosar knew this for a fact. He had spent the past three months campaigning around the state for the president—attending rallies, knocking on doors, handing out flyers. Enthusiasm for Trump was off the charts. Meanwhile, Gosar did not encounter a single voter who claimed to support Biden. And as Gosar would later write in a letter to his constituents, "We all remember when candidate Joe Biden held a rally in downtown Phoenix and precisely zero people attended. Nada. Zilch."

In fact, the Biden event referred to by Gosar was *not* a public rally but instead a private meeting in a museum with Arizona tribal leaders. Somehow, Gosar's mind failed to capture this information. In similar fashion, he had managed not to know that the Sharpie pens being handed out in Maricopa County's polling stations on Election Day were in fact disseminated to *all* voters, not just Republicans, and that the Sharpie ink could reliably be read by the Dominion voting machines that the Republican-dominated Maricopa County Board of Supervisors had approved for use in the 2020 elections. It was apparently far easier for Gosar to imagine a dark conspiracy of election theft than to consider the possibility that his door-to-door sampling of voters fell somewhat short of scientific.

As it would soon become clear, Paul Gosar's suspicions were shared by tens of millions of conservative Americans. That their beloved Donald J. Trump might somehow be a historically unpopular president—one whose Gallup approval rating never topped 49 percent at any point during his four-year term—was a reality from which right-wing media and self-segregation had thoroughly buffered them.

At the same time: that Democrats, led by a career politician Trump termed "Sleepy Joe," might be diabolical enough to cheat their way to victory? This was an eventuality for which the same influencers had fully prepared them.

The following day, November 4, Congressman Gosar's longtime chief of staff, Tom Van Flein, reached out to Mike Cernovich, the forty-three-year-old right-wing activist who had promoted the "Pizzagate" conspiracy theory in which Democrats were said to be operating a pedophilia ring in the basement of a Beltway pizza parlor.

Cernovich's lunatic-fringe claims were hardly disqualifying in certain circles. His social media following was immense, dwarfing that of Congressman Gosar. Van Flein therefore recruited him to publicize a march that Gosar intended to stage that night, from the State Capitol in Phoenix to the Maricopa County Recorder's Office. Cernovich vowed to do so, and to drive from California to be present himself.

That same post-election evening, Gosar drove from Flagstaff to Phoenix. With an aide dutifully recording the episode on her iPhone, the congressman trudged slowly but purposefully through downtown in a navy jacket and baggy jeans, clutching a white megaphone in his left hand. A few staffers and allies walked alongside him. One carried the American flag. Another brandished a flag bearing Trump's name. Others fell in with the entourage. A few trucks bearing Trump signs whizzed past, honking encouragement. Someone else in a passing car yelled at Gosar, "Racist!"

Several hundred Trump supporters had already gathered in the parking lot of the Recorder's Office. Someone announced that the congressman had a few words to say.

Through his megaphone, Gosar hollered out: "Patriots! They're not gonna steal this election from us, are they?"

PAUL GOSAR'S EVENT IN DOWNTOWN PHOENIX RECEIVED ONLY CURSORY AT-tention at the time. Three days later, on November 7, every major network would call the election for Biden. The notion that any such countermovement would gain meaningful traction did not take hold until the day Gosar stood at the Ellipse on January 6, 2021.

In fact, Gosar's ad-hoc protest was the first "Stop the Steal" rally in America. Several others would soon be staged by Gosar's friend, the right-wing agitator Ali Alexander, in Georgia, Pennsylvania, Wisconsin, and Nevada—all contested states that Biden had carried but each of which now seethed with elaborate counternarratives in which the president had been robbed of legitimate victory.

Gosar was at the vanguard of these counternarratives as well. On the evening of November 7, as the streets of the nation's capital filled with Democrats celebrating Biden's victory, Tom Van Flein sped to a private airstrip two miles from Phoenix's airport. He was there to meet a right-wing "citizen-journalist" named Ryan Hartwig. Earlier that day, Hartwig had attended two "Stop the Steal" rallies in which Trump supporters breathlessly speculated about election theft. Hartwig then received word that a Korean Air chartered jet had landed on the Phoenix airstrip—crammed with "illegal" ballots, according to a flight attendant who had seen them but whose name and whereabouts no one seemed to know. Hartwig asked a friend to transmit the information to Gosar's chief of staff, knowing the Arizona congressman's concerns about the election.

At the airstrip parking lot, Van Flein, Hartwig, and a few other like-minded sleuths watched as two large black sedans arrived at the tarmac. Several men in suits emerged from the vehicles. They loaded what appeared to be one or two large boxes onto the plane. The men in suits drove off, after which the Korean plane departed, bound for Seattle. Van Flein photographed the license plates of the two black sedans, which belonged to a Phoenix limousine company.

And after that? Dark intimations swirled. The plane's cargo records had been scrubbed from the flight manifest. One of the men in suits had a drug record. A Federal Express worker in Seattle was aware of ballots being unloaded. The CEO of a major South Korean semiconductor company was possibly involved. Oprah Winfrey was possibly involved as well.

Or none of this was the case, and the proper reaction was the one provided that evening of November 7 by a Phoenix police officer when he was dispatched to the scene and was told that Tom Van Flein, Ryan Hartwig, and the others believed they had seen illegal ballots being loaded onto a Korean airplane.

"The cop," Hartwig later recalled, "laughed in our faces."

Still, it was fitting that Paul Gosar would come to be associated with the first of several international conspiracy theories of the 2020 election. The congressman maintained an operatic fever pitch about sweeping fraud from his very first rally, when he declared to a right-wing journalist, "We will not allow Biden and his thugs to steal this election"—adding, "God is on our side."

On Twitter, Gosar urged Trump's attorney general, Bill Barr, to seize Arizona's ballots and search for "stolen votes." Gosar's fellow election protesters, he wrote, were "beautiful people saving their beautiful country."

On November 18, he tweeted: "THIS ELECTION IS A JOKE!"

And on December 7, he published "An Open Letter to Arizona" that began with a rhetorical question: "Are We Witnessing a Coup d'État?"

(Gosar wrote the latter missive while self-quarantining. A week earlier, on November 30, he had attended a ten-hour "election hearing" in Phoenix organized by Trump's lawyer, former New York City mayor Rudy Giuliani. In the futile hopes of halting the official certification of Arizona's election that same day, a procession of supposed experts and witnesses to election fraud offered their testimony. Even Gosar found some of their claims to be dubious. He ducked out several hours early—but not before contracting the coronavirus, just as Giuliani did, though Gosar never acknowledged his affliction publicly.)

On the afternoon of Monday, December 21, Gosar and several other Trump allies in Congress met with the president in the White House. The topic was no longer rallies. The group was there to discuss January 6, 2021, when Congress would meet for the pro forma ratification of the final Electoral College tally. Trump and his legal adviser, Giuliani, wanted to know if there was an appetite within the House Republican Conference to mount a vigorous objection to the election results. Gosar and the others assured the president that the appetite to do so was indeed strong.

But every attendee at the White House meeting well knew that the January 6 certification challenge would not be taking place in a hermetically sealed vacuum. Indeed, two days before the meeting, Trump had tweeted: "Big protest in D.C. on January 6. Be there, will be wild!"

Subsequently, Gosar himself would amplify Trump's invitation: "I'll be in DC with @Ali and the rest of America."

"Every American who wants to take a stand against a Technology Coup and protect the lawful victor of the election should join us. Biden is an illegitimate usurper."

"Patriots: The time is now. HOLD THE LINE. Join me in DC January 6th. #FIGHTFORTRUMP."

"Patriots start your engines."

THE MORNING IN AMERICA HAD ARRIVED. PAUL GOSAR STOOD FOR A MOMENT on the north side of the Washington Monument while his chief of staff, Van Flein, took the photograph. Then the two men walked across the Ellipse, where the rally's organizer, Amy Kremer, ushered them through security and into the VIP section.

Gosar took his seat among the Make America Great Again semi-elite: big donors, current and former cabinet members, loyalist agitators like Overstock CEO Patrick Byrne and General Mike Flynn and still others who had contrived their own way in. It was cold and Gosar had reason to feel bittersweet. His place in the speaking lineup had been scuttled at the last minute. Likely this had occurred because of his closeness to Ali Alexander, whom the other organizers had decided was too unpredictable.

Thus relegated to the audience, Gosar took in the soundtrack, familiar to any MAGA rally-goer. "YMCA" by the Village People, "Bohemian Rhapsody" by Queen, "Tiny Dancer" by Elton John. He dutifully tweeted his approval of the early speeches. He sat through music from Michael Jackson, Céline Dion, and the Backstreet Boys. He gamely sang along to a chorus of "Happy Birthday" to Trump's son Eric at the direction of the latter's wife, Lara. Gosar endured speeches by Eric and his older brother, Don Junior, along with their significant others.

But as more songs of Elton John and the Village People blared through the cold air and across the Mall, it became apparent to Gosar that he would not be able to wait around long enough for President Trump to address his supporters. He excused himself and snaked his way through the crowd of over 25,000 to the edge of the Ellipse, where a car awaited him.

Back in his Capitol office, Paul Gosar gathered his thoughts. In less than two hours, he would be giving the only historic speech of his career to date: an attempt to overturn the election results in his state of Arizona, in hopes of restoring Donald Trump to the presidency.

IT WAS JUST AFTER ONE IN THE AFTERNOON IN THE HOUSE CHAMBER OF THE Capitol. In the alphabetical recitation of each state, Alabama's and Alaska's electoral tallies had been certified without objection.

The presiding officer that day, Vice President Mike Pence, then asked, "Are there any objections to counting the certificate of vote of the state of Arizona that the teller has verified appears to be regular in form and authentic?"

Pence had not completed his question when a tall and wispy-haired man with a star-spangled mask pulled down below his chin stood and briskly made his way toward the podium. "Mr. Vice President, I, Paul Gosar, from Arizona—I rise up for myself and sixty of my colleagues to object to the counting of the electoral ballots from Arizona."

"Is the objection in writing and signed by a senator?" intoned the vice president.

Looking to his direct right, at the Texas senator Ted Cruz, Gosar declared, "Yes, it is."

Standing as well, Cruz said, "It is."

An audible groan from the few Democrats in the chamber—their numbers limited at the request of House Speaker Nancy Pelosi because of COVID-related social distancing—was quickly drowned out by applause. The Republicans, who had defied Pelosi's social distancing request, stood and clapped for Gosar and Cruz. For the first time in American history, a U.S. senator had joined a U.S. congressman to object to a state's presidential election result.

Gosar had held the line. The senators filed out of the chamber. Subsequently, the two legislative bodies separately debated the Gosar/Cruz objection. In the House chamber, Gosar sat with quiet satisfaction while a half dozen members from each side of the aisle argued for or against the Arizona matter.

Then it was Gosar's time to speak again. "Madam Speaker, I rise in support of my objection," he began. In a somewhat stumbling cadence, his head swaying about from his unnamed neurological disorder, the Arizona congress-man demanded "a forensic audit" of the Arizona election—analogizing it to a football game, where "a slow-motion review from multiple angles" would likely reveal fraud. Gosar then proceeded to recite a litany of already-discredited claims. That Dominion machines had "a documented history of enabling fraud." That a court-ordered audit determined "a 3 percent error rate against President Trump" but was then mysteriously halted. That "over 400,000 mail-in ballots were altered" to Biden's favor.

He was just getting to the part in his speech where he would falsely assert that "over 30,000 illegal aliens voted in Arizona." But a growing din had over-taken the room. It was 2:17 P.M., and members had just received a system-wide text from the U.S. Capitol Police, instructing all Capitol staffers to "move inside your office . . . find a place to hide or seek cover . . . remain quiet and silence electronics."

Gosar had been looking down at his prepared remarks and thus had not seen the text. Neither had he seen the presiding officer, Speaker Pelosi, third in line to the presidency, being ushered off the House floor by Capitol security agents.

"Madam Speaker," Gosar protested. Then, seeing that the person now holding the gavel was the Democratic chairman of the House Rules Commit-tee, Jim McGovern, he started again: "Mr. Speaker, can I have order in the chamber?"

It was 2:18 P.M. Fifteen minutes later, Paul Gosar would be fumbling to open his gas mask.

Vice President Mike Pence (center), January 6, 2021

Chapter Two

INSURRECTION

T wo hours before Paul Gosar objected to the Arizona tally on the House floor, Liz Cheney sat in the Cloakroom adjacent to the House chamber, putting the finishing touches on her own written remarks. As the chairwoman of the House Republican Conference, it was the Wyoming congresswoman's job to articulate and promote a central message for the benefit of her Republican colleagues. The problem for Cheney was that the central message advocated by most House Republicans was Gosar's—namely, that the 2020 presidential election results should be discarded. The chairwoman believed that such an action could prove ruinous to American democracy.

She had said as much, forcefully, on a House Republican Conference call on New Year's Day—to the annoyance of several of her colleagues, one of whom, Jeff Duncan of South Carolina, conveyed his exasperation in a text to House Minority Leader Kevin McCarthy. Typically, McCarthy kept silent while the conference chair ran the proceedings. This time, he interjected. "Her opinion is her opinion," he said. "Liz isn't speaking for the Conference."

Three days later, on January 4, Cheney disseminated a twenty-one-page memo in hopes of swaying her colleagues to drop their objections to the 2020 election results. The memo methodically addressed the argumentative flaws in each of the six states—Arizona, Georgia, Pennsylvania, Michigan, Wisconsin, and Nevada—whose results were being challenged. "By objecting to electoral slates, members are unavoidably asserting that Congress has the authority to overturn elections and overrule state and federal courts," she wrote.

"Such objections set an exceptionally dangerous precedent, threatening to steal states' explicit constitutional responsibility for choosing the President and bestowing it instead on Congress. This is directly at odds with the Constitution's clear text and our core beliefs as Republicans."

But the words in Cheney's memo fell on deaf ears. The following day, Tuesday, the fifth of January, the House Republicans held a final meeting before Wednesday's vote. To the chairwoman's chagrin, Leader McCarthy implicitly encouraged his 208 colleagues to challenge the election outcome. As Jeff Duncan would recall the day after the meeting, "Kevin was pretty clear that the American people are expecting their voices to be heard. They're frustrated, and the mainstream media isn't reporting on this. He felt the people wanted us to have this debate."

Cheney's implacable expression hid her disappointment. The stoicism was among the traits she had inherited from her father, Dick Cheney, the former vice president—though the latter had not bothered to disguise his concern when he called his daughter while she sat in the Cloakroom on the early afternoon of January 6, about two hours before Gosar began speaking. Dick Cheney had been watching Trump on television. Addressing the tens of thousands of supporters on the Ellipse, the defeated president was midway through a bitter, delusional tirade about the "stolen" election when he said: "And we got to remember, a year from now, you're going to start working on Congress and we got to get rid of the weak Congress, people, the ones that aren't any good, the Liz Cheneys of the world. We got to get rid of them."

Dick Cheney wanted his daughter to be aware that many of the rally-goers were departing the Ellipse and heading on foot toward the Capitol. And so when Paul Gosar asked for order in the House chamber, Liz Cheney deduced that the commotion was coming from a few Trump supporters who had managed to find their way into the premises. She watched Capitol officers escort Speaker Pelosi from the chamber, though Pelosi's cell phone still sat at the rostrum.

The Speaker pro tempore, Jim McGovern, had declared the House in recess at the instruction of the Capitol Police. The moment he did so, a Democrat seated in the House gallery—Dean Phillips, ordinarily a mild-mannered Minnesotan—sprang to his feet and yelled at Gosar: "This is because of YOU!"

Speaker Pelosi's floor manager, Keith Stern, stood to quiet the Democrats: "Please, this isn't helping." Plainclothes Capitol officers, suddenly more of them than before, moved briskly across the floor, making sure that all the doors in the chamber were securely closed. One of them took McGovern's place at the rostrum. He informed the House members that the Capitol had been breached and that the chamber was in lockdown. Four other House leaders—Majority Leader Steny Hoyer, Minority Leader McCarthy, Majority Whip Jim Clyburn, and Minority Whip Steve Scalise—were hustled out.

McGovern checked his phone and saw that there were several texts from his nineteen-year-old daughter, who had been watching the news. *You should leave*, she had written.

After eight minutes, Capitol security officials indicated to McGovern that the chamber was secure. He gaveled the House back into session and signaled for Paul Gosar to continue, thinking: *Let's get this guy over with; he's like listening to fingernails on a chalkboard.*

Gosar returned to the podium: "Mr. Speaker, as I was saying . . ."

Cheney edged up to Stern. Though she was already on the list of speakers, she now wanted to be moved up. Pointedly, she said to Pelosi's floor manager, "I think we need to hear from a member of Republican leadership."

Stern proceeded to slot Cheney as the next Republican to speak. But before McGovern could acknowledge the next speaker after Gosar, a member of the Capitol Police interrupted him. The officer said that a crowd of protesters were now in the Capitol Rotunda and headed toward the House chamber. He added that everyone needed to reach under their seats and locate their gas mask.

Gosar pulled out the bag under his seat containing the air hood. He tugged at it for a moment before saying to the person closest to him, Liz Cheney: "How do I open this?"

Cheney tore the bag open and handed it back to Gosar. One of the few Democrats on the floor, Ruben Gallego, a former Marine, could see several members struggle with their air hoods. Gallego went from one to the next to give instructions before finally standing on a table and telling everyone wearing an air hood to breathe normally so as not to pass out from hyperventilation.

From the gallery, a Democrat, Steve Cohen of Tennessee, drawled loudly to the Republicans below: "Call Trump! Call off the dogs!"

Four Republican members—Markwayne Mullin, Tony Gonzales, Pat Fallon, and Troy Nehls—proceeded to barricade the doors of the chamber with bookshelves. A Republican from Georgia, Andrew Clyde, stood behind the other four, hollering in panic while his fellow Georgian Jody Hice dismantled a hand-sanitizer stand, presumably to use as a club. Up in the gallery, Democrats Jason Crow and Tom Malinowski sealed all the doors shut. It was 2:40, and the mob coming from the Rotunda had reached the main doors to the House chamber. Their shouts and pounding could be heard by everyone inside.

"Let's go, let's go!" the Capitol Police suddenly yelled as they motioned for the members on the floor to evacuate through the Speaker's Lobby. The rush to do so created a bottleneck in the lobby. One of the last to leave, Jim McGovern, looked over his shoulder. He could see the mob pressed against the opposite doorway, separated only by a few feet and several police.

"I don't think they're here to protest," McGovern said to one of the other members. "I'm pretty sure they're here to hurt us."

Gallego, carrying the only weapon he could find, a ballpoint pen, ran across the floor one last time to make sure that no one was left behind, crouching under their seat. Mullin was still at the chamber door piled up with furniture. He was trying to reason with the mob.

Gallego, Mullin, and Eric Swalwell were the last to leave the chamber. At the marble staircase just outside the Speaker's Lobby, Swalwell heard Liz Cheney talking on the phone.

"Dad, I'm OK," she was saying.

From up in the gallery, Michigan Democrat Diana DeGette stood and leaned over the railing, addressing the last of the Capitol Police on the floor: *"WHAT ABOUT US?"*

Two dozen Democratic members, several members of the press, and three Capitol Police were left stranded in the upper deck. Most of them lay sprawled out on the floor or against the wall. Two of them, Lisa Blunt Rochester and Val Demings, held hands while Blunt Rochester loudly prayed—calling up the spirits of her enslaved ancestors, her deceased husband, and her iconic former colleague, the late John Lewis.

"Someone needs to radio that we're up here," said Jason Crow to one of the officers. Crow, an Army Ranger and sharpshooter, had just finished calling his wife to tell her that he loved her and that it looked like they might have to fight their way out. He eyed the three officers and wondered which one he should ask to surrender their firearm to him. Surveying the scene, he hollered for everyone to take off their member pins. Pramila Jayapal, an émigré from India, thought to herself, *What good will that do me? They'll know by the color of my skin that I'm not one of them.*

A loud noise prompted one of the officers to yell, "Everybody down!"

"Jackie," said Brad Schneider of Illinois to his California colleague, Jackie Speier. "That was a gunshot. Wasn't it?"

"Yes," replied Speier, who as a congressional staffer four decades ago had been shot five times while investigating the cult at Jonestown, Guyana. It was now 2:45 P.M., and a thirty-five-year-old air force veteran and Trump supporter named Ashli Babbitt had just been killed by Capitol police officer Michael Byrd one level below them.

Five minutes later, someone banged loudly on the gallery doors. An officer drew his gun and with his free hand reached for the doorknob. The rescue team had arrived. The members and reporters scrambled out the west doors of the gallery and down the stairs. One floor below them, they encountered a half dozen men lying facedown on the marble floor while a SWAT team stood over them.

As soon as the members had safely evacuated—down another flight of stairs, then down a hidden spiral staircase that led to the Capitol basement, and from there to the tunnel leading to the House Longworth Office Building—the SWAT team rushed back toward the Rotunda to assist other officers.

The rioters lifted themselves up from the ground and walked away free.

ABOUT FOUR HUNDRED HOUSE MEMBERS AND STAFFERS HAD WEDGED THEM-selves into the House Ways and Means Committee Room in the Longworth Building. The House chaplain led them in prayer. Then Sergeant-at-Arms Paul Irving stepped up to the rostrum.

"We ask that everyone in this room wear a COVID mask," he said.

Two groups of maskless Republicans ignored Irving. Pennsylvania congressman Brian Fitzpatrick, a moderate Republican, offered to talk to them. His efforts proved fruitless. Another Pennsylvania Republican, Mike Kelly, refused a Democrat's offer of a fresh mask. "I can't breathe" was his explanation.

Lisa Blunt Rochester, who moments earlier had been praying on the floor of the House gallery, thought to herself, *We just escaped gunshots. And now we're in a superspreader event.* With a handful of masks, she strolled up to one of the groups, which included the ultra-conservative House Freedom Caucus chairman Andy Biggs and the freshman from Georgia, Marjorie Taylor Greene.

"Wouldn't you like a fresh, clean mask?" Blunt Rochester cheerily asked as she extended her hand.

Greene smiled, held her arms tightly around her chest and pretended not to notice the Democrat from Delaware. Markwayne Mullin, who earlier had helped barricade the House chamber doorway, knew Blunt Rochester from working together on the House Energy & Commerce Committee. "Let's not get political here," Mullin said as he waved her off.

"No, it's not," Blunt Rochester replied. "It's about our health."

Mullin turned to Greene and said of Blunt Rochester, "This is a nice woman." Greene maintained her tight smile and said nothing.

"I tried," sighed Blunt Rochester to Pramila Jayapal, who thought angrily: *Damn, I'm going to get COVID here.* (She did.)

Another announcement went up—this time from GOP Conference chairwoman Liz Cheney. "Right now, there is someone in this room giving a livestream interview and describing our current whereabouts," she said—sternly adding that this was endangering the lives of everyone in the committee room.

Cheney went on to say that she had been in touch with Senate Minority Leader Mitch McConnell, who concurred with her that Congress would not let the rioters prevail and would instead finish its business that night. Republicans and Democrats applauded—though at least one of the latter, Annie Kuster, wondered to herself if many of the former had privately been hoping for a delay in the electoral count. She wondered as well if any other Republican Conference chairperson would have been so insistent that they return to their urgent work.

After Cheney stepped down from the dais, Kuster approached her. "Your father would be very proud of you," she said.

Most of the Capitol media had been turned away from the committee room by the Capitol Police, but three reporters had managed to gain entrance. One of them, Matt Fuller (then with the *Huffington Post*, though he would leave for the *Daily Beast* two months after the riot), happened to be sitting between two New York legislators, GOP freshman Chris Jacobs and Democrat Paul Tonko. Jacobs was fretfully rethinking his stated intention to object to the election results. "I am sickened by this," he texted to a staffer. (Jacobs ultimately voted against certifying the election results.)

Tonko leaned over to see the video Fuller was looking at on his laptop. It was President Trump's long-awaited message to the rioters. Tonko listened to the monologue: "It's a very tough period of time. There's never been a time like this, where such a thing happened, where they could take it away from all of us—from me, from you, from our country. This was a fraudulent election. But we can't play into the hands of these people. We have to have peace. So go home. We love you. You're very special . . ."

"Un-fucking-believable," muttered Tonko.

Another reporter, Jonathan Tamari of the *Philadelphia Inquirer*, sidled up to the maskless Pennsylvania legislator Mike Kelly. "We look more like a banana republic now than the United States of America," Kelly lamented.

But, he hastened to add, this was not Trump's doing. "We know what caused this and what's kept this boiling," Kelly said. The riot, he maintained, was the media's fault.

A Republican freshman from Michigan, Peter Meijer had been sworn into office only three days beforehand and was at pains to comprehend the events he had just experienced—having been turned away from an elevator during the House evacuation by a Capitol officer who said, "This is an active crime scene," and realizing later that this had been the area where Ashli Babbitt was shot.

And yet arguably more discombobulating were several texts Meijer was receiving from his supporters back home. One of them read: "You better not buckle and wimp out to the liberals. Those who stormed the Capitol today are true American heroes, this election was a fraud. And you know that that's true, Peter, don't sell us out."

What had crept into his party, Meijer would later reflect, was "a psychosis of denial."

But the House Democrats, to a person, could not see this wave of denialism gathering strength. They were unaware that Republicans like Peter Meijer were already hearing from their constituents that—as one of the latter actually said on the phone to Meijer—"Let's not get bent out of shape over a couple of broken windows."

Instead, the Democrats' assumption was that being engulfed in a violent attempt to overturn the election results would jar the Republican lawmakers into sobriety. As Michigan Democrat Dan Kildee would later say, "Honestly, at that point, I assumed erroneously that this was it. That this ends now. End of the bullshit. They're not going to pursue this. That what could have been the worst-case scenario happened right before our very eyes. And we were not just witnesses, but victims of it. And my full expectation was, okay, even the nuttiest of these people won't continue to cling to this fantasy."

But Liz Cheney knew differently. Throughout the afternoon in the Ways and Means Committee Room, she was sending staff intermediaries to speak with members of the House Freedom Caucus, imploring them to desist from objecting to the election results. The Freedom Caucus would not budge.

Meanwhile, Cheney conferred with her Democratic counterpart, conference chairman Hakeem Jeffries. She urged Jeffries and his fellow Democrats to immediately begin drafting articles of impeachment.

The president, she told the Democrats, was "a threat."

WHILE NEARLY ALL THE HOUSE MEMBERS WERE LOCKED DOWN FOR FOUR hours in the secure committee room, their counterparts in the U.S. Senate were confined to the Senate Judiciary Committee Room in the Hart Building. Among them were two wayward House Democrats, Kathleen Rice and Stephanie Murphy, who had intended to wait out the afternoon's droning speeches in the Capitol basement hideaway office of their friend Senator Kyrsten Sinema. Instead, the rioting outside the western side of the building had left them temporarily trapped until Sinema dispatched Capitol officers to retrieve them. Sprinting with Rice and the police through the Capitol tunnel, Murphy later concluded, bore an eerie kinship to her own Vietnamese parents' fleeing the violent authoritarianism of the Viet Cong.

Others in the Capitol were far less fortunate. Unlike Sinema's hideaway, Senator Patty Murray's Capitol office had a window and was therefore visible to the rioters, who pounded on the glass while Murray's husband held the door shut with his outstretched legs. Meanwhile, in the Lindy Boggs Reading Room adjacent to the House chamber, Democrats Lois Frankel and Grace Meng were barricaded for five hours while a disembodied uproar persisted on the other side of the door.

The Capitol staffs of Speaker Pelosi, Majority Leader Hoyer, and Senate Minority Leader McConnell were all barricaded in their innermost offices while the rioters pillaged the outer rooms. In the case of Hoyer's staff, their retreat to the inner enclave occurred eight minutes before the rioters broke in, after first bashing to bits the placard of John Lewis at the office entrance. Several of the staffers were persons of color; some of them were calling their parents to say goodbye.

A thin and amply tattooed young man who went by the nickname T.Y. and who worked as a contractor in the Capitol mailroom was walking with his mail cart through the Rotunda when a group of rioters approached him. "Hey, take that diaper off your face," one of them said, referring to T.Y.'s pandemic mask.

When the worker reached Statuary Hall, the rioter confronted him again: "Didn't I tell you to take that fucking diaper off your face?" The rioter then ripped it off with such force that it left scars on T.Y.'s neck.

But one habitué of the Capitol was far more sanguine about the day's events: Paul Gosar.

The Arizona congressman had split off from the other House members and made his own way back to his office in the Rayburn Building. There he sat for hours with his chief of staff, Tom Van Flein, sending out deliriously contradictory statements on the congressman's various social media accounts. On Parler, they posted a photograph of rioters' scaling the Capitol walls with the caption: "Americans are upset."

On Twitter, they fixed the blame for the violence on Arizona's secretary of state: "Is @KatieHobbs satisfied with her obstructionism now? For weeks the people have demanded transparency. Instead they got lies and cover up."

But they also tweeted that the riot bore "all the hallmarks of Antifa provocation" and jeered at an antagonistic journalist that the rioters were "All Antifa—your little buddies."

Still, a friend of Tom Van Flein's who called that afternoon to express concern over his and the congressman's safety received an oddly reassuring reply. The chief of staff and Gosar had nothing to fear, Van Flein said.

He explained, "These are our people."

Mob inside the Capitol

Chapter Three

TRUTH AND THE WEST TERRACE

I n fairness to Gosar and his chief of staff, the truth on January 6, 2021, was both on visual display to the entire world and at the same time unfathomable to the naked eye.

The previous afternoon, I had walked to the Capitol grounds to pick up my updated press badge. After the past nine months of a pandemic-induced lockdown that had turned Washington, DC, into a deserted movie set, it was remarkable to see the area hotels suddenly overflowing with visitors. What made the spectacle especially surprising was that seemingly every one of the out-of-towners wore Trump regalia. The sighting of a single MAGA cap in liberal DC was an exceedingly rare occurrence. Now the city was awash in red-clad Trump supporters. I wondered what that portended.

At about 12:45 on the afternoon of January 6, I was getting a sandwich in the Capitol's basement cafeteria when I noticed three Capitol police officers huddled around a squawk box. A "bomb-like device," I could plainly hear, had been discovered a few blocks away, near the headquarters of the Republican National Committee. The three officers hustled out and disappeared into the tunnels. I made my way upstairs, toward the House of Representatives, where the official counting of the electoral votes was soon to begin.

I arrived just in time to watch the slow, regal procession of U.S. senators making their way southward across the Rotunda to the House chamber. That they all wore COVID masks lent them an air of priestly inscrutability as their footsteps echoed in the marble corridor. The sight of them in aggregate, in step to the tempo of this moment in American history, was arresting in a way that I hadn't anticipated. To witness the ritualized transfer of power is to experience a connectedness not only to America's democratic principles but to all civilized societies where the voice of the people is sacrosanct.

One of the senators, Republican Kelly Loeffler of Georgia, walked alone in a kind of daze; she had just been defeated in a runoff the previous evening. The Republican leader, Mitch McConnell, also walked in solitude, seemingly lost in his thoughts—among which was surely the somber fact that Loeffler's defeat, along with that of her fellow Georgian David Perdue, meant that McConnell was no longer the Senate majority leader. Meanwhile, Ted Cruz was cheerfully bending the ear of a Democratic colleague, Chris Murphy—exhibiting no sign, apart from his telegenic purple tie, that he and Paul Gosar were minutes away from bringing the pro forma ceremony to a screeching halt.

Once all the senators were inside the House chamber, I headed upstairs to the press gallery—only to be informed that, owing to social-distancing mandates, no seat would be available for me. I tried the visitors' gallery. A Capitol officer waved me away: the gallery was occupied by House Democrats.

I headed back down the marble stairs and strolled to the Rotunda. No one was there, not even a single security officer. It was ten minutes past one. I decided to take the western staircase to the first floor and look out the doorway of the terrace to see if any Trump supporters were gathered out on the grass in protest. As I did, a Capitol police officer ran up the staircase in the opposite direction—brushing past me, seemingly not noticing I was even there. I proceeded down the path that he had come from, toward the basement level of the Capitol's West Terrace.

I got there just as the doors to the terrace flew open and a half dozen police officers staggered inside. Their faces were red. Their eyes were swollen. They were searching for water to flush out their eyes. One of them sprinted down the corridor, banged on the door of the women's restroom, and then disappeared inside.

I stood in the hallway as a young officer leaned against the wall a few feet away. His chest was heaving. He tore open an aluminum bag and pulled out a gas mask. I assumed that they had been spraying protesters for crowd control and that some of the gas had blown back at the officers. When I wondered aloud if this was the case, the officer shook his head vigorously.

"They're throwing containers at us," he said. "All sorts of stuff."

Gasping for breath, the officer added, "I don't know who they are."

I edged toward the doorway and looked outside. A frothing sea of protesters encircled a badly overmatched armada of police officers. Flags and fists flew in a haze of smoke. The cacophony was overwhelming to the senses. Above them, dozens of men clung to the scaffolds that had been set up for the inauguration of a new president two weeks hence. I had never seen a riot up close before. But already I could tell that this was something worse than a riot.

I stepped away and followed a few officers into the Capitol Service Center, where the center's manager, Robert Johnson, was gathering up plastic ice buckets from a supply cabinet and filling them with water. Without so much as a hello, he handed a full bucket to me, which I took back to the terrace entrance and placed on the ramp of the baggage-inspection machine. Johnson and I ferried a few more buckets to the makeshift water station, where officers were now hunched over, washing the chemicals out of their eyes.

The terrace doors flew back open, and two officers strode in, pulling a young man with them. He was sandy-haired and wore a beard and paramilitary gear from head to toe. His wrists were zip-tied behind him. One of the officers was carrying the man's bulging camo backpack. On the left side of his chest was a patch that read FUCK ANTIFA.

The officers set him on a leather bench by the staircase. One of them asked the man if he was injured. Somewhat out of breath, he managed, "I got tased, but I'm OK."

They left him on the bench. I stared at him for a while, seeking to memorize his face so that I might interview him in jail later. But I never saw the young man in any booking photo—neither on January 6 nor in the weeks and months to come.

More officers poured in through the doorway of the West Terrace. I noticed that one of them, badly beaten and with mucus pouring out of his nose, was not a Capitol officer but instead was from the DC Metro Police. Reinforcements had arrived, but not nearly enough of them. Less than ninety minutes later, two other DC officers, Michael Fanone and Jimmy Albright, would lead a valiant but futile effort to hold these same terrace doors shut against the crazed force of hundreds of insurrectionists on the other side. When Fanone tried to appeal to their humanity, telling them through the crack of the door that there were injured police being treated inside, they responded with doubled rage. Someone pulled Fanone outside and dragged him down the terrace steps, where a member of the mob shocked him with the officer's own Taser at least a half dozen times and beat him until he lost consciousness. Fanone was still unconscious when his partner Albright managed to retrieve him and drive him to a hospital.

By that time, Robert Johnson would be wrapping paper towels around the bloody knuckles of police officers and giving them a fan to pull out into the hallway to disperse the tear gas. The police would run out of nonlethal ammunition. The corridor would be littered with crutches, flagpoles, shoes, and a foot-long knife blade.

I did not stick around to see any of this. Having assessed the enormity and intensity of the mob outside, and the likelihood that within minutes they would be where I now stood, I decided to head for the Capitol tunnels. I found my way to the House Rayburn Office Building, where I exited through the basement garage and out into the street.

The air was cold and the sidewalk surprisingly uncluttered—at least, on the east side of Independence Avenue. Among the first people I saw were several men in paramilitary gear. They moved with brisk intentionality, but not toward the Capitol across the street. Instead, they spread their ranks out on either side of the Longworth Building, where nearly all the members of Congress were sequestered. Fourteen months later, the leader of the Proud Boys, Enrique Tarrio, would be arrested and his house searched by federal agents. Among the materials confiscated from Tarrio's house was a fifty-page document that included plans to occupy all six House and Senate office buildings.

I made my way over to Constitution Avenue and crossed the street, with my back to the Supreme Court and the half dozen or so officers standing on its steps. For several minutes, I stood facing the eastern front of the Capitol Building, surrounded by thousands of Trump supporters, conspicuous in my suit and my COVID mask. Sirens raged. A few stun grenades were discharged. A chant went up: *USA! USA! USA!* But the more persistent noise was a disordered, visceral clamor.

As I watched, the crowd pulsed with heightened fervor. The Capitol steps swelled with onrushing Trump supporters. The East Terrace had been breached. The rioters were pushing their way through. *"My fucking God,"* I said out loud.

Police scrambled about—not to any tactical end, but more like passengers on a ship bucking against a gale. I saw that their vehicles on the north side of the building had been abandoned. Standing next to the squad cars were young men with backpacks and Trump flags, talking urgently among themselves. At that moment, violence felt like an inevitability. As a journalist, I had been in Mogadishu, watching Al-Shabab take over one block after the next. I had dodged Taliban roadblocks in northern Afghanistan. I had been placed under house arrest by the Yemeni intelligence service. I had been held up by young men brandishing AK-47s on the Congo River. None of this had prepared me for the sight of America in a state of domestic siege.

"Where's Antifa?" I heard someone ask.

Another said, "There. Those guys. They're Antifa!"

I followed their gazes but could not see anyone standing out from the crowd. It was then that I began to understand why so many of the Trump supporters were wearing backpacks that afternoon. They were anticipating something more protracted and fraught than a two- or three-hour rally. Later, I would learn about the right-wing message boards and their incessant drumbeats urging the MAGA throngs to gird themselves for conflict—though not against Pence and Pelosi and the other cowardly DC swamp creatures.

Instead, so it was warned, the battle would be joined by the swamp's strange bedfellows: Antifa, the black-garbed anarchists who had set fire to businesses and police stations in Minneapolis and Portland the previous summer while protesting racism, who had allegedly waylaid innocent pro-Trump demonstrators in Washington a month earlier. In MAGA theology, repeated as daily catechism across the conservative media ecosystem, it was never *we* but rather *they*—Antifa, Black Lives Matter, the paradoxically effeminate and easily-brought-to-tears socialist left—who resorted to deadly violence. This, despite the omnipresence of heavily armed Proud Boys and Oath Keepers and

Three Percent Militia, whose plans for combat today would later be a matter of public record.

The cognitive dissonance of January 6 was therefore so jarring that only a circular logic could ease the confusion. The enemy was nowhere in sight. It was, in fact, not there at all. But because violence was there, so was Antifa, by definition.

I continued to roam the perimeter. Nearly all of those who maintained a distance from the Capitol steps were no different from any other Trump rally attendee I'd encountered as a reporter. Others displayed a flair for the burlesque. Two individuals wore hooded overcoats made entirely of tin foil. Four women, bedecked in robes in the manner of some obscure religious order, chanted out a prayer as they skipped along the perimeter. Farther afield, on a patch of grass between the Capitol and Union Station, a man belonging to something called the Great American Patriot Party stood on a miniature stage and ranted to an audience of perhaps fifty about COVID's being a Chinese bioweapon.

But what struck me, almost as profoundly as the earlier sight of all those beaten officers staggering inside from the West Terrace, was the recognition that almost none of the people around me lived anywhere near DC. As I surveyed the outskirts of the Capitol grounds, I studied the nearby parked cars with their license plates: West Virginia. Kentucky. Tennessee. To say nothing of the thousands who had arrived by airplane or bus. I struggled to contemplate the emotional kinetics that would draw so many, from so far, to a single city on a single day, in the furtherance of an objective that their leader never once made explicit, beyond a simple promise: "Will be wild!"

And yet the objective was manifestly clear. The enemy—Democrats, the deep state, Liz Cheney, Mike Pence, me and others in the media—had stolen the country from Donald Trump and his "silent majority." Now they were here to take it back by force.

As I turned away from the Capitol grounds, I saw a man in his forties, garbed in red but otherwise entirely unremarkable, talking to two teenage boys who were likely his sons. What drew my attention to the man was how his voice quavered loudly.

"Freedom isn't free," he said to the boys. "Sometimes you have to fight for it, like our forefathers did. And I think today is that day."

The three fighters moved past me and made their way toward the Capitol.

THREE HOURS LATER AT 5:40 P.M., 150 MEMBERS OF THE NATIONAL GUARD arrived at the Capitol. House Speaker Nancy Pelosi was soon notified that the Capitol was secure. Law enforcement officials erected a barrier on the west side of the building that would soon extend to the full perimeter of the Capitol complex. Washington fell under a citywide curfew.

Just before nine o'clock that evening, the House and Senate returned to the House chamber. Before entering, Liz Cheney decided to take a detour. She walked down the north–south corridor connecting both legislative chambers. She stopped in the Rotunda.

Dozens of police officers were stretched out on the marble floor. They had been fighting the insurrectionists for hours, hand to hand, and had won. Still, they lay there silently like ghosts, or like men and women who had seen ghosts.

Cheney thanked the officers. Democracy had held. Now the House and Senate would do their part.

Hours earlier, she had spoken to Minority Leader Kevin McCarthy by phone. He told Cheney that he had prepared some remarks that he would deliver as soon as they reconvened. McCarthy added that it would be "a speech about America." Cheney took that as a hopeful sign that the minority leader intended to join the Republican chairwoman in bringing to a halt this dangerous exercise in democracy subversion.

At 9:02, Speaker Pelosi gaveled in the proceedings. The Democratic leader exercised her privilege to deliver a speech. In a voice of almost eerie calm, she began: "It is my responsibility to validate the election of Joe Biden and Kamala Harris."

Then came Majority Leader Steny Hoyer, who surprisingly devoted the last half of his speech to reciting the remarks that GOP Senate Minority Leader McConnell had given hours earlier, before the insurrection. "If this election were overturned by mere allegations from the losing side," McConnell had said, "our democracy would enter a death spiral."

Hoyer paused, then added, "How presciently he spoke."

When it was McCarthy's turn, he began by delivering according to his promise to Cheney. "We saw the worst of America this afternoon," the Republican House leader said. "Yet, in the midst of violence and fear, we also saw the best of America." He commended the police, as well as House members like Jason Crow and Markwayne Mullin, who had helped protect their colleagues.

But then McCarthy said, "We solve problems before our nation not through destruction but through debate. That is the heart of this democracy. I know what we debate today is tough, but it is just. It is right."

Cheney was stunned. Even after a deadly insurrection, Kevin McCarthy was once again giving his approval for members of his party to attempt to overturn the election. Even after a riot stoked by lies, the truth was literally up for debate.

She walked off the floor, not wanting to hear the rest of McCarthy's speech.

PART TWO

THE POWERS SOON TO BE

Representative Marjorie Taylor Greene

Chapter Four

"HARDER THAN ANYONE"

L ast night and into the early morning hours was probably one of the saddest days of my life," reflected Marjorie Taylor Greene on the afternoon of January 7, 2021.

Greene had been a member of the 117th Congress for only four days. She sat in a corner of her office in the Longworth Building, next to a lampstand that was adorned with a USA STRONG cap. Her office walls were bare; unpacked boxes were strewn about. The person interviewing her, Katie Hopkins, was a British white nationalist who had been banished from most social media outlets for her Islamophobic rants.

In the weeks before she was sworn into office, Greene was widely regarded within the national Republican Party as a marginal character who had won her Georgia district through fluke-ish circumstances that Washington would thereupon course-correct. She would quickly be relegated to outlier status, positioned at the party's *Star Wars* bar next to Paul Gosar of Arizona, Louie Gohmert of Texas, Matt Gaetz of Florida, and other misfits. She would be trounced in the next cycle and quickly forgotten. The thought that Marjorie Taylor Greene would, within a year's time, be a dominant force within the Republican Party—would in fact be the party's loudest and most memorable messenger outside of Trump himself—was too dubious a proposition to serve even as a bad punch line.

She arrived in Washington for freshman orientation the previous November on a red tide of grievance. On Twitter, Greene complained that because of the COVID pandemic and what she termed "Democrat tyrannical control," no local gyms were open. ("There is literally a gym around the corner from the hotel she is staying at," replied Ruben Gallego on Twitter.) She upbraided fellow Republican member and former Navy SEAL Dan Crenshaw for showing a "loser mindset" and not challenging the 2020 election results, prompting Crenshaw to fire back: "You're a member of Congress now, Marjorie. Start acting like one."

During orientation, Julie Conway, the director of the prominent women's conservative political action committee VIEWPAC, hosted a reception at the GOP-affiliated Capitol Hill Club for the thirty or so House Republican women it had endorsed. A single uninvited guest arrived, one who happened to be the only maskless person in the room.

"Julie," whispered one of the women in Conway's ear, "she's coming right at you."

Marjorie Taylor Greene introduced herself. Then she added, in a voice both hurt and defiant, "I know that you and VIEWPAC weren't supportive during the campaign."

Looking around at some of the other prominent Republicans in attendance, Conway replied, "Well, to be fair, no one here was. But look, Marjorie, you're part of the team, if you want to be. It's a legislative body. If you don't want to work together, well, that's your choice."

At her swearing-in, the House floor managers had requested that she take her oath of office while wearing a COVID mask like everyone else. Greene initially refused to do so. After finally performing her oath, she had departed the House floor with her new colleagues and down the steps of the Capitol outside, surrounded by her all-male entourage of young staffers, one of whom happened to notice the Democrat Eric Swalwell, who had recently disclosed that in 2014 he had unwittingly received fundraising help from the Chinese spy Christine Fang.

"Hey, China boy!" the staffer called out.

Already, Greene had caught the eye of the most powerful man in the world. The next day, the fourth of January, the Georgia freshman rode on Air Force One with President Trump to the Fourteenth Congressional District of Georgia, which she now represented. She and Trump were attending a rally in Dalton that evening for the benefit of Republican senators Kelly Loeffler and David Perdue, both of whom were facing runoff elections the following day.

Trump had come to Greene's district at her strong urging. A month earlier, at what was intended to be a congratulatory visit in the Oval Office with some of the newly elected Republican women—among them Lauren Boebert of Colorado and Yvette Herrell of New Mexico—the Georgia freshman "owned that room with Trump," one of the White House senior staffers recalled. Greene was using the face time for a specific purpose. From conversations with her new constituents, she could tell that all the conspiratorial talk about Biden's stealing the election—talk that Greene was herself loudly spreading—was likely to discourage Republican voters from taking part in the Senate runoffs. In particular, Greene told the president, she worried about her own lawyer, Lin Wood, telling fellow Georgians that it made no sense to "go back and vote in another rigged election."

"Lin Wood is not being helpful," Greene warned Trump. "I'm concerned that the mixed messages could result in people in my district staying home. You need to come there."

He had done so. And midway into his speech, Trump said, "Come up here," beckoning Greene. As the gun-toting new congresswoman beamed and made her way toward the stage in her bright-red coat, he hollered out in warning, "Don't mess with her! Don't mess with her!"

Greene, for her part, pledged to the audience, "And we're going to fight for President Trump on January 6!" She intended to do precisely that—vowing, in a brief video outside her office building on the evening of January 5, "to object to the stolen Electoral College votes." Greene concluded by urging her fellow patriots to "get ready to fight for America tomorrow."

On the morning of the sixth, Greene was a conspicuous sight on the Capitol grounds as she paraded briskly down the Longworth hallway dressed all in black, accompanied by her usual male entourage—the only maskless individuals in the House office building corridor. Walking beside her was a fellow freshman, Michael Cloud of Texas, and they were discussing the legislation that the House Democrats would soon be bringing to the floor—abominations like the Green New Deal and H.R. 1, a comprehensive voting rights package.

"Unbelievable," Greene declared in disgust. Then, seeing several Capitol police officers stationed by the west doorway of Longworth, she grinned at them, offering a chirpy "Thank y'all" before swiveling back to Cloud: "OK. So . . ."

The House GOP leadership had assigned each freshman a senior mentor. Greene's was Paul Gosar. Like the Arizona congressman, Greene intended to challenge Georgia's presidential election results that afternoon—telling a *Newsmax* interviewer, "This is our 1776 moment." Senator Loeffler had already pledged that she would join Greene in objecting to the state's electoral tally, as Cruz would join Gosar for the Arizona challenge.

But then the mob engulfed the Capitol. Momentarily trapped in the House chamber with her colleagues, Greene texted White House chief of staff Mark Meadows, "Mark I was just told there is an active shooter on the first floor of the Capitol." She added that President Trump needed to say something that would calm the rioters.

By the time Greene had been ushered into the Longworth Building's Ways and Means Committee Room, her composure had returned. At 3:45 P.M., Trump campaign senior adviser Jason Miller texted Meadows and Trump's social media director Dan Scavino with a messaging idea: "Bad apples, like ANTIFA or other crazed leftists, infiltrated today's peaceful protest about the fraudulent vote count." Miller's suggestion immediately circulated in right-wing circles and took on the guise of fact. Just seven minutes later at 3:52 P.M., Greene—who had been conferring with her conservative colleagues and, like them, receiving messages from the outside world—texted Trump's chief of staff, "Mark we don't think these attackers are our people. We think they are Antifa. Dressed like Trump supporters." She spent the remainder of the afternoon in the overcrowded room defiantly maskless, assuring her fellow Freedom Caucus members that she would lead the charge in decertifying Georgia's election results.

That plan would be scotched, however. Unnerved by the riot, Kelly Loeffler reversed her decision to be the freshman's Senate co-signatory, and Greene was left that evening to join in the challenge of Pennsylvania—a futile but long-winded effort that, along with the rioting, had caused an ordinarily ceremonial legislative procedure to drag on until 3:44 in the morning.

Now here was Greene just a few hours later, sitting in the House office she had barely moved into, while across the street in the Capitol, laborers wearing air hoods were vacuuming the tear gas from the carpets. To Katie Hopkins, who was interviewing her for a right-wing YouTube show, the Georgia freshman reflected somberly on "just having our Capitol attacked, being blamed on the president that I love, and I know it's not his fault. . . . Watching basically the certification of the Electoral College votes for Joe Biden and Kamala Harris, even though we know the election was stolen . . ."

Hopkins listened attentively, face knotted with anguish. Then she observed, "It's almost as if you're one of them—you're almost like one of those who could've been at the rally."

"I *am* one of those people," Greene said emphatically. "That's exactly who I am."

Hastily, she added, "I'm *not* one of those people that attacked the Capitol yesterday. I completely condemn that. I completely condemn attacking law enforcement; I support our police officers. And I thank them for their courage yesterday in keeping us safe. I know there were bad actors involved and investigations are under way—and it's Antifa."

At the close of the interview, Katie Hopkins became emotional as she considered her fellow spunky Trump fan. "On behalf of so many of us that look to this place for hope, and look to Trump for hope, you *are* that," she effused. "And what you did was so brave and made a difference to so many people. And I personally want to say: thank you for being that person."

"Thank you, Katie, thank you so much," Greene replied, and reached over to squeeze the British white nationalist's hand. "That's so kind of you. Yeah, that was a hard thing we did yesterday, but I wouldn't do anything else. I wouldn't do anything else. And I would love to trade you for some of our people here who have no appreciation for our country! And I'm grateful. Truly grateful," she finished as her eyes welled.

"I'M NOT A POLITICIAN," MARJORIE TAYLOR GREENE HAD TOLD HOPKINS. LIKE much of what she said during their interview, this statement was not altogether accurate. Her precocious gift for offending and demonizing qualified her as a natural for the trade, at least as the trade had come to be reimagined by Trump and others of his performative ilk.

It was, however, the case that she was new at it. The Georgian who had identified herself on a 2019 FEC donor form as a housewife had decided to run for elective office less than two years earlier, to represent the state's Sixth Congressional District, where she resided. On May 17, 2019, Greene attended the state Republican Party convention in Savannah. She had recently injured her leg and was trundling along the convention hall with the aid of a scooter. A mutual friend introduced her to Travis Klavohn, an Atlanta construction-firm owner and GOP activist. Greene informed Klavohn that she, too, came from a construction family: her father, Robert Taylor, had founded Taylor Commercial, which she and her husband Perry Greene bought from him in 2002.

As they talked, it became evident to Klavohn that the woman had not devoted deep thought to the issues of the day. Though she claimed to be a devotee of the Bible, he would later say, "I don't think she's ever read it or understands it." He was particularly struck by her loathing of Muslims.

Still, Klavohn saw that Greene possessed certain desirable traits. She had a pithy "America First" agenda. She also enjoyed a sizable social media following, owing to the plethora of videos and self-authored articles and videos she had posted on Facebook during the previous two years. (Klavohn found some of these to be a bit wacky, though he suspected that they were just stunts to ratchet up her audience size.)

Most of all, Marjorie Taylor Greene was determined. She had already loaned her nascent campaign $100,000 of her own money (and would soon add another $400,000) and hired a respected local political consultant, Mark Rountree. Travis Klavohn agreed to sign on as an additional adviser.

The day after the Savannah convention, an Atlanta photographer, Chris Savas, showed up to the sprawling Greene country home in Milton to shoot photographs for her campaign website. After the usual poses with family and at Taylor Commercial, Savas—who had decades of experience photographing politicians—suggested that she might want to grab a few people of color from her office to add a little diversity to her web page.

"We don't have any," she replied matter-of-factly.

Though Rountree had carefully scripted an elaborate campaign rollout—a trip to Washington to meet with GOP kingmakers at the Capitol Hill Club, an interview in the *Atlanta Journal-Constitution*—Greene had her own notions. Without telling her consultant, on May 30, 2019, Greene announced her candidacy on a conservative talk radio show, followed by a Facebook Live post.

A local political journalist, Lawton Sack, happened to catch the announcement as it was taking place. Wondering who Greene was, Sack started searching the internet. He came upon several of her videos—including one posted two years earlier in which Greene suggested that the October 1, 2017, mass shooting in Las Vegas had been staged by leftists as a pretext for seizing everyone's guns. Sack filed a story on GeorgiaPol.com that same afternoon with the headline "Las Vegas Shooting Conspiracist Running in GA-6."

Sack's piece went unnoticed. Despite Marjorie Taylor Greene's preternatural talent for attracting attention, her obscurity in the political world worked somewhat to her benefit in the early months. Rountree and Klavohn both left her campaign after the first weeks, deeming her unmanageable. "I felt like I was talking to a sheet of glass—nothing sticks, no changes made," recalled Klavohn. "She ended up being exactly what we were trying to keep her from being." (Greene did, however, tone down her form-fitting wardrobe as Klavohn had advised her to do.)

Greene proceeded to work through a succession of other professional consultants, discarding each of them as being out of sync with her pugnacious affect. She settled on Isaiah Wartman, a young Ron Paul devotee from Kentucky with little campaigning experience but a gift for digital fundraising, to be her campaign manager. She handed her mass-mailing responsibilities over to Patrick Parsons, who had never worked on a political campaign—but who, as president of the right-wing Georgia Gun Owners Association, was skilled at the art of provocation. Rounding out her cast were Justin Kelley, a thirty-three-year-old army veteran who served as an all-purpose aide, and Jamie Parrish, an unpaid adviser who also ran a cheerleading camp.

Greene's principal competition in the Sixth District's Republican field was its former congresswoman, Karen Handel. From the start, the novice styled herself as the Trumpiest candidate in the primary: "Everyone knows I support @RealDonaldTrump. Always have, right from the start!" The latter sentence was untrue: Greene had not bothered to vote in the 2016 primary, nor had she contributed to Trump's campaign until after he had already been elected president.

What was true was that "right from the start" of her own campaign, Marjorie Taylor Greene was telling local Republicans that she intended to run just as Trump had: all heat and hyperbole, reliant on small online donations and her personal wealth rather than establishment Republicans who wanted nothing to do with her anyway. Like Trump, she described herself as a successful business owner. Similar to his 2016 campaign slogan "Make America Great Again," hers was "Save America Stop Socialism." She praised her "favorite president" lavishly, even lasciviously—going so far as to rub the crotch area of Trump's cardboard likeness at a campaign event of conservative women.

In October 2019, Greene paid a visit to Washington and managed to score an appointment with White House political director Brian Jack, a fellow Georgian. Greene was seeking Trump's endorsement. This, Jack explained to her, was an impossibility: Karen Handel was a consistent supporter of Trump. The meeting lasted only a few minutes but was long enough for the president's political director to recognize that Marjorie Taylor Greene was absolutely determined to do whatever it took to win.

Few believed she could—probably not against Handel, and almost certainly not in the general election against incumbent Democrat Lucy McBath. Then Greene received a decisive break in her new career. On December 5, 2019, Tom Graves, the GOP congressman representing the Fourteenth District in northwest Georgia for the past decade, stunned the political world with the announcement that he would not be running for another term. A new seat, in a district that Trump had carried by 75 percent in 2016, was suddenly up for grabs.

A fundraising consultant, Tom Hammond, had introduced Greene to his longtime client House Freedom Caucus cofounder Jim Jordan. The Ohio conservative had already conveyed to Greene that while it would be difficult for him to support her over his old House colleague Handel, he would certainly do so if she found another district to run in. And now here it was. Though Greene had frequently made a virtue of her residency in the Sixth District—

even telling a radio interviewer just a couple of days before Graves's surprise announcement, "I understand my district uniquely, because it's where I've lived for so many years"—she would now cheerfully eat her words and run as a carpetbagger. On December 13, 2019, Marjorie Taylor Greene became the first declared candidate to succeed Tom Graves.

Instantly, her political fortunes changed. Greene received pledges of support from Jordan and Debbie Meadows, the wife of Trump chief of staff Mark Meadows. Greene's campaign staff immediately printed a flyer highlighting Jim Jordan's seal of approval. Feeling her oats, Greene loaned her campaign another $200,000. On December 27, 2019, the House Freedom Caucus political action committee kicked in $5,000 as a down payment; by the end of March 2020, the organization would contribute a total of nearly $200,000 to Greene's campaign, far and away her largest donor apart from herself.

Set loose in a deeply conservative region, Marjorie Taylor Greene seemed unbound. Her first campaign ad in the Fourteenth District began with "AOC wants to plunge us into Communism" (referring to the liberal New York congresswoman Alexandria Ocasio-Cortez) and ended with "President Trump needs more support in Congress." In early February 2020, she visited Trump's resort Mar-a-Lago for the first time. She paid hundreds of thousands of dollars to a far-right media consultant, Rick Shaftan, who once asserted that the NAACP was "the black KKK, only more violent and dangerous."

By March, the pandemic had locked down most campaigns, but not Greene's. She masklessly attended several gun shows and Second Amendment rallies throughout the district—posing with members of the Georgia Three Percenter militia and, unwittingly, former KKK leader Chester Doles. On June 2, she released a campaign message, accompanied by the image of her holding an AR-15 assault rifle: "Here's my message to ANTIFA terrorists: Stay the HELL out of NW Georgia. You won't burn our churches, loot our businesses or destroy our homes."

Almost none of Greene's antics received media coverage in real time. Stretched to capacity with two Senate races to cover, the Georgia press took little notice of the congressional race in the state's northwestern corner—much less of the kooky rich lady who didn't even live in the district. (Just after announcing her candidacy, the Greenes acquired a residence in Rome, Georgia.)

Her inroads were there to be tracked, however. A Beltway-based consultant, Chris Wilson, had designed a predictive analysis model identifying upward of 100,000 households in the Fourteenth District most in alignment with the candidate's conservative views. Greene made it her mission to visit thousands of them. In daylong death marches, she went door to door, impressing upon her new constituents that she and they were one and the same: pro-God, "pro-life," pro-gun, pro–border wall, anti–everything Democratic. Perhaps the only meaningful difference between them—apart from her wealth, obviously—were the sacrifices Greene was willing to endure as their champion. Among these were the "countless death threats from ANTIFA terrorists" she claimed to be receiving. (Whether those who had supposedly threatened Greene had identified themselves to her as "Antifa terrorists" was unclear.)

Even had the media seen fit to cover her, they might well have snickered at the novice's unartfulness. At a candidate debate, the moderator offered Greene a softball: Would she be willing to reach across the aisle to get things done in Congress?

Greene did not hesitate. "Well, if needed—but here's the deal," the candidate replied. "We know who the Democrats are. The Democrats are now the anti-American party. Their policies of the Green New Deal, which would be a takeover of our economy and the energy sector, and then their government takeover of the health-care system, which they're calling Medicare for All, will see the destruction of massive parts of our economy. See, I think the problem is the spineless Republicans who won't stand up to the Democrats and constantly give in. So when it comes to policies like that, no, I will *not* work across the aisle with the Democrats. I'll fight hard—harder than anyone—to stop them."

Was she kidding? Hadn't Greene heard from Beltway reporters and think tanks that voters craved unity and reflexive bipartisanship?

From her doorstep conversations in the Fourteenth District, Greene knew otherwise. No one was laughing in her face for describing AOC and Antifa as enemies of America. No one lectured her on the imprudence of wielding an assault rifle in campaign ads. On the contrary: walking door to door throughout northwest Georgia, Marjorie Taylor Greene could see, very early on, that its constituents saw the world through the same dark lens that she did. Within days, she knew that the majority of these voters would be hers.

On June 9, 2020, Marjorie Taylor Greene came in first in the GOP primary, 19 points ahead of the establishment Republican everyone figured would win, Rome-based neurosurgeon Jon Cowan. The Tweeter in Chief issued his praise to her: "A big winner. Congratulations!"

The runoff between Greene and Cowan would take place in August. She was now the undisputed frontrunner. All of a sudden, the rival campaigns that had offered in the past to share their opposition research files on Marjorie Taylor Greene began receiving desperate entreaties from the national media.

Eight days after the primary, *Politico* unleashed its bombshell oppo-file story, headlined "House Republican Leaders Condemn GOP Candidate Who Made Racist Videos." One paragraph in the piece summarized a few of Greene's previous posts: "The candidate, Marjorie Taylor Greene, suggested that Muslims do not belong in government; thinks black people 'are held slaves to the Democratic Party'; called George Soros, a Jewish Democratic megadonor, a Nazi; and said she would feel 'proud' to see a Confederate monument if she were black because it symbolizes progress made since the Civil War."

Reaction in the political world was swift and brutal. Republican leaders Kevin McCarthy, Steve Scalise, and Liz Cheney condemned Greene's remarks. The conservative KochPAC demanded that its onetime donation to her campaign be refunded.

But a funny thing happened—or, rather, did not happen—back in the Fourteenth District. Greene's remarks did not seem to make a dent in her standing. If anything, the appearance of a tell-it-like-it-is Georgia warrior being bullied by the "fake news" and the equally fake Republicans inured to her benefit. On August 11, Greene thrashed Cowan by 14 points. At her victory party in Rome that evening, the exultant winner said of Speaker Nancy Pelosi, "We're going to kick that bitch out of Congress."

The next day, Greene received a congratulatory phone call from McCarthy, who later told a confidant, "Clearly, I'm going to have to sit her down and tell her that you can't call the Speaker a bitch." Greene in fact tripled down. The day she heard from Minority Leader McCarthy, the winner memorialized her "kick that bitch out of Congress" sentiment on Twitter. The day after that, she told a Georgia radio interviewer, "I did call her a dirty name. But I don't back down. I don't apologize."

Greene did offer up a single penitent gesture. Shortly after her victory, she sought a meeting with the mayor of Rome, Bill Collins, who is Black.

"I just want you to know, Mr. Mayor, that I'm not a racist," Greene said to Collins by way of introduction.

She added, "I have some very good friends who are Black."

President Donald J. Trump

Chapter Five

THE ART OF THE LIE

I t's true, you know," said Donald Trump to me, sotto voce.

It was a March evening in 2016, and the Republican presidential candidate and I were dining with his wife, Melania, at Mar-a-Lago, surrounded by other members of Trump's private club who fawned over him like vassals of a feudal lord. Trump was referring to a story that had recently been published in the *National Enquirer* alleging that his chief Republican rival at that moment, Senator Ted Cruz, had conducted multiple sexual liaisons over the years with various female staffers.

More specifically, Trump was claiming to me that he knew it to be true that one of the women named in the story, Katrina Pierson—who was now on candidate Trump's payroll as a campaign surrogate—had indeed slept with Cruz. I found this very difficult to believe while also feeling utterly confident that Trump had himself planted the story. After all, Trump was buddies with the *Enquirer*'s publisher, David Pecker. A few weeks later, the candidate would also apparently feed Pecker's tabloid the preposterous claim that Cruz's father had been involved in the assassination of John F. Kennedy. The story failed to get traction, to Trump's chagrin. "Why isn't the media picking up on this?" he later asked me.

That evening at Mar-a-Lago had been replete with gossip. Trump was an avid consumer of other people's foibles, while correspondingly he lapped up praise from others. His ears were still ringing from the compliments lavished upon him a couple of hours earlier by the Fox host Lou Dobbs. ("He's been so nice to me," Trump said.)

But he remembered those who had slighted him most of all. About an hour after we parted company, the candidate would retreat to his bedroom and from there retweet an unflattering photograph of Cruz's wife, Heidi, juxtaposed against a glamorous image of Melania.

That day in March 2016 was the first of several I would spend with Trump for a *New York Times Magazine* cover story on the presidential candidate. What I learned from that first day, and then from a half dozen subsequent days talking to him one on one aboard the candidate's private plane, enabled me to see Donald J. Trump in a way that none of his worshipful followers ever could.

Trump was not the first con artist I had spent time with as a journalist. He was, however, the wealthiest among them, and certainly the most famous. By these measures, then, his con—meaning, his ability to inspire confidence in the furtherance of a swindle—was far and away the most successful of any to which I'd been exposed.

Every con artist relies on the same tactic, and Trump was no different: they reveal themselves, or at least enough of themselves, to convince a mark that they are utterly transparent and so despite their best efforts are simply incapable of deception. This was Trump's greatest talent. Lacking in raw charisma, he drew people close with his all-too-humanness: the boasts, the whining, the flattery, the voracious neediness. So encompassing was his pathos that one could lose sight of his malevolence, until the moment when it seemed to swallow up the sun.

Understanding Trump's weakness as his great strength was at times a bewildering exercise. He was an Olympian-level hyperbolist, compulsively multiplying every approval rating or crowd size by five or ten, moving so quickly from one specious assertion to the next that it felt all but impossible to keep up. His need to be adored was palpable. His disinterest in anyone but himself was undisguised.

While he worked overtime to project an image of wealth, power, and indomitability, Trump was astoundingly vulnerable. He feared germs; the Purell hand sanitizer never left his side. He scoffed at a news story that suggested his private Boeing 757 airplane was in rickety condition. Why would Trump tempt fate like that? "I hire the very best pilots on the planet," he told me—adding, with a feeble smile, "and then the rest is up to God." He did not bother to conceal his paranoia. According to a former employee of his, Trump was convinced that union mobsters had put a price on his head.

He embraced quaint superstitions: twice on his plane, I saw the candidate toss salt over his shoulder before he ate. Famously, Trump consumed Kentucky Fried Chicken and McDonald's hamburgers—and one day, he told me why: it was a way to avoid getting sick. "You go into a nice restaurant and order a hamburger, you get food poisoning and you're done," he explained. "You get food poisoning at a McDonald's, there's a class-action lawsuit and *they're* done."

The MAGA faithful adored their emperor-without-clothes. At rallies, they wore T-shirts or carried flags with Trump in the image of Rambo, or a hunky celebrity, or a Founding Father, or Jesus. But they also seemed to love that he was a crass, overweight TV junkie whose diet was a coronary waiting to happen and whose face was lacquered with tanning makeup, crowned by a swirling comb-over of hair.

Trump himself seemed in awe of his stranglehold on his followers. On the afternoon of July 21, 2016, as Trump's private plane was hurtling over downtown Cleveland a few hours before he was to deliver his acceptance speech at the Republican National Convention, he called me to yell about a story I had just published about him. He interrupted his tirade to say, "Robert, are you outside? You gotta get outside! We're just about to land—there's a crowd for me like you've never seen before, it's *yuge!*"

That a Manhattan developer was drawing crowds of this size in Ohio, Alabama, and South Carolina—states he otherwise knew only by the quality of their golf courses—was itself an astonishing feat. Trump was correct: I had seen nothing like it, and neither had anyone else since the hordes that greeted Abraham Lincoln after his election. Still, Trump knew better than anyone that their loyalty to him rested on a most precarious fulcrum—that is to say, a lie. The lie was Trump's professed allegiance to what he termed "the forgotten men and women of our country."

Coming from other candidates such stated fidelity to the commoners might not have seemed like such of a whopper. In truth, Trump loved nothing so much as being in the company of the rich and famous—while correspondingly he recoiled from the campaign rope line, where God only knew how many proletarian germs awaited. The off-the-record anecdotes candidate Trump shared with me on his private plane centered on O. J. Simpson, Frank Sinatra, and Megyn Kelly. Mostly, he talked about himself. Trump did, of course, gloat over his immense crowds. But he preferred to see these "forgotten men and women" in aggregate, as a referendum on his fabulousness rather than as individuals who might be experiencing pain and despair.

Still: in the political arena, they could make or unmake him. Like all practitioners of con artistry, Trump assiduously tended to the care and feeding of the confidence he had engendered in his following. Few presidential candidates in American history were as attuned to applause lines as Trump or as fearful of losing their audience. While it was certainly the case that his followers seemed unbothered by Trump's pliable ideology, his feral intelligence could sense whenever he had crossed a line.

In the spring of 2016, after blurting out in an interview that "there has to be some form of punishment" for women who had abortions, he quickly recognized that even some of his diehard followers regarded this as a bridge too far. Lamely, Trump walked back the position, telling me later that he "didn't mean punishment for women like prison—I'm saying women *punish themselves*." Throughout his presidency, Trump would apply similar ex post facto recalibrations when it came to immigration reform, gun control, condemning racism, and halting the spread of the coronavirus.

At times, Trump's insincerity was so brazen and lacking in nuance as to suggest the psychodynamic of a serial felon who half wishes to be caught. At the CPAC conference of conservatives in 2020, the president bizarrely smothered an American flag with hugs and kisses to emphasize his patriotism. Later that same year, he famously stood in front of a church near the White House, in the wake of a Black Lives Matter demonstration that had been dispersed with the use of tear gas, and wordlessly held up a Bible as if it were a bumper sticker that read: PLEASE VOTE FOR ME, EVANGELICALS! His everyday fables of personal greatness became a running joke in the media. As a tell that the CNN reporter Daniel Dale first seized upon, Trump's most dubious anecdotes tended to be of the "sir" genre: ones in which some random rough-hewn man—a cop, a marine, a farmer—would approach the president and, with tearstained cheeks, offer profuse gratitude or fealty and unfailingly call him "sir."

"We're going to win so much, you're going to get tired of winning," Trump promised his rally-goers. The audience invariably laughed and cheered along, knowing full well that it was unlikely to become reality. Never did they hold Trump to his cartoonish claim that "I alone can fix it." Never did they clamor for specifics as to how he would improve their lives.

What mattered was that Trump was fighting—and not even necessarily *for* them, so long as he fought *against* their shared enemies. And not necessarily to any lasting end. Performance, the star of *The Apprentice* well knew, mattered more than results. Tapping into their reservoir of grievance, Trump unleashed a counterculture of vendetta: "liberal tears," vowing to make Mexico pay for a border wall, smashing to bits everything with President Obama's name on it even if that left millions without health care . . .

Trump doused their resentments with gasoline. As the Stanford social psychologist Geoffrey Cohen would observe of the president's behavior, "A key tool in the demagogue's tool kit is to vilify or demonize the other side." Never, before Trump, had there been an American president who described his perceived adversaries as being something less than American ("enemies," "traitors") or even less than human ("swamp creatures," "human scum"). In doing so, Trump gave permission for his followers to hate as he hated, which in turn deepened their abiding devotion to a Manhattan billionaire who returned their love by tirelessly playing golf on private courses and watching himself on TV.

Trump especially encouraged them to hate the mainstream media, even as he continued to preen for the latter's attention. Hot and cold though his sentiments ran toward the press, President Trump never stopped doing business with them. He sat for innumerable interviews, including many with avowed foes like the *New York Times* and the *Washington Post*. Trump tended not to acknowledge this fact during the obligatory moment at every MAGA rally when the president would gesture to the riser in the back and orchestrate a whirlwind of booing while he condemned the "very, very dishonest people" and ridiculously claimed that their TV cameras were making the crowd look much smaller than it actually was.

Trump's calculus was easily deduced. But he was also happy to share it, albeit off-camera, with famed *60 Minutes* correspondent Lesley Stahl in 2016, just after clinching the nomination. As was the case with most media figures, Trump had known Stahl for decades. Given that fact, Stahl wanted to know: why was he persisting with these tired evocations of "fake news"? What was the point of it all?

"You know why I do it?" Stahl would recall Trump replying. "I do it to discredit you all and demean you all, so that when you write negative stories about me, no one will believe you."

"DON'T ENCOURAGE HIM," MELANIA TRUMP SAID IN HER BRITTLE SLAVIC AC-cent to the other guests seated nearby at the White House Correspondents Dinner on the evening of April 30, 2011. Trump, at the time toying with the idea of running for president, was bragging to his table mates about the fervent applause he had received over the past few days in New Hampshire and Nevada.

In particular, Trump was pleased with how the audiences had responded to his lines about China's exploitation of President Obama's timidity. "I'm telling you, the China stuff sells!" he crowed.

A few of his fellow guests laughed. Melania repeated her half-hearted plea: "Don't encourage him."

That night would, of course, become famous for Obama's merciless needling of Trump, who for the previous few weeks had been claiming that the president's birth certificate was phony—that Obama was perhaps not a true American citizen. The "birther" conspiracy theory had gained traction among conservatives, for the same reason that Trump's "China is raping this country" worked. Both portrayed an opponent as "the other," as a cunning deceiver. The implicit if not overtly stated racism winked at his overwhelmingly white, grievance-afflicted audiences.

Birtherism and China-bashing fed the belief that "regular, patriotic Americans" were not to blame for their lot in life, that they were in fact getting screwed over by the elites. In turn, their allegiance to Donald Trump wedded them to a prominent campaign leitmotif in 2016—namely, that anytime Trump did not win it was only because the other side had cheated.

This tendency to deflect blame harked back to Trump's business days, when his casinos in Atlantic City went bankrupt and he faulted two executives who had been killed in a helicopter crash. As upstate New York congresswoman Kathleen Rice would later tell her Republican colleagues, "Look, I've known this man for over twenty years. He's *always* been a sore loser."

Trump began his political career by losing and then immediately asserting otherwise. On the evening of February 1, 2016, Trump learned that he had been defeated in the Iowa GOP presidential caucus by his archrival, Ted Cruz. Trump's private response was to blame his campaign staff; Trump screamed at them on his private plane the entire flight home from Des Moines to New York, I was later told. His public response was to claim that Cruz "stole it." Later, Trump lost the caucuses in Wyoming and Colorado to Cruz and again cried foul, telling an audience in Indiana, "It's all rigged by the professionals, it's all rigged by the bosses, and it's a disgrace." Even in victory over Hillary Clinton that November, president-elect Trump sniveled that "thousands" of Massachusetts voters had been bused into New Hampshire to ensure that Clinton would carry the state.

A week before Trump's inauguration, the Senate Select Committee on Intelligence began an investigation into the Trump campaign's possible links to Russia. Already it had been assessed by the U.S. intelligence community that Russia had favored Trump over Clinton—a preference Vladimir Putin would later publicly confirm—and that it had aggressively meddled in the election in hopes of achieving that end. It was also known by the FBI in the summer of 2016 that a Trump campaign foreign policy adviser named George Papadopoulos had claimed to know that the Russian government had damaging information about Clinton that it was willing to share with her Republican opponent. The *New York Times* would later break the news that on June 9, 2016, a Russian intelligence agent met at Trump Tower with Trump's son Don Junior, his son-in-law Jared Kushner, and the campaign's chairman, Paul Manafort, after an intermediary had promised that the Russian had dirt on Clinton. "If it's what you say, I love it," Don Junior had replied to the intermediary via email.

Central to MAGA theology was the belief that Democrats had instigated what Trump would describe, with characteristic overstatement, as "the single greatest witch hunt in American history." The president had been hounded day and night by the "Russia hoax," in which his foes claimed collusion where there was none. The incessant persecution of President Trump stood as proof that the only meaningful collusion was between the Democrats and the news media—and that both could only be trusted to lie. The "collusion hoax" would repeatedly be deployed by Trump and his supporters: to justify his paranoid vindictiveness, to demonize his antagonists, and to establish a rationale for embracing "alternative" sources of information from within the MAGA ecosystem.

Inconveniencing this narrative was the fact that it was a Republican, Senate Majority Leader Mitch McConnell, who had given the investigative task to the Senate Intelligence Committee, which was chaired by Richard Burr, also a Republican. The staffs of both Burr and the ranking Democrat, Senator Mark Warner, conducted nearly all of the two hundred or so interviews by themselves, without any other member of either party present.

In the early months of the investigation, Chairman Burr received dozens of unsolicited phone calls from President Trump. "These were not check-in calls," said someone with knowledge of the conversations, but instead Trump seeking to work the ref. His constant refrain to Burr was, "I did nothing wrong."

In the end, the Intelligence Committee did not pronounce Trump innocent. Instead, according to the committee, the available evidence could not decisively prove that an organized conspiracy existed between the Trump campaign and Russian officials to game the 2016 election. This conclusion was not intended to serve as exoneration. Rather, it reflected the belief that the Trump campaign was incapable of organizing a one-car funeral, let alone a clandestine transcontinental conspiracy. Nonetheless, as the committee's members would unanimously agree in their final report, the numerous contacts between Russian actors and Trump surrogates like Paul Manafort "represented a grave counterintelligence threat." In other words, the investigation had been justified (though many media accounts of the Trump-Russia connection lapsed into hyperbole).

But Trump had his story and was sticking to it. That story, as he told a Minneapolis audience in October 2019, was that "from day one, the wretched Washington swamp has been trying to nullify the results of a truly great and democratic election, the election of 2016."

It therefore followed logically that the wretched Washington swamp would attempt to do the same in 2020.

By the pandemic-stricken spring of 2020, Trump was spinning a yarn about how his foes were scheming to rob him of a second electoral victory. For those paying close attention, his conspiratorial prediction bore familiar echoes of 2016, when he warned of a "totally rigged election." Back then, Trump had all sorts of ideas as to how such rigging would occur, which he helpfully shared at rallies and in interviews. Dead people would vote. Living voters would vote twice in different states. The lack of a photo ID requirement in some states meant, Trump warned *Washington Post* reporter Dave Weigel, that "we may have people vote 10 times." Three weeks before the 2016 election, the Republican nominee tweeted: "Of course there is large scale voter fraud happening on and before election day! Why do Republican leaders deny what is going on? So naïve!"

No such fraud occurred, of course. Trump continued to insist inaccurately that double voting had cost him a win in New Hampshire. Four months into his presidency, Trump convened an Advisory Commission on Election Integrity, chaired by the Kansas secretary of state and fraud fabulist Kris Kobach. The commission found little to back the president's claims. Trump passed on the opportunity to advocate sweeping election reforms during his term. After all, the passage of such reforms would remove from his campaigning toolkit a crucial line of attack.

Instead, by early 2020, Trump had a new fact-free refrain to peddle. "I think a lot of people cheat with mail-in voting," he told a reporter on April 3. He elaborated during a coronavirus briefing four days later: "Now, mail ballots, they cheat, OK? People cheat. Mail ballots are a very dangerous thing for this country because they're cheaters."

In fact, there was precisely zero evidence to suggest that mail-in balloting was more prone to election fraud than any other voting process. For example, in Arizona, which Trump had won in 2016 by 3 points, early voting had existed since 1992; about 80 percent of Arizona's voters did so by mail, and most who did so were Republicans. It was "difficult if not impossible to cheat" in Arizona elections, Governor Doug Ducey told Trump and his deaf ears on August 5, 2020, three months before the election.

By then Trump had repeated his fact-free prediction literally dozens of times, even though he had cast his own vote with a mail-in ballot in Florida. He continued to rail against imminent fraud, all the way up to the night before the election, at a rally in Kenosha, Wisconsin, where he incanted: "It's going to be cheating. It's going to be cheating."

On Election Night, following the prediction by the Fox News Channel and the Associated Press that Biden had won Arizona, a somewhat shell-shocked Trump addressed his supporters. "I want to thank the American people for their tremendous support—millions and millions of people voted for us tonight," he said. "And a very sad group of people is trying to disenfranchise that group of people and we won't stand for it. We will not stand for it."

At that moment, Donald Trump had ensured for himself a special place in American history. His presidency might otherwise have been judged, a half century hence, as a single term of sound and fury with a handful of accomplishments marred by an ugly appeal to the underside in the nation's character. Now, as the first sitting president ever to refuse to concede electoral defeat, Trump had asserted himself as being above American democracy. And he had done so by insisting, without a shred of evidence, that he was the true winner that night.

All those years spent perfecting the art of the lie had led Donald Trump to this moment, this apogee of untruth. For the Big Lie was his wildest and most dangerous con yet. And tens of millions of people believed it.

ON THE AFTERNOON OF SUNDAY, JANUARY 2, 2021, WHEN A DEFEATED PRESI-dent Trump should have been focused on transitioning the American government to the next president, he chose instead to ring up Georgia's Republican secretary of state, Brad Raffensperger.

Trump knew that Biden had carried Georgia by fewer than 12,000 votes out of nearly 5 million cast. It was Raffensperger who saw to it that all

Georgians received applications for mail-in ballots for the November election. His rationale for doing so was concern for safety, owing to the pandemic. But the secretary of state was also a loyal Republican, and his new mail-in policy would have the effect of leveling the playing field for conservative rural areas, because the liberal urban counties already had the funding to disseminate ballots widely. "If that hadn't been done," said a Georgia Republican of Raffensperger's decision, "the president would have lost by 100,000 votes instead of 11,779."

The question Trump wished to explore was whether Raffensperger's loyalty to his party's leader was greater than his fidelity to the facts. The conversation began with a brief introduction by White House chief of staff Mark Meadows. He then yielded to the president. For the next twelve minutes, Trump spewed forth a fusillade of confected statistics, by no means limited to mail-in balloting. Signatures had been forged. Dead people had voted. Others had voted twice. Illegal votes had been cast from out of state. Trump fantastically claimed that ballots from his voters had been shredded or otherwise invalidated. And because in other states Trump's people had found what he termed "tremendous corruption with Dominion machines," it stood to reason that the voting machines were likewise problematic in Georgia as well. Trump then provided his own fanciful projection: he imagined that he had carried the state "by half a million." He knew this from the tremendous size of his rallies.

"It's just not possible to have lost Georgia," he said. "It's not possible."

For the Georgia Republicans on the call, Trump's monologue was at the same time shocking and all too familiar. Each of his assertions had been bouncing around right-wing internet and talk radio for days if not weeks. But this was not a professional fabulist from *Infowars*. This was a sitting president, seemingly in the thrall of proven lies.

"Well, Mr. President," the secretary of state replied evenly, "the challenge that you have is the data you have is wrong." Raffensperger proceeded to rebut Trump's notions one by one.

Sitting with Trump in the Oval Office was a Republican lawyer named Cleta Mitchell. Four months before, on September 9, 2020, Mitchell and a few other conservative activists had received an election security briefing from the Department of Homeland Security's cybersecurity director Chris Krebs.

Or rather, that was the briefing Krebs intended to give. As it turned out, Mitchell and her colleagues seemed to have no interest in election infrastructure and how the DHS was working to combat foreign interference. Instead, they wanted to find out the best way to prevent undocumented immigrants from voting. The meeting broke up early.

Now it was January 2, 2021, and Cleta Mitchell was suddenly evincing great interest in election security. She quizzed Raffensperger on multiple ballot scans, on improper signature verification, on flawed voter rolls. Again, Raffensperger and his general counsel, Ryan Germany, refuted each bogus claim.

Losing patience, Trump grew plaintive. "Fellas," the president said, "I need 11,000 votes. Give me a break."

He added, "I'm not looking to shake up the whole world."

Raffensperger and the two staffers on the call listened with numb horror. But they would not give Trump his votes.

Four days later, he shook up the whole world.

House Minority Leader Kevin McCarthy

Chapter Six

THE ENABLER

A mong the most commonly used descriptors of Donald Trump's rule over the GOP is that he "hijacked" the party. The term connotes several dynamics at once. First, that Trump overtook the Republicans through force and by surprise. Second, that the party was fully functioning and purposeful, with a clear direction in mind, before the hijacker waylaid it. And third, that the GOP bore no responsibility for the crime committed against it.

Each of these notions is false. What made the Republican Party such an easy mark for Trump was that it had already been playing the con on a less bombastic level for years. It had reveled in the personal demonization of Democratic leaders like Nancy Pelosi and Barack Obama. It had compulsively cast the opposition party not just as wrongheaded but as one that stole votes and was consciously bent on the country's destruction. And in doing all this, it had happily encouraged lies, as long as they netted political results.

As the table-setter for Donald Trump, no Republican went to greater lengths to enable him than Kevin McCarthy.

In the spring of 2011, I flew to Bakersfield, California, to report on the early life of McCarthy, whose colleagues had recently elected him to be the Majority Whip, the third-most-powerful leadership position among the House Republicans. Slick and supple-minded, McCarthy's every pore oozed ambition. This latter trait, I was soon to learn, had been with him since his youth.

The Republican whip had suggested I call Marshall Dillard, the principal of a local elementary school, who had known McCarthy since the two were teammates on the Bakersfield High School Drillers football team from 1979 to 1983. Dillard, the team's star running back, told me that McCarthy had been something of a free spirit whose locker room antics grated on their old-school coach. "He was always outgoing, always trying to make people feel good," recalled Dillard. "But he was smarter than he let on."

And he was determined. McCarthy developed a crush on a girl in biology class named Judy Wages. A dozen years later, she became Judy McCarthy. He became active in Young Republicans and was eventually elected its national chairman, while also serving as district director for Bakersfield's U.S. congressman, Bill Thomas, who would groom McCarthy to replace him in 2006. Though the unctuous Californian was perfectly suited for politics, he fancied himself an entrepreneur. "He was always business-savvy," Dillard told me. "He always thought about how to make the least go the furthest. I remember him saying, 'Don't buy a new car. Always buy a good used one. Don't buy the biggest house on the block. Buy the smallest among the biggest.'"

And, recalled Dillard in 2011, "One person that he always talked about back then was Donald Trump. He talked about him all the time. I don't recall if he met him, but he talked about him a lot in our early twenties."

"WELL, KEVIN," PRESIDENT TRUMP SAID TO MCCARTHY BY PHONE SHORTLY before three in the afternoon on January 6, "I guess these people are more upset about the election than you are."

"More upset?" McCarthy yelled back incredulously, according to an account he gave a few hours later to a Republican colleague. *"They're trying to fucking kill me!"*

After evacuating the House chamber, the Republican minority leader had retreated into his office suite with a fellow member, Bruce Westerman of Arkansas. The minority leader's security detail then insisted that he be moved to Fort McNair, an Army base in southwest DC. McCarthy assented, leaving behind Westerman, who would spend the next two and a half hours crouched on the toilet in McCarthy's office bathroom while rioters barreled through the suite, shattering windows, leaving behind zip ties.

On the heels of the insurrection, the House Democrats drew up an article of impeachment against President Donald Trump. Six days after the attack on the Capitol, the House GOP's chairwoman, Liz Cheney, announced that she would vote to impeach. "There has never been a greater betrayal by a President of the United States of his office and his oath to the Constitution," her statement read.

Other senior Republicans—among them John Katko of New York, Adam Kinzinger of Illinois, Fred Upton of Michigan, and Jaime Herrera Beutler of Washington—also said that Trump deserved to be impeached. So did the first-termer Peter Meijer of Michigan, who had been warned by a Republican supporter on the sixth, "You better not buckle and wimp out to the liberals."

In all, ten House Republicans voted to impeach Trump on January 13— and a month later, seven Republican senators would vote to convict him. Each of them did so while knowing that death threats would ensue and their political careers would be jeopardized. Though the GOP's Senate leader, Mitch McConnell, voted against convicting Trump, his language was unsparing. The rioters, he said on the Senate floor, "did this because they'd been fed wild falsehoods by the most powerful man on Earth because he was angry. He lost an election." McConnell added, "There's no question, none, that President Trump is practically and morally responsible for provoking the events of the day."

Kevin McCarthy was somewhat more measured in his public criticism of Trump. Still, on January 13—as House members debated the article of impeachment, one week after the insurrection and with a week still to go before Joe Biden's inauguration—McCarthy stated on the House floor, "The President bears responsibility for Wednesday's attack on Congress by mob rioters. He should have immediately denounced the mob when he saw what was unfolding. These facts require immediate action by President Trump: accept his share of responsibility, quell the brewing unrest and ensure President-elect Biden is able to successfully begin his term. The President's immediate action also deserves congressional action, which is why I think a fact-finding commission and a censure resolution would be prudent."

That same day, McCarthy also offered an exclusive to his hometown paper, telling John Cox of the *Bakersfield Californian* that he had spent an hour on the phone with President Trump two days earlier, urging him to acknowledge defeat, meet with Biden, and leave him the customary welcome letter in the Oval Office desk. (McCarthy said that Trump would not commit to doing any of this.)

Discerning McCarthy's calibrations did not require a political science degree. He yearned to be Speaker of the House. Fulfilling that ambition necessitated first regaining the House majority in the 2022 elections. Accomplishing that feat required, among other things, money. By January 12, over fifty major corporate donors had announced that they were pausing their donations to the 139 House Republicans who had voted on the late evening of January 6 to object to the results of the presidential election. Kevin McCarthy had been one of the 139 objectors, despite his stated belief that the fraud-crazed rioters were "trying to fucking kill" him.

The minority leader therefore wished to project to corporate America an aura of sobriety and order. At the same time, to win back the House required, in McCarthy's belief, continued allegiance to Trump. The GOP establishment might well despise the disgraced president behind closed doors, but their base still loved him. McCarthy believed he needed both to win the Speaker's gavel.

And so when McCarthy later learned that Trump felt betrayed by his words on the House floor on January 13, he did what he had to do. On January 24, he clarified his earlier statement that Trump "bears responsibility" for the January 6 riot. To TV host Greta Van Susteren, McCarthy stated, "No, what I said—I thought the president had *some* responsibility when it came to the response." But when it came to inciting the mob, he said, "I also think everybody across the country has some responsibility."

Four days later, on January 28, while traveling through Florida on a fundraising trip, the minority leader made a pit stop at Mar-a-Lago. There, for the first time since his departure from Washington eight days prior, Trump emerged into public view, wearing a hearty grin as he posed for a photo with Kevin McCarthy. "Today, President Trump committed to helping elect Republicans in the House and Senate in 2022," a statement from the minority leader's office said.

In other words, Kevin McCarthy had gotten what he came for, at the small cost of his pride, though at the somewhat greater price of his party's integrity.

EVEN BEFORE DONALD TRUMP CLINCHED THE REPUBLICAN NOMINATION IN May 2016, Kevin McCarthy sought to align himself with the man whose bestselling (and ghostwritten) book *The Art of the Deal* had once been given to him as a Christmas gift by McCarthy's then-girlfriend, Judy. "You think I can win California?" the nominee said to McCarthy one day in 2016.

It was an early indicator to McCarthy of just how steeped Trump was in sycophancy. A man of his ego could suffer only so much real talk. Still, McCarthy was enraptured by the man's self-belief. Though he claimed to have dissuaded Trump from thinking that he could possibly win California, McCarthy would later say to me in amazement about Trump, "I don't believe there's anything he thinks he can't do."

He told me this in early 2017, at the dawn of Trump's presidency. McCarthy was the House majority leader, second in command to the Speaker, Paul Ryan, whom Trump often referred to as a "Boy Scout," not meaning it as a compliment. Trump knew that Ryan had denounced him after the infamous *Access Hollywood* video clip (in which Trump bragged that a celebrity such as him could assault women with impunity) surfaced in October 2016. He also knew that it was Kevin McCarthy who had urged Ryan to temper his condemnation. McCarthy privately was of the belief that anytime Trump decided to turn on the Republican-controlled House, the president could take them all down with little effort. McCarthy therefore saw it as his mission to convince Trump that the House GOP Conference was his friend. He urged Ryan to do some road trips with the president—not as a favor to the Speaker, but because the majority leader was biding his time, riding the tiger that was Trump for as long as it took until it was Kevin McCarthy's turn at the Speaker's rostrum.

McCarthy was convinced that he had what it took to tame the tiger. After all, he had performed more or less the same stunt as minority leader in the California legislature with another celebrity turned politician, Governor Arnold Schwarzenegger. Evidence piled up early in 2017 that McCarthy was dealing with a different sort of beast, however. He urged Trump to appoint Mitt Romney, a frequent Trump critic, as his secretary of state, saying that the pick would be "Lincoln-esque." It did not happen. He viewed the New York developer as a "builder" and therefore was certain that Trump would pull off a major infrastructure deal. It did not happen. "He's good at relationships—he'll build relationships with Democrats," McCarthy predicted to me. It did not happen.

Instead, Trump bent the conservatives in the Republican House to his will. The hardline House Freedom Caucus—established in 2015 by a rump group that believed then-Speaker John Boehner was compromising too much on fiscal negotiations with the Obama administration—quickly came to see that President Trump did not share their ideological purity. When it also became evident to them that voters back home were far more wedded to Trump than to conservative orthodoxy, the Freedom Caucus wasted little time rebranding itself a populist club of Trump mini-mes.

Teaming up with Trump took some of the wind out of the Freedom Caucus's ideological sanctimony. Throughout the forty-fifth president's term, he would oversee a 36 percent increase in the federal debt, the fastest rate of any presidency in U.S. history. For all Trump's boasts that he was single-handedly "draining the swamp" in Washington, his cabinet—which at given times included defense, oil, and coal lobbyists, in addition to several former corporate executives now put in charge of overseeing their former industries—was unambiguously swampy. And though Freedom Caucus members fulminated about Obama's "imperial" behavior in having signed 129 executive orders during his second term, the same group fell strangely silent when Trump issued 220 such orders during his one term.

McCarthy himself did not fault the Freedom Caucus for their pliability. Quite the contrary: he saw them as survivors, much as he was. Like Trump, McCarthy was a transactionalist, never one to be weighed down by policy minutiae or core values. Like the president, he craved human interaction, albeit of a more communal sort, habitually forming exercise groups and dragging junior members along with him to dinner.

And as with Trump, McCarthy was hardly above sublimating facts in favor of narrative. He enjoyed telling reporters like me his too-good-to-fact-check origin story—that of the Bakersfield fireman's son who won a $5,000 lottery ticket, used it to start a sandwich shop at the age of nineteen and in turn devoted the proceeds to paying his college tuition after first encountering onerous government regulations on small business. (Alas, *Washington Post* reporter

Glenn Kessler did check it. McCarthy was twenty-one when he started his business, not nineteen. He did not "open" a shop but rather worked out of his uncle's yogurt store. He did not pay business taxes. His college tuition was free.)

McCarthy once claimed to a Bakersfield audience in my presence that he broke from his family's Democratic Party allegiances upon reading in the *Weekly Reader* that, in his words, "Jimmy Carter put a sweater on and told America to turn down the temperature [on their home thermostats] because America's best days were behind it." This was, of course, reductive to the point of caricature. But McCarthy knew that the brand mattered more than the facts. In Obama, he saw a community organizer, union activist, and lawyer—or as McCarthy preferred to frame him, "a redistributor who never created wealth."

By early 2018, Paul Ryan had wearied of Trumpism. He announced that, as one does, he was retiring at the age of forty-eight to spend more time with his family. (Ryan subsequently joined two corporate boards, formed a non-profit, and became a faculty member at Notre Dame.) Ryan had been around town long enough to anticipate what was coming. After a rough 2018 midterm election cycle, the House GOP fell back into the minority.

Kevin McCarthy was now the top Republican in the House. From his perch, he had seen that the man he'd admired from young adulthood had not lived up to his billing as a consummate dealmaker. If anything, Trump seemed uniquely unskilled at working with the legislative branch. He could only govern through executive order. The GOP base nonetheless remained loyal to him. He piled up debt and bashed America's allies and it did not matter. The party was whatever Trump said it was. Meanwhile, McCarthy's friend and predecessor Ryan had been unable to fake his approval of Trump's performance. Ryan had headed for the exits, and now McCarthy presided over a disgruntled minority.

It was time for him to shine. He did so by enabling the man who referred to McCarthy as "my Kevin."

A COMPLIMENT THAT MCCARTHY OFTEN BESTOWED ON REPUBLICANS HE favored was that the elected official in question was a "happy warrior." He left it to others to deduce that McCarthy was the quintessence of that label: always fighting the good fight, always with good cheer.

The term, originating in an 1806 poem by William Wordsworth, was first applied in American politics to Hubert Humphrey, the Democratic Minnesota senator and Lyndon Johnson's vice president. But in Humphrey's case, "happy warrior" was not a performative label. He was nobody's idea of a charismatic figure. As Johnson's vice president, he had been consigned to insignificance. He ran for president in 1960, 1968, and 1972 and was defeated each time.

But Humphrey had stood for something greater than a winning image and professional advancement. He had fought tirelessly for civil rights, going back to his speech at the 1948 Democratic convention, at a time when many in his party resisted equal treatment for Black Americans. He had fought for labor unions and for the poor. Humphrey's sunny disposition was not that of a cocksure pugilist. It was the outward image of a committed idealist whose credo was "Never give in and never give up."

Kevin McCarthy was a very different kind of happy warrior. Though his transactional nature well equipped him for a career in politics, one could just as easily see him as an aspiring Hollywood studio titan, or Wall Street barracuda, or real estate mogul like his early hero Donald Trump. Committed belief was inconvenient. Truth was important to know but not so important to tell.

Adam Schiff learned this about McCarthy through painful firsthand experience. The Los Angeles–area Democrat was just beginning his fourth term in the House in early 2007 when he and the newly elected Bakersfield Republican sat together on the long flight from Washington back to LAX. As they chatted, Schiff shared a few thoughts about their House colleagues with the freshman. McCarthy promptly disclosed tidbits to the local media.

When Schiff confronted McCarthy on the House floor to tell him that members should not betray such confidences, the freshman shrugged. "That's just politics," he said with a grin.

Nine years later, McCarthy was the House GOP's majority leader when a defense-spending bill came to the floor. Included in it was an amendment offered by Democrat Sean Patrick Maloney and cosponsored by moderate Republican Charlie Dent that would remove language that could enable discrimination against LGBTQ members of the military. The bill seemed certain to pass, until Majority Leader McCarthy extended the voting time. Furtively, he ushered Republican members who had voted for passage into the Cloakroom and urged them to defeat the Democratic measure.

A Democrat, Dan Kildee, saw what was going on. Accosting McCarthy, he said angrily, "Just let them vote their conscience."

The happy warrior coolly replied, "If you want to talk to me, make an appointment." The amendment was defeated.

For McCarthy, happiness came with little effort but was also a tactic, a veneer that disguised his zeal for partisan warfare. A book I wrote about the 2010 "Tea Party class" of the House of Representatives received considerable attention for disclosing that a group of Republicans had gathered on the night of Obama's inauguration at a Washington steakhouse, where they schemed to thwart the new president's agenda. In truth, I would not have known about this secret meeting except that Kevin McCarthy had enthusiastically told me all about it, on the record, in 2011. In his telling, McCarthy had been among the most pugnacious participants at the 2009 dinner, saying of Obama's Democrats, "We've gotta challenge them on every single bill and challenge them on every single campaign."

Four years after offering me that happy-warrior anecdote, McCarthy bragged in an interview with Fox News Channel host Sean Hannity about the true objective of a House committee set up ostensibly to understand how the U.S. embassy in Benghazi, Libya, came to be attacked in 2011. "Everybody thought Hillary Clinton was unbeatable, right?" he said of Obama's secretary of state, who was the putative favorite in the 2016 Democratic presidential sweepstakes. "But we put together a Benghazi special committee. A select committee. What are her numbers today? Her numbers are dropping."

The Republican chairman of the Benghazi committee, Trey Gowdy, had taken its work seriously and was infuriated to see it debased by McCarthy's boast. Hoping to be John Boehner's heir apparent as Speaker, McCarthy instead watched his support within the conference evaporate. Beset as well by unsupported rumors floated by political adversaries in his own party that he had been having an affair with a Republican congresswoman, McCarthy withdrew from the race and backed his friend Paul Ryan.

Then he waited. It did not take long. Three years after his loose mouth had cost him the Speaker's gavel, Kevin McCarthy was again the leader of the

Republican House. With Trump's ascendancy, the terms and methods of battle had changed dramatically. But in the end, Trump shared with McCarthy a key objective: beating Democrats.

In courting Trump's support to help the GOP edge closer to regaining the House majority in 2020, McCarthy was up to the task in a way that former Republican leaders like Ryan and Boehner were not. It required living inside the president's scrambled universe, where objective truth was sublimated in accordance with Trump's outsized needs.

McCarthy seemed to enjoy the game. Knowing how proud Trump was that not a single House Republican had voted to impeach him in early 2020, McCarthy convinced him to reward the loyalty of every GOP House incumbent now facing a primary challenge with a Trump endorsement. Knowing as well how much Trump loved to see a former antagonist later kiss his ring, McCarthy arranged for the endorsement of Florida candidate and onetime Never Trumper Carlos Giménez.

McCarthy understood that Trump wished to side with winners above all else. He also understood that Trump would want full credit after victory was assured. He recognized that the president's moods were tempestuous, and so McCarthy secured back-channel connections with Trump's top two White House lieutenants: his son-in-law, Jared Kushner, and his social media director, Dan Scavino.

McCarthy was a new kind of friend for Trump, whose tastes ordinarily ran to fellow billionaires, authoritarian foreign leaders, and Fox News Channel hosts. For all his bravado, however, the president did not understand how Washington worked, and neither did most of the White House yeasayers around him. McCarthy knew his place, but he also knew his way around town. Additionally, the House Republican leader comprehended the vagaries of the 435 congressional districts better than almost anyone. If "my Kevin" steered him to a good bet, the president unfailingly took it.

McCarthy, in turn, bet that the prognosticators were wrong—that even in an election season that did not favor Trump, the president's support could still turn out low-propensity voters in several contested congressional districts. In all, Trump made over fifty calls on behalf of House Republican candidates during the 2020 cycle. The very last presidential activity Trump undertook before testing positive for COVID on October 2 were three "tele-rallies" in which he endorsed Jeff Van Drew, Scott Perry, and Burgess Owens by video. After emerging from his sickness on October 9, his first order of business was to conduct tele-rallies for Yvette Herrell, Stephanie Bice, and Nancy Mace. Each of these candidates ended up winning, several of them by close margins.

Still, there was a price to being Trump's political Rasputin. On November 2, the day before the election, a confidant asked Kevin McCarthy, "What are you going to do if Trump doesn't concede?"

"Well," predicted McCarthy, "of course he's going to want to say the thing was stolen and the whole thing was rigged. There are going to be stages of grief."

In a very low voice, the minority leader then said, "There will come a point where McConnell and I would need to come out and issue a joint statement."

But this did not occur. On December 14, 2020, the Electoral College officially confirmed that Joe Biden had won the presidency with 306 electoral votes. The next day, Mitch McConnell publicly issued congratulations to Biden. McCarthy held his tongue, however.

"I'm trying to get through to him," he said of Trump to his confidant. "I'm trying to give him time."

McCarthy of course knew that Trump had lost. The president's first debate performance, his condemnation of mail-in voting, and his failure to project empathy after contracting COVID had combined to doom him, in McCarthy's view. At least the House Republicans had picked up a dozen seats, though not quite enough to win back the majority.

"Don't you think we're headed down a dangerous road here?" asked McCarthy's confidant—referring to Trump's continuing refusal to acknowledge the election results.

"Maybe," said McCarthy. "Maybe so." To the confidant, the Republican House leader did not sound especially bothered by this possibility. Instead, Trump's chief enabler was looking ahead, to a new Democratic president who was likely to encounter a rebuke by voters two years into his term.

"The silver lining," Kevin McCarthy said, "is that I have a pretty good chance of being Speaker in two years."

Representative Liz Cheney

Chapter Seven

CLIO AND THE CHAIRWOMAN

Three weeks after the Capitol riots, it was abundantly clear that there were two distinct and mutually incompatible views as to how the Republicans could return to power in Washington. One of them was espoused by House Minority Leader Kevin McCarthy. His view held that the GOP could not regain the House without the help of Donald Trump. Such a path would require indulging the ex-president's incessant claims that the 2020 election had been stolen from him. It would mean enabling a seditious lie for the sake of power.

The other view was held by Liz Cheney, the third-ranking Republican House member. Far from regarding Trump as the party's savior, Cheney's position was that the former president was a lead anchor around the GOP's neck.

Cheney had not anticipated that this belief would prove to be profoundly unpopular within the Republican Party. Prior to the events of January 6, 2021, it had never occurred to her—nor, likely, to anyone—that the events of that day would alter her political persona more dramatically than that of any officeholder in America, including Trump. This nearly overnight transformation occurred without Liz Cheney's changing her opinion about any single issue or behaving in any way previously thought to be scandalous. Quite the contrary: she had merely cast a vote of conscience and thereafter refused to back away from it.

An empirical logic supported Liz Cheney's argument that the party needed to move on from Trump. In four short years, the Republicans had lost the House in 2018, and then the Senate and White House in 2020. Politically, it made no sense to tether the party's fate to a certified loser.

For Cheney, however, the matter went even deeper. Her family had served in government for a half century. The Cheneys had always been Republicans. They were conservatives who believed in limited government, but also democratically elected government. The party Liz Cheney grew up in simply could not embrace insurrection as a means of maintaining power. She was a party leader, and she would not allow it to happen.

In her view, the impeachment vote on January 13 represented a golden opportunity for the Republicans to move past Trump once and for all. But by traveling to Palm Beach to pay obeisance to the ex-president, McCarthy had squandered that opportunity. The minority leader had implicitly confessed to the entire world that the twice-impeached president who had refused to concede defeat was still their party's leader and that the Republicans could not move forward without his help.

McCarthy had not given Cheney a heads-up that he intended to have lunch at Mar-a-Lago with Trump on January 28. Then again, the conference chairwoman had not informed the minority leader about her intention to vote to impeach Trump until he read her press statement on January 12. Cheney hadn't thought it necessary to clear the matter with McCarthy. He had already told the entire House GOP Conference that the decision about whether to impeach Trump was a "conscience vote" that Republican leadership would not attempt to influence.

But of course, Liz Cheney was not just any member. She was one of the Republican Party's top leaders. Her last name was one of the most prominent in American politics. When Liz Cheney said something, people noticed. And if what she said was, *The leader of the Republican Party is a threat to our democracy and needs to be impeached,* one could bet that the Democrats would pounce on it.

Which they did. "Good for her for honoring her oath of office," declared Nancy Pelosi when informed of Cheney's statement, which Rules Committee Chairman Jim McGovern promptly entered into the *Congressional Record.* Pelosi and McGovern were using Cheney's moral clarity to shame the other Republicans for their moral failure.

On the evening of February 2, 2021, Cheney was summoned to the minority leader's office. With her and McCarthy were Steve Scalise and Patrick McHenry, a forty-five-year-old congressman from North Carolina who served as the ranking member of the House Financial Services Committee and was widely viewed as a strong candidate to be majority whip if the Republicans retook the House in 2022. McHenry brought up the next day's conference, where members intended to vent their unhappiness with Cheney's impeachment vote.

"Liz, I'm not asking for an apology," McHenry said. "But I think members would benefit from hearing that you understand that they had to answer for your words. Some contrition, in other words."

Cheney stared at McHenry and said nothing.

"OK, maybe contrition's not the right thing," he said. "Maybe saying you understand that it was a challenging vote for them as well."

Again, Cheney did not respond. McHenry said, "OK, how about this? Tell them it was not your intention that they have to answer for your vote of conscience."

When again she said nothing, McHenry tried to contain his exasperation. "OK, can I ask you a question?" he said. "Let me ask it this way: Did you intend for members of our conference to have to answer for your statements that you made about your vote?"

"No," Cheney said.

"OK," said McHenry. "Can you say that? Can you acknowledge that? I think that would help."

Then Scalise interjected. "Liz," the minority whip said, "I think you've got, like, one-third of the conference that wants to hear that you have some empathy for them. That when you put out your statement, it made things tough for them. They want to know that you get it."

"The vote I took was the right vote," Cheney evenly replied. To the chairwoman, empathy was beside the point. Yes, her statement had been a strong and unambiguous one. That was what the situation had called for. And yes, she understood quite well that there were political consequences to casting a vote to impeach Trump. She was from Wyoming, after all. No state was more supportive of Trump than hers. It was precisely because her view was inconsistent with that of her constituents that her statement had to be *above* politics.

Left unspoken by Cheney was what she did get—which was the role that fear played in the impeachment vote. Had it been a secret ballot, Cheney was confident that far more than ten Republicans would have voted to impeach the president. She knew this because several members had said so to her. Those same members feared their own constituents. They feared for their physical safety.

But before she was a congresswoman, Liz Cheney in the 1980s had worked for the State Department and had served overseas in countries like Poland and Czechoslovakia that did not have peaceful transitions of power. She had also read Ted Widmer's book *Lincoln on the Verge: Thirteen Days to Washington*, which recounted the president-elect's dramatic train trip from Springfield, Illinois, to the nation's capital to take the oath of office in 1861. As the nation teetered on the brink of civil war, Lincoln avoided two assassination attempts on the journey, while the counting of Electoral College votes in the Capitol was preceded by fears that someone might seize the mahogany box containing the ballots and thereby undo Abe Lincoln's presidency before its inception.

Cheney had shuddered to think what would have happened had the mob gotten their hands on the mahogany boxes on January 6, 2021. Democracy was not a given, not even in America. And when she later viewed the Capitol security video footage of Vice President Mike Pence's being hustled out of the building, immediately she thought of Vice President Dick Cheney's being whisked away to the White House bunker by Secret Service agents on the morning of September 11, 2001.

So, no: Liz Cheney was not going to apologize. She was not going to show contrition or project empathy. If the Republican Conference preferred a leader who wasn't going to vote her conscience, then by all means, they should replace her with someone else.

That was Cheney's dare to her fellow Republicans, leading to the special conference to vote on whether to remove her as chairwoman on February 3, 2021.

APART FROM AGE AND GENDER, THERE WERE FEW IF ANY MEANINGFUL DIF-
ferences between Dick Cheney and his elder daughter. She was a foreign policy hawk who continued to defend the decision to invade Iraq decades after
most had ceased doing so. On all other matters, she was at least as conservative as the former vice president was—and even, during her unsuccessful campaign for the U.S. Senate in 2014, announced her opposition to same-sex
marriage, contrary to the views of not only her father but also her sister Mary,
who was gay. (After dropping out of the race, Cheney privately acknowledged
that her stance had been an ill-advised ploy to win over conservative voters.
Some who were close to Liz Cheney later speculated that this lapse in principle had guided her determination to oust Trump from the party.)

It was understood that the fifty-year-old woman who had won Wyoming's at-large congressional seat in 2016 by 32 points would never be viewed
as a back-bencher. The chairman of the House Freedom Caucus, Jim Jordan,
approached her at the outset of her first term and asked her if she would like
to join. "We need a woman," Jordan added.

Unimpressed by the sales pitch, Cheney declined. Her energies were more
focused on matters before the Armed Services Committee. But after winning
a second term in 2018, she decided to run for conference chair, a position her
father had held three decades earlier. The Republicans had just lost the House,
and it was understood that one sacrificial lamb would be the current chairwoman, Cathy McMorris Rodgers—though in truth, no messaging wizardry
by House Republican leadership during the midterm cycle could have overcome suburban voters' increasing distaste for Trump. It was not lost on some
in her conference that Cheney, in campaigning for the post, openly criticized
the ineffectual branding that had taken place under McMorris Rodgers.
Though she won easily, it should have been evident that assuaging a colleague's injured feelings was not something viewed by Liz Cheney as part of
her job description.

Now she was in the leadership chain. No other Republican woman possessed her national profile, and the broad assumption was that she would not

let it go to waste. McCarthy correctly regarded her as a rival for the Speaker-ship. In early 2019, the minority leader was asked at a public gathering who among the House Republicans was destined for greater things. McCarthy volunteered the name Liz Cheney—then quickly added, "I think she'd make a great secretary of defense."

Complicating Cheney's ambitions was her relationship with Wyoming's favorite Republican, Donald Trump. Though Trump had never missed an op-portunity to take a swipe at Bush and Dick Cheney for going to war in Iraq ("one of the worst decisions in the history of this country"), he appeared to regard Liz Cheney as political royalty. His feral instincts also seemed to rec-ognize that a Cheney was unlikely to be intimidated by him. She in turn viewed Trump as a president she would endeavor to find a way to work with regardless of his questionable character. Cheney supported Trump policies 93 percent of the time. She was an occasional guest at the White House. When the House Democrats moved to impeach Trump over his attempt to strong-arm Ukraine's president into digging up dirt on Joe Biden, it was Republican Conference chairwoman Liz Cheney who led the charge in opposing the effort. The real villains, said the chairwoman on the House floor, were the Demo-crats and their "partisan, reckless, and dangerous Articles of Impeachment"—which, if passed, "may permanently damage our Republic." According to Cheney, it was not Trump but rather the Democrats who "will be held accountable by history for what they are doing."

In truth, the chairwoman's messaging was never a defense of the president. Privately, Cheney found Trump's behavior in the Ukraine matter to be appall-ing. She nonetheless sought refuge in a process argument. The Democrats, she asserted, were impeaching Trump based on secondhand testimony and circum-stantial evidence, rather than on firsthand accounts from White House aides (who were in fact refusing to testify). Of course, Cheney did nothing to encour-age deeper investigation into the conduct of her party's leader. She did not decry the stonewalling by potential key witnesses like chief of staff Mick Mulvaney, national security adviser John Bolton, and Vice President Pence. After Trump ranted on Twitter about Marie Yovanovitch, the former U.S. ambassador to Ukraine, while the latter was testifying, the chairwoman said to the press, "I don't think the president should have done that." Otherwise, she said nothing about the president's misconduct. If anything, Liz Cheney's condemnation of the Democrats was thoroughly consonant with Trump's insistence that he was the victim of "the greatest witch hunt in American history."

The breaking point for Cheney was the coronavirus. Trump's cavalier insistence that the virus would soon disappear "like a miracle" struck her as profoundly irresponsible, all the more so because her father, who had suffered multiple heart attacks over the years, was in a high-risk category. She publicly defended the scientific experts whom Trump had contradicted. In the past, her disagreements with the president over troop withdrawals in Germany and Afghanistan could be viewed as minor differences in ideology. By criticizing Trump's statements on the coronavirus, however, Cheney was in effect saying that Trump was grossly mischaracterizing scientific reality for the sake of his political future. Implicitly, she was accusing Trump's allies—her Republican colleagues in the House—of the same misconduct.

On September 23, 2020, President Trump was asked at a press briefing whether he would commit to a peaceful transition should Biden defeat him. His answer was, "Well, we're going to have to see what happens," followed by his oft-repeated lie that "the ballots are a disaster." When word of Trump's remark reached Cheney, she responded on Twitter: "The peaceful transfer of power is enshrined in our Constitution and fundamental to the survival of our Republic. America's leaders swear an oath to the Constitution. We will uphold that oath."

We? Liz Cheney appeared to be speaking for her entire conference—or perhaps *to* them. Either way, the breach between them was growing.

ON THE MORNING OF FEBRUARY 3, 2021, LIZ CHENEY GATHERED WITH OTHers in the Capitol Rotunda to honor Brian Sicknick, the Capitol police officer who had collapsed and died a day after battling the rioters on January 6. The Wyoming congresswoman stepped up to the urn containing Sicknick's remains and bowed her head for a moment. A mother of five herself, she embraced Brian's mother, Gladys Sicknick. "Whatever I can do, let me know," she said. "We won't forget what he did for us."

Later that day, Cheney walked to the Capitol Visitor Center.

It was just after four in the afternoon. More than two hundred of her Republican colleagues were seated inside the conference room. The chairwoman stood in front of them and remained standing, as she always did during their conferences. But those meetings typically lasted one hour. This one would exceed four hours.

"Madam chairman," said Dan Bishop of North Carolina, "I have submitted a resolution of no confidence in the chair."

Staffers were instructed to leave the conference room. "Let's make this as friendly as possible," McCarthy then said.

Agreed Scalise, "Let's talk in a civil way." Referring to Biden's Democrats, the GOP whip then said, "Let's resolve this here and let's go out there and kick their ass on the things they're trying to do to destroy this country."

Now Liz Cheney had the floor. "Most of you know of my love for the House," she began. "But I have to tell you, I'm really deeply, deeply concerned about where we are as a party."

Invoking the image of some of the Capitol rioters who wore Neo-Nazi emblems, the chairwoman said, "That can never be us. We are the party of Lincoln. We're the party of Reagan. We believe in honor and courage, limited government and low taxes. We believe in a strong national defense. And most of all, we believe in fidelity to the Constitution of the United States."

She realized that several members wanted her to apologize for her vote to impeach Trump or, at minimum, for the statement she had put out. "I cannot do that," Cheney said. "It was certainly not my intention to cause anybody pain in their district. But I had an absolute obligation to do what I thought was right."

Instead, Liz Cheney doubled down. "If you walk through Statuary Hall," she said, "you'll see a statue over the north door: Clio, the muse of history. And she's there with a book, looking down at what was the House chamber. And she's taking notes. She's there to remind us that what we do will be recorded by history. What we do here in the Republican conferences has huge consequences for our party, and for our nation going forward. And we have to get it right."

Concluded Cheney, "We have to be worthy of the mantle of Lincoln. Thank you very much."

The line to the microphone was, by the standards of these conferences, extraordinarily long. The freshman from Montana, Matt Rosendale, minced no words. "On the eve of impeachment, the conference chair responsible for messaging put out a statement that the mainstream media and the Democrats used against us," Rosendale said in a loud and angry voice. "She made our lives harder. You cannot have unity in this conference without trust. And we do not have trust in the current conference chair."

Mike Kelly followed Rosendale. He likened the experience to a football game: "You look up into the stands and see your girlfriend on the opposition's side—that's one hell of a tough thing to swallow."

"She's not your girlfriend!" a female member interrupted.

"Yeah, I'm not your girlfriend," Cheney concurred. Otherwise, she remained stoic as House Freedom Caucus chairman Andy Biggs sputtered, "You didn't protect us, Liz. I'm not fine with you out there providing aid and comfort and top-cover to the opponent." Echoed Scott Perry of Pennsylvania, a retired National Guard brigadier general, "This is about the aid and comfort that you offered to our enemy, used as a cudgel on me."

Several standing in line voiced support for Cheney. Adam Kinzinger of Illinois, who had also voted to impeach Trump, did not bother to conceal his disgust. "This party has lost its damn mind," he said. "You look at the fact that Liz Cheney, one of the most conservative members of Congress, casts a vote of conscience after a frigging *insurrection* that killed a Capitol police officer under the name of *our* party, *not* Antifa. . . . Maybe you should blame President Trump—who, by the way, if we don't say a word after this meeting, is the *only* voice speaking for us. I'm not going to take it anymore. I'm all for unity—but not unity under the Trump banner."

Peter Meijer, the freshman from Michigan who had also voted to impeach, observed in a shaking voice, "If Liz Cheney is the person who suffers the most for what happened on January 6, we're in a dark, dark place."

Another impeacher, John Katko of New York, suggested that Cheney's conservative critics were being hypocritical by complaining that her words and deeds had caused them political heartburn. "I have a D plus-5 district," Katko said, "and the things you put up on the right side of the party are *crushing* to me. I've never *once* gone to the media."

Back and forth they went. Defenders and detractors alike cited Scripture in support of their view. Allusions were offered to football, hockey, cattle branding, hog farming, auto sales, the Alamo, Aesop's fables, and dysfunctional families. The true "enemy," they reminded one another, were the Democrats. Unity, they concurred, was the ideal.

But the obstacle to unity was not just Liz Cheney—or even just Cheney and Trump. For though the February 3 special conference was intended to focus on Cheney's future as the conference chair, another immediate issue loomed—one that, like the Cheney problem, forced upon them the existential question: *What matters to us as a party, apart from victory?*

It was Marjorie Taylor Greene, the freshman from Georgia, who was also prompting this question. A week earlier, CNN's Em Steck and Andrew Kaczynski had unearthed an additional tranche of Greene's past musings. Among these was the sentiment expressed by Greene two years earlier that Nancy Pelosi should be executed. The liberal group Media Matters had additionally surfaced writings reflecting Greene's views that the 2018 Marjorie Stoneman Douglas High School shooting in Parkland, Florida, was staged and that a wildfire in California that same year had been instigated by a laser beam shot from space by a prominent Jewish family, the Rothschilds. Such delusions were commonly featured in the community of QAnon followers.

Indignant Democrats were now demanding that Greene be stripped of her committee assignments. McCarthy refused to do so. As he said at the beginning of the special conference, "They're going after Marjorie for things she said before she even got here." And, the minority leader warned, "They won't stop with her. . . . They're coming at you next."

What Kevin McCarthy proposed was a sidestep from the Republican Party's existential inquiry. To the question *What matters to us?* the answer would simply be: *unity.* That meant protecting both Greene *and* Cheney, for the sake of togetherness.

This was why, just over an hour into the conference, Jaime Herrera Beutler of Washington—a moderate who also had voted to impeach Trump—stepped up to the microphone and said: "Marjorie Taylor Greene is *not* the moral equivalent of Liz Cheney."

Continued Herrera Beutler, "Now, I'm willing to give Marjorie Taylor

Greene a chance. She wasn't a kid when she made those comments, all right? It was recent. And Liz Cheney is standing up against the most powerful man in the world *and* our entire leadership team—and *you* assholes are chewing her out and making her out the same as Marjorie Taylor Greene? *Excuse me!*

"This isn't a conversation about whether Liz stays in her chair or not," she emphatically concluded. "This is about the direction of the future of our party. It really is."

Representatives Paul Gosar, Andy Biggs,
Marjorie Taylor Greene, and Thomas Massie

Chapter Eight

=========

"I FIND IT VERY INTERESTING"

Midway into the four-hour conference to argue over removing Liz Cheney from leadership, the other elephant in the room spoke.

Marjorie Taylor Greene stepped up to the microphone. The freshman from Georgia did not have anything to say about Cheney, or even about—as Jaime Herrera Beutler had put it—"the future of our party." She was there to talk entirely about herself.

"Well," she began, "many of you I've enjoyed getting to know in my one month in Congress. But there's also more of you that I haven't gotten to get to know, and you haven't gotten to get to know me. Some of you attack me every single day, and usually I find that the ones who attack me every single day don't know me, and that's unfortunate."

Greene then proceeded to tell her life story, and how it was that she came to embrace the conspiracy theories of the QAnon community that now scandalized the Republican Party and jeopardized her political career. But for that one blemish, the freshman told them, "I'd have a résumé that probably would've beaten most of yours. Because most of my life I'd done everything right."

This, like much of what she would recount, was an artisanal blend of truth, untruth, and omission. Marjorie Taylor was born in 1974, in the town of Milledgeville, which had been Georgia's capital during the Civil War. Her father, Bob Taylor, was an ingenious self-promoter who had founded a construction firm and later penned a book analyzing the supposed effects of gravity on the stock market—a theory he dubbed the Taylor Effect and for which, he frequently claimed, he had been nominated for the Nobel Prize in Economics in 2000.

This was an exaggeration: a few friends had sent a letter "nominating" Taylor to the Nobel Committee, much like a far-right Norwegian politician would "nominate" Trump for the Nobel Peace Prize two decades later. Bob Taylor would also say that his theory had been peer-reviewed in a paper published in the *Harvard Business Review*. This claim was entirely false: a paper cowritten by Taylor was published in the *Journal of Private Equity* and mentioned only briefly in the *Harvard Business Review*, but it did not discuss the Taylor Effect, and a coauthor of the paper, when I contacted him, said that he had never heard of either the theory or its inventor.

Marjorie Taylor, named for her grandmother on her mother Delle's side, grew up comfortably, a reasonably good student with a manageable attention deficit disorder. She received one scare in 1990, when a fellow high school student walked into a classroom with four firearms and, by the congresswoman's recounting to her Republican colleagues, "we were held hostage and were on lockdown for five hours." (Only nine were held hostage, Marjorie not among them, and the school was not on lockdown but instead evacuated, after which the police peacefully relieved the mentally ill student of his weapons.) She attended the University of Georgia, becoming the first in her family to graduate from college. While on campus, she met Perry Greene, whom she married just after graduation. Perry begged his father-in-law for a job and eventually took over Bob Taylor's construction firm in 2002. Two years later, they purchased a sprawling 6,000-square-foot, five-bedroom house in the exclusive Atlanta suburb of Milton.

In 2011, Marjorie was baptized at North Point Community Church, but, according to a church official, she ceased to be active in the church three years after her baptism. The year 2011 was also when Greene became deeply involved in what she would term "this underground cult fitness thing called CrossFit." In the summer of 2012, the thirty-eight-year-old mother of three young children moved out of the house and filed for divorce.

These personal details were left out of the "résumé that probably would've beaten most of yours" she recited to her Republican colleagues on the afternoon of February 3, 2021. And in telling them that she'd "run a hell of a successful construction company," Greene was taking credit for her husband's success, because, as a friend of the Greenes would tell me, "Perry built that whole fucking thing." What Marjorie Taylor Greene *did* build with the help of a friend, after returning to her marriage in November 2013, was a gym, CrossFit Passion—though, as she conceded in an interview in 2015, "We're experts at coaching people . . . but the business part we weren't good at."

Up to this point in her life, Greene did not publicly espouse political views. During the 2014 midterm election, she did not vote at all—instead writing on her CrossFit blog, "Today was just one of those days, where someone was saying my name every minute and there wasn't enough time and just stressful." But through the obsessive CrossFit community, Greene had become very active on Facebook, especially once she sold CrossFit Passion in 2016 and suddenly had an abundance of idle time.

"I was upset about Russian collusion conspiracy lies that I was seeing on the news every day," Greene recalled to her colleagues. "So I looked into the internet—and I was like, 'What is going on?' And I stumbled upon something like QAnon. Yep, I did. I read about it, posted about it, I talked about it, and I asked questions about it."

Here, more precisely, is what she did:

By the summer of 2017, she had made contact online with a counselor in the New York public school system who shared Greene's affinities for both President Donald Trump and dark conspiracy theories. She began writing for the counselor's online publication, *American Truth Seekers*, that August, under the pen name Elizabeth Camp, which happened to be the name of her great-grandmother.

Somehow the "Russian collusion conspiracy lies" had created a permission structure for Greene to believe that a Democratic staffer named Seth Rich had been murdered by Hillary Clinton's top adviser, John Podesta, in order to cover up the fact that it was Rich, not Russia, who had leaked Democratic emails to WikiLeaks. (Later, Greene would modify this conspiracy theory: it was the Latino gang MS-13, "the henchmen of the Obama administration," who had murdered Seth Rich.) It allowed Greene to believe that Robert Mueller, the special counsel investigating Trump's ties to Russia, was actually a "white hat" protagonist who was quietly working to bring down the Clintons. It allowed her to believe that "many in our government actively worship

Satan." It allowed her to believe that Trump was singlehandedly battling evil—that "thousands of Pedophiles and Child Traffickers have been arrested since Trump was sworn in." This "Global Evil," she was allowed to believe, was all being funded by the Saudi royals in concert with two Jewish billionaires: George Soros and the Rothschild family. Marjorie Taylor Greene believed all this not only because the media had made up lies about Trump but also because in some dark corner of the internet, some anonymous patriot claiming to have military intelligence "Q clearance" had said so.

In her speech at the special conference, she acknowledged that she had been misled by QAnon. "And when you have a source that puts out true things and false things, that's very dangerous," Greene said, adding, "And that's what CNN does every day too! Right?"

But Greene did not elaborate on why she found CNN less trustworthy than an anonymous source on the internet that claimed Democrats raped and cannibalized babies. Nor did she discuss with her fellow Republicans the other pet theories that had *not* been alleged by Q but were still embraced by Greene and other Anons, because those theories buttressed the foundational view that the other side was incorrigibly evil. Among these was her belief that the mass shooting in Christchurch, New Zealand, was a false flag operation to prompt strict gun laws in the United States. (That John Podesta had been in New Zealand a few days before the shooting was a factoid Greene found "very, very interesting.") She also believed that the attempted mail bombings of various Democratic officeholders and CNN's headquarters in 2018 by Trump supporter Cesar Sayoc were "a deflection" and an "interesting October surprise" perpetrated by the Democrats to influence the November midterms.

Of Obama, Greene said, during a conference of right-wing activists in December 2018, "Yes, I do believe he's a Muslim, and Valerie Jarrett is too." (Neither was true.) In the same speech, she brought up Hillary Clinton's Senate run and the false claim that John F. Kennedy Jr. was also a candidate: "And yes, I could dive into Kennedy's plane crash, because isn't it interesting he'd just announced he was going to run for Senate just before he died in a mysterious plane crash—that's another one of those Clinton murders, right?"

To the Republican House members, Greene shrugged and said, "I don't know what Jewish space lasers are—I've never said that term myself." This was literally true but materially a lie: what she had not said but instead written of the California wildfires, in 2018, was that "oddly, there are all these people who have said that they saw what looked like lasers or blue beams of light causing the fires." Noted the author, "I find it very interesting" and "I do find it really curious" that such technology was allegedly made by a company with ties to another company that had a board member who was also the vice chairman of the international investment banking firm Rothschild Inc., owned by the prominent Jewish family. "But what do I know?" Greene had mischievously concluded. "I just like to read a lot."

For that matter, in videos that she began to post online in 2018 (and did not mention to her Republican colleagues in the special conference), Greene offered views that were not so much conspiratorial as racially offensive. In decrying the removal of Confederate statues, she said, "If I were a Black people [sic] today and I walked past one of those statues, I would be so proud! Because I'd say, 'Look how far I've come in this country. Look at what my people have overcome. And these are good things, not bad things.' But no."

And in her 2018 speech, she felt moved to opine that the white people who "felt like it was time for America to have a Black president" were "the most racist people in America, because you voted for someone based on their skin color." Later on, in a YouTube video, she spoke of her fears, as the mother of a teenage boy, that he would be "the last one on the list that'll be accepted into college, because he's a white male." (Her son was accepted by the University of Mississippi, his first choice, in the summer of 2022.)

By the end of 2018, Marjorie Taylor Greene had been suspended from social media for her postings so many times that she had resorted to opening four different Facebook pages in an attempt to elude what she termed "Facebook jail." But the dawn of 2019 found Greene to be more determined and more politically committed than ever. On January 13—ten days after she watched with disgust as Pelosi reclaimed the Speaker's gavel—Greene put her manifesto to rhyme: "What is This Generation? Are you not entertained? While you slumber and play, the creature has you chained. . . . Socialism, Communism, One World Government they try. Death to Tyrants and

Traitors, is our battle cry! For We are The People, the giant within! We are going to make them pay for their sin!"

She spoke notably less that pivotal year about QAnon, apart from occasionally posting in Facebook comments the cult's covert battle cry, "WWG1WGA (Where We Go One, We Go All)." But its key tenets remained hers. Trump was the greatest president of her lifetime. The Democrats, the deep state, and the fake news media were evil. Greene and her fellow Trump supporters were patriots. The stakes in this battle for America were existential. Children all over America were gravely at risk.

She attended Trump rallies across America, beginning with the first of his reelection campaign, in El Paso on February 11, 2019. Shimmying to Michael Jackson's "Beat It," Greene hollered out, "We're telling the illegals to beat it, baby!" In a video that Greene posted on Facebook, she gleefully recalled the treatment a protester had received inside El Paso County Coliseum: "Oh it was awesome, one guy totally tackled a guy, pulled his sign away—it was great!" (She did not mention that an apparently drunk Trump supporter had shoved a BBC cameraman nearly to the ground while screaming, "Fuck the media!")

Meanwhile, outside the coliseum, the former Democratic presidential candidate and El Paso resident Beto O'Rourke had organized a counter-rally. When Greene and her friends had emerged from the arena and saw the large crowd, she declared to her Facebook Live viewers that it was a "major Antifa protest" and that "they're trying to attack us," though the video revealed no such thing.

More significantly, in early 2019 Marjorie Taylor Greene began showing up in Washington, DC. On February 22, she and three other right-wing YouTube hosts visited the office suite of Speaker Nancy Pelosi. Greene presented the receptionist with a petition to impeach Pelosi for the supposedly treasonous act of supporting sanctuary cities. "Lock her up!" the four of them chanted before leaving the Speaker's office suite.

To Greene's delight, the post of her harassing Pelosi's staff garnered 2.6 million views. Realizing that she was onto something, Greene and her YouTube friends Anthony Aguero, Will Johnson, and Ben Bergquam dropped in on Congressman Adam Schiff, chairman of the House Judiciary Committee, and taunted a young male intern. When Johnson, who is Black, insisted that the intern shake his hand and the latter replied pleadingly that he was just trying to get some work done, Greene hissed, "Racist. Racist."

They barged into the office of Rashida Tlaib, the Palestinian-American congresswoman from Michigan, wanting to denounce her for believing in Sharia law. Instead, they encountered a transgender staffer, prompting a lecture from Greene: "You're a man. I'm a woman. God only created male and female."

But Greene and her gang saved their chief torments for Alexandria Ocasio-Cortez, the young progressive firebrand from New York. They arrived at her office to find the door locked. But Bergquam waggled his fingers through the door slat while he and Greene called out, "We know you're in there!" After receiving no answer, Greene and the others contented themselves with rearranging the Post-it notes that were stuck along the right side of the congresswoman's door ("almost like a high school locker," Greene later said with disgust), before a couple of Capitol officers requested that they leave.

"We were terrifying everyone," she would recall with relish.

Still, these exercises in what Greene called "confrontational journalism" were formative. For as one of her most infamous videos would memorialize— her harassment of the eighteen-year-old Parkland High School shooting survivor David Hogg as he made the rounds in the Senate to lobby for gun reform—Greene's antics were going ignored where it counted. Facing the camera after Hogg tuned out her taunts and disappeared from view, the Georgia millionaire protested, "He got to talk to thirty senators . . . and I got none. NONE. I had *zero*. Guess what: I'm a gun owner. I'm an American citizen, and I've got *nothing*. But this guy, with his George Soros funding, and his major liberal funding, has got *everything*. I want you to think about that."

Greene was certainly thinking about it. She was thinking about it as she got turned away from the offices of Republican senators like Marco Rubio, Ted Cruz, and her own Georgia senators, David Perdue and Johnny Isakson. ("I couldn't get past a low-level staffer," she would later recall.) She was thinking about it as she stood in a line in March 2019 to attend a Senate Judiciary Committee hearing to consider gun legislation—a lone opponent surrounded by gun-safety groups. "I've been feeling really outnumbered and really sad standing in this line," she confided to her Facebook Live followers.

And a month later, Greene vented to a fellow right-wing YouTuber: "Conservatives have to get over themselves. Conservatives are so selfish in so many ways. We will spend, spend, spend on our very nice handbags, and on our golf clubs." Meanwhile, she confessed, not all the progressives she encountered were funded by Soros. Many of them, like her, "were just showing up. Took off work too. Conservatives have to stop making excuses."

Less than a month after that April interview, Marjorie Taylor Greene had filed her FEC paperwork to run for Congress. It was a story she would tell friends—how she, a taxpayer and job creator who cared about the Constitution, was turned away by Republicans and Democrats whose salary she paid. That was why she decided to run for Congress.

And now, February 3, 2021, the freshman defiantly told her new colleagues: "I'll tell you what I do want. I want Republicans to *compete*. I'm very competitive. I'm a terrible loser."

She concluded with an admonition: "Let's just make sure we keep our eyes on the enemy. Because they're really wanting to take *all* of us out."

About a third of her colleagues rose to applaud her as she took her seat among them.

NOT EVERYONE IN THE CONFERENCE WAS WOWED. "THE HEADLINE TONIGHT," warned South Carolina freshman Nancy Mace, "is that we kicked out Liz Cheney, but we gave a standing ovation to Marjorie Taylor Greene."

Tom Reed, a moderate from New York, was even more pointed. "I'm committed to winning the majority," he told his colleagues. "So how is it going to look if we kick out Liz Cheney and keep Marjorie Taylor Greene? How is it going to play across the U.S.? How am I going to stand in front of my kids? 'Dad, you kicked out the person who stood up for principle. And you retained'—and this is what the perception's going to be, and Marjorie, I don't mean to offend you—[the person] 'that stood for white supremacy, that stood for believing that a laser in the sky was controlled by the Jews to start a fire in California?'"

Finally, it was Kevin McCarthy's turn to speak. "Some of you hate me because I saw Donald Trump," the minority leader said, referring to his visit to Mar-a-Lago the previous week. "Some of you hate me because I don't agree with one thing Marjorie said beforehand.

"But by damn, I'm not letting Dems pick us off one by one," McCarthy vowed. "I'm your leader. You elected me leader. *Let. Me. Lead.*"

Said McCarthy, motioning to the chairwoman, Cheney, and the whip, Scalise, "I believe this is the team that can get us to a majority." He added, "Let's turn this corner. Let's spend the next 96 percent of our time kicking the crap out of *them* and earning the majority back once and for all."

The applause was loud and sustained. The Republican conference voted against the resolution to remove Liz Cheney, 145 to 61. The chairwoman held a brief press conference with the Capitol media, not letting on how exhausted she was after standing for four hours and weathering the scorn of a third of her colleagues.

She ate at her home in McLean, Virginia, that night. For the time being, at least, Cheney's status was secure.

Greene, on the other hand, would be facing a vote in Congress the next day. She spent that evening at the BLT Prime steakhouse in the Trump Hotel, ringing up a tab of $1,892.40 that she would later charge to her campaign as a travel expense.

"I GOT MY MOJO BACK!" MCCARTHY LATER TOLD SEVERAL PEOPLE, INCLUDING me. He believed that his speech had made the difference in ensuring Liz Cheney's position in leadership.

The question now was whether he could save Marjorie Taylor Greene's committee assignments. The subject of her placement on committees had been a source of angst since the Republicans on the Steering Committee had first met to decide where to put the freshman, knowing her penchant for making noise. Ultimately, they decided to assign Greene to the House Budget Committee, which was a backwater for those members in the minority; and the Education Committee, because the ranking member, Virginia Foxx, was known to be a tough lady who stood the best chance of keeping Greene in line.

But then CNN and Media Matters posted the latest excavation of Marjorie Taylor Greene's lunatic-fringe posts. That very day, January 28, Republican members voiced their anger on a conference call held by their fundraising arm, the National Republican Congressional Committee. Greene was on the call as well. Responding to the bemoaning about how each of them would have to answer for the freshman's words, she responded as any well-heeled American might. Greene promptly pledged to donate a whopping $175,000 of her own campaign funds to the NRCC. (She later made good on the promise.)

She had also met with McCarthy in his office. What Greene had to say fell short of contrite. Some of QAnon's postings had turned out to be true, she maintained. Others, not. Outside of Greene's presence, the minority leader conferred with Steve Scalise and Patrick McHenry. McCarthy wondered if he could split the baby—just remove her from the Budget Committee and leave her with Education. Both of them counseled the minority leader that this was a bad idea. "You'd look weak," warned Scalise. It would be better for McCarthy to exhibit leadership and remove her from both committees altogether.

McCarthy continued to wobble. The day before the February 3 special conference to discuss Liz Cheney's status, he contacted House Majority Leader Steny Hoyer—the only Democratic leader with whom he had a relationship, as Pelosi could not abide him—and asked, "What if we just put Marjorie on the Small Business Committee?"

Hoyer warned McCarthy that this would probably not fly with the Democrats. On the morning of February 3, just before Officer Brian Sicknick's memorial service in the Capitol, the Republican leader called Hoyer. The Democratic majority leader conveyed his caucus's view that if McCarthy wasn't going to take care of his party's mess—meaning, strip Marjorie Taylor Greene of her committee assignments—then the Democrats intended to do so.

McCarthy was apoplectic. "You mark this down in the history books," he yelled, threatening that once the Republicans took back the majority, they would strip Democrats of committee assignments with impunity.

"Kevin," Hoyer replied, "*you* mark this day down. This is the day I told you that your pandering for Trump is bad for your party, bad for the country, and bad for your career."

The two hung up angrily. They checked in again on the morning of February 4. Hoyer's Democrats had not changed. "Trust me," McCarthy vowed to Hoyer, "I won't forget this when we're in the majority."

That afternoon, as the House voted on whether to strip Marjorie Taylor Greene of her committee assignments, the Georgia freshman took to the House floor. During her first month in office, she said, "I haven't gotten to know any of my Democrat colleagues"—not adding that she had not bothered to reach out to any of them, because she considered them enemies of America. Instead, she framed herself as the very portrait of victimhood—a patriot who bypassed the fake news media and therefore undertook to explore the internet, where she "was allowed to believe things that weren't true."

Greene, as always, understood who her audience was. The day before, it had been her Republican colleagues. Today, it was her conservative following. After acknowledging that "school shootings are absolutely real" and "9/11 absolutely happened," Greene then lamented that "big media companies can take teeny, tiny pieces of words that I've said, that you have said, any of us, and can portray us as someone that we're not."

She apologized for nothing, just as she had been unrepentant in her speech to the Republican Conference less than twenty-four hours beforehand. When Steny Hoyer claimed his floor time, the Democratic majority leader reminded viewers that Greene had proclaimed herself in a 2020 campaign ad "the Squad's worst nightmare," her AR-15 hoisted at the ready—and then added that the aforementioned "Squad" of four Democratic women were actual people, in some cases mothers like Greene herself.

Eleven Republicans joined the unanimous Democratic vote to strip Marjorie Taylor Greene of her two committee assignments. Only three of them had voted to impeach Trump. For the other eight, Marjorie Taylor Greene represented a new and potentially even more toxic elixir for the GOP than the former president. After all, they no longer had to answer for Trump's deeds.

Greene, on the other hand, was just getting started. The day after the vote to remove her from committees, the freshman held a press conference in front of the Capitol. For a defiant twenty-two minutes, Greene declared herself unbowed. She made a point of saying exactly what no one in her party at that moment would wish to be the Republican message—namely, that the twice-impeached ex-president still called the shots: "The party is his. It doesn't belong to anybody else."

But this amounted to a rare show of modesty on Marjorie Taylor Greene's part. A month into her career as an elected Republican, the party now belonged to her. Newcomer to politics though she was, Greene already understood a significant portion of the GOP base in a way that party leaders like Kevin McCarthy and Liz Cheney did not. She understood that in sizable swaths of Middle America, numerous ordinary citizens—including successful and reasonably well-educated folks such as herself—believed in a truth that could not be found on CNN or in the *New York Times*. The truth, to these Americans, was that their country had been stolen from them. They believed that Hillary Clinton was, for once, speaking truthfully when she referred to them all as "deplorables." They wore the label as a badge, like the blood of Christ as they armored themselves against the evil they knew was capable of anything.

After all, there was a reason why, when Greene declared her candidacy in May 2019, she elected not to take down the countless social media postings that the mainstream media and party leaders predicted would spell her doom. The reason she did not do so was simple. She knew the things that she had said and written would not hurt her political chances.

She believed, in fact, that the QAnon posts would help her win.

PART THREE

AGAINST THE CRAZY

House Democratic leaders Steny Hoyer, James Clyburn, and Nancy Pelosi

Chapter Nine

====

THE GALLERY GROUP

Mchenry! Come over here!"

The North Carolina Republican Patrick McHenry looked up from the House floor to see the Democratic majority leader, Steny Hoyer, motioning for him to cross the aisle from the west side of the chamber, where the Republicans traditionally sat, and visit with Hoyer on the east side, where the Democrats normally congregated. It was a slow day in late February 2021, with only a few members in the chamber. McHenry walked over to see what Hoyer wanted.

Hoyer was holding court with a couple of other Democrats in the front row, near the center aisle. Silver-haired and toothy, with an aquiline nose and upright carriage that projected a sort of antique nobility, the Maryland Democrat had served in Congress for forty of his eighty-one years. He prided himself on his ability to get along with any serious legislator, regardless of party affiliation. McHenry, the ranking Republican leader in the Financial Services Committee, certainly qualified in Hoyer's mind as a serious legislator.

"Is she dangerous?" Hoyer asked.

McHenry smiled. "Is *who* dangerous?"

"Oh, come on. Greene. From Georgia."

The North Carolinian could see that the Democratic majority leader wasn't kidding. "In a lot of ways, yes," he replied. "Not the way your members think she's dangerous, though."

"What do you mean?" asked Hoyer.

"I mean, it's not going to be a physical assault," McHenry said. "But she *is* dangerous in a lot of ways. And all you guys have done is help give her added stature."

Patrick McHenry was referring to the vote three weeks earlier to strip Marjorie Taylor Greene of her committee assignments, an unprecedented show of force by a House majority that had made the freshman an object of sympathy in some quarters—not an easy task, given Greene's offensive past utterances.

"Yeah, I understand that," the majority leader sighed. An institutionalist who revered the House's traditions, Hoyer would have been much happier if Kevin McCarthy had disciplined his fellow Republican rather than leaving it up to the Democrats to do so. One of Hoyer's members, Jimmy Gomez of California, had even circulated a resolution to have Greene expelled from Congress altogether. In a leadership meeting, Hoyer had argued strenuously against such a power play, protesting, "She hasn't even had a hearing. Hundreds of thousands of people voted for this woman." Nancy Pelosi and majority whip Jim Clyburn ultimately concurred that stripping Greene of her committee assignments was the proper recourse.

"She's different," Hoyer said of Greene to McHenry—then corrected himself: "No. She's *crazy*. We've all had our crazies. But she's really set a new standard."

Hoyer's fellow Democrats were genuinely concerned about their physical safety in Greene's presence. They didn't say such things about Jim Jordan, the former wrestling coach who bellowed at witnesses during committee hearings and seldom wore a suit jacket, as if spoiling for a brawl. They never expressed fear of Louie Gohmert, the former judge from east Texas whose innumerable floor speeches were sometimes accompanied by visual aids depicting a labyrinth of Obama/Clinton conspiracies.

"What about—Bubble? Bubbler?" Hoyer said, not remembering how to pronounce the name of Lauren Boebert, the freshman from Rifle, Colorado, who had launched her campaign following a confrontation between her and presidential candidate Beto O'Rourke in which Boebert recited O'Rourke's earlier pledge to confiscate AR-15 semiautomatic weapons and then declared, "I am here to say, 'Hell no, you're not.'"

"She's a gun nut," McHenry replied. "I don't know that she's crazy across the boards, though."

But this characterization hardly assuaged Hoyer's concerns. Boebert's stated view of Democrats was only a couple of degrees less incendiary than that of Greene's. Meanwhile, the freshman from Rifle—whom some Democrats referred to as "Annie Oakley"—claimed that she routinely carried a Glock with her on the Capitol grounds. She had protested a new ban on firearms being brought into committee hearings by suggesting that Democrats might next ban Bibles.

Like Greene, Boebert had tweeted on the morning of January 6, "Today is 1776." Democrats had not forgotten how the freshman that day tweeted in real time, "The Speaker has been removed from the chambers"—whether out of glee that 1776 had arrived or to provide information to the insurrectionists it was yet to be established.

Hoyer's colloquy with McHenry represented more than an exercise in killing idle time. His sentiments reflected an unexpected turn in the career of an establishment Democrat who had perennially been viewed with suspicion by progressives, not least because of his chumminess with the opposition. But Republican friends—Fred Upton of Michigan, Roy Blunt of Missouri, long-departed pals like John Boehner and Robert Michel—had ceased to be the voice of the GOP. The violence-tinged antics of Greene and Boebert deeply offended Hoyer, who correspondingly became the unlikely protector of their chief targets: the female left-wing Democrats known as the Squad. Following Hoyer's thundering denunciation of Greene on the House floor when she was stripped of her committee assignments, Alexandria Ocasio-Cortez tearfully thanked him, while Ilhan Omar later tweeted that she "even gave him a hug."

Pelosi, too, could understand why the Democrats in her caucus were genuinely fearful. After all, the rioters had repeatedly called out the Speaker by name. They had terrorized her staffers. And now the 117th Congress included a freshman Republican who had asserted that Nancy Pelosi should be executed for treason. The Speaker therefore ordered that a magnetometer be installed at the main entry of the House chamber. A few Republicans sought to circumnavigate the metal detectors; for each offense, $5,000 was deducted from the member's salary. One Republican, Andy Harris of Maryland, lit up the magnetometer as he walked through it. The offending object was a hand-gun inside Harris's jacket pocket.

One senior Democratic staffer summed up the fears toward the House GOP felt by many in her caucus in a memo to colleagues. "I have a Member on my Committee who brags about hiding guns in his wheelchair to sneak into the Capitol grounds on Jan. 6th," the staffer wrote, referring to freshman Congressman Madison Cawthorn of North Carolina. "I have another Member who assaulted a Black female officer who was operating the metal detectors off the House Floor so he could avert the no-guns-on-the-Floor policy. I have a Ranking Member who told a Capitol police officer, 'Good thing no one stopped me,' after she ran through the magnetometer to go to the Floor to vote. I have a Member with familial ties to the 3 Percenters [far-right militia] and quoting Hitler being right about the youths. The only reason MT Greene is not on Education & Labor is due to early outcry. With every passing day, it is becoming clear that these Members are not anomalies."

The Democratic staffer requested that Democratic members enforce Occupational Safety and Health Act workplace safety guidelines to protect Capitol employees from hazard. Her memo concluded: "The threat is real!"

LONG AFTER PATRICK MCHENRY AND STENY HOYER'S LATE-FEBRUARY CONVER-sation on the House floor, Democrats remained shaken and angered by the January 6 insurrection. A number of them, as well as their staffers, exhibited persistent symptoms of PTSD. Annie Kuster of New Hampshire, a sexual assault victim during her college years who had also been mugged while working on the Hill as a staffer four decades before, found after January 6 that she could fall asleep only under a weighted blanket. Even so, Kuster was now beset by night terrors, where she often screamed herself awake.

Kuster had been among the two dozen or so Democrats who were trapped in the House gallery and temporarily abandoned after the floor was evacuated. In the weeks to follow, many of them participated in therapy sessions via Zoom with a counselor. They called themselves the Gallery Group and in text chains checked in on one another. A few formed a "Go Deeper Group" to discuss more intimate details of their trauma. Others sought help on their own.

But what could not be helped—what the Democrats had absolutely no control over—was the cavalier dismissiveness with which their Republican colleagues had glided past the seismic travesty that was January 6. Thousands of Trump supporters had apparently become convinced that the election was stolen and attempted to overturn the election results by force. Democrats wondered: Would the mob have succeeded had the 1776-fevered Republican party of Marjorie Taylor Greene and Lauren Boebert been in charge of the House proceedings that day?

Jim McGovern, the chairman of the Rules Committee, had been elected to his third House term in 2000 when Al Gore won the popular vote but ultimately lost to George W. Bush by 537 votes in Florida and a 5–4 Supreme Court decision. "When Al Gore said, 'It's over,' we said the same thing—we went on with life," he would recall. "People were upset. But the idea that we would somehow plan an insurrection or a coup? No one even *thought* like that."

On the early evening of January 6, while sequestered with the other House members in the Longworth Building, McGovern was one of the vast majority of Democratic members who felt certain that what all of them had just been through would surely bring them together. That had been the case on September 11, when McGovern joined fellow Democrats and Republicans on the Capitol steps, locking arms as they all sang "God Bless America."

McGovern had spoken to one Republican member in the Longworth Building who told the Rules Committee chairman that his mind had been changed by the riot. He would be voting to uphold the election results. But by the time the vote had occurred, the Republican had changed his mind again. This member explained to McGovern, "I won't come back otherwise."

It was a sentiment Democrats had heard being voiced increasingly during the Trump years. In early 2020, Denver Riggleman, a GOP member from Virginia who was popular on both sides of the aisle, was gently chided by Democrat Sean Casten for bashing the Green New Deal as "radical." Riggleman replied that he was already skating on thin ice with Republican voters for having officiated a same-sex wedding the previous summer.

"Look, Sean, if I come out strong on climate change and gay marriage,"

Riggleman confided, "I *will* get a primary challenge. And you will *not* like the guy who beats me."

Riggleman was prescient. A few months after their conversation, he lost in the primary to Bob Good, an athletic director at Liberty University who had termed the coronavirus "a phony pandemic." Casten could therefore see that Riggleman had a point. It reminded him of something the Illinois Democrat had been told in early 2019 by the majority whip James Clyburn, shortly after Casten had defeated a senior GOP House leader, Peter Roskam.

"You probably think that the guy you just beat was a real right-winger," Clyburn had said to Casten. "And well, by the standards of the Republican Party in the mid-'90s when Roskam came in, he was. By the standards of today, he was one of the few left who hadn't gone off the edge."

Sean Casten had developed a spreadsheet that he shared with any Democrat who was interested. It tracked the votes every House Republican had cast that related to the 2020 election or its ugly aftermath—beginning with the 126 members who, in December 2020, had signed onto an amicus brief in support of a lawsuit by the Texas attorney general to overturn the election results in several contested states. After January 6, Casten added to the spreadsheet the names of the House Republicans who had voted to overturn the Arizona election results before the riot (121) and those who had objected to the Pennsylvania results following the riot (138).

Casten's vow was that he would no longer do business with *any* of those Republicans on his spreadsheet. He would, however, make an exception for a Republican who publicly acknowledged his or her mistake. The stringency of Casten's test was made evident in late February, when a couple of Republican bills were submitted for House consideration under suspension rules (in which a two-thirds majority is required for passage of a particular bill or resolution, and no amendments are permissible). This was one of the few remaining procedures in Congress that encouraged bipartisanship: suspension bills were uniformly innocuous so that they could clear the two-thirds threshold and tended to be passed by voice vote rather than a roll call.

The two GOP bills in question were very much of this ilk. One would rename a Mississippi post office after a prisoner of war. Another would rename a South Carolina post office after Joseph Rainey, the first Black congressman in American history. Democrats, including James Clyburn of South Carolina, were particularly eager to honor Rainey with a perfunctory voice vote. But Sean Casten demanded that each vote be recorded, so that Republicans would see that at least some Democrats intended to hold them accountable for their past sins. Casten's move struck several of his fellow Democrats as excessive.

A Democratic colleague of Casten's, Brad Schneider of Illinois, held to a more lenient principle, which his staff dubbed the "Schneider Standard." If a Republican who had voted to overturn the election conveyed to Schneider, either directly or via staff, that he or she accepted the election results, regarded Biden as lawfully elected and would cease claiming otherwise, they could continue to work together.

One such semi-reformed Republican, Schneider concluded, was Jody Hice of Georgia. Hice remained an ardent defender of Trump, had claimed after November 3 that the election had been stolen, and had voted to decertify the results on the late evening of January 6. Since then, however, Hice's language seemed more restrained. The Georgia Republican indicated through his staff to Schneider's staff that he acknowledged Biden as the legitimately elected president. That was enough for Schneider to partner with Hice on a bipartisan bill to monitor potentially cancer-causing ethylene oxide emissions. They announced the measure on May 28, 2021.

The next day, a CNN reporter happened to corner Schneider's Republican cosponsor and ask him if he still believed Trump won Georgia. Replied Jody Hice, who would soon after announce his candidacy for Georgia secretary of state: "I believe if there was a fair election, it would be a different outcome. Absolutely."

Rules Committee chairman Jim McGovern, for his part, had always felt that the minority deserved an airing of its views. After January 6, he modified his stance. When one of Lauren Boebert's flurry of nonsensical amendments turned out to be reasonable, McGovern refused to let it go to the House floor for consideration. A Republican member of the committee asked why.

As McGovern would recall it, his response was, "We have a new rule in the Rules Committee. If you're batshit crazy, you're not getting an amendment. I'm sorry. We're not doing this. We're not doing this. I'm not going down that road. I'm not going to be part of any effort to legitimize people who are fucking lunatics."

Even the Democrats most inclined to bipartisanship—the two dozen or so members of the Problem Solvers Caucus—could not simply overlook the vote to decertify the 2020 election results as if it were a mere spasm of political calculation. Four of the Republican members of the Problem Solvers Caucus were among the 138 who had objected to the election results. At a caucus meeting in February, two moderate Democrats—Stephanie Murphy of Florida and Abigail Spanberger of Virginia—argued that the four should be expelled from the group.

The Republican leader of the caucus, Tom Reed of New York, had voted to certify the results but nonetheless took umbrage on behalf of the four who had not. "Well," Reed said, "if you're going to start judging people for their votes, then I don't see how we can commit to our mission of working in a bipartisan way. I mean, *you* take votes I don't agree with. I don't try to cancel *you*."

Ultimately, Murphy took the view that the people of Florida had elected her to work on their behalf. Ceasing to do business with two-thirds of the Republicans, even for so unconscionable a vote as the one they took on January 6, would make it impossible for her to do right by her voters.

Still, Stephanie Murphy would look back on that conference call with the Problem Solvers "as maybe when the gaslighting begins. With the shaming. That use of the word: 'You're just trying to *cancel* us.' The gaslighting began there."

THE GASLIGHTING AND SHAMING COMMITTED BY REPUBLICANS AGAINST Democrats was, in effect, an act of self-absolution. Whatever sin had been committed by their party's leader to stoke an insurrection, whatever their complicity and cowardice, could and should be forgiven for a simple reason: the other side was worse. Apocalyptically worse.

Behind closed doors in caucus meetings, Democrats sometimes characterized their counterparts as wrongheaded, greedy, craven, callous, and spineless. These were all character flaws for which rehabilitation was not necessarily out of the question.

What Stephanie Murphy did not know was how Republicans described even moderate Democrats like her when no one else was listening. In the February 3 conference to discuss whether to remove Liz Cheney, it was not just Marjorie Taylor Greene saying the quiet part out loud about how Democrats were devious socialists bent on destroying the American way of life. It was not just Louie Gohmert with his addled-uncle vibe saying to his colleagues, "I mean, we're facing real evil here."

It was also Burgess Owens, the Utah freshman who was one of the House GOP's two Black members, who said of Democrats, "They love mobs. They love to rev up hate. They love to destroy people without due process."

And, too, it was Mario Díaz-Balart, the ten-term congressman from Florida, who half-jokingly compared his fellow Republicans in the room to the Democrats somewhere outside: "*These* are patriotic Americans. *Those* are Commies."

QAnon and the Capitol riot

Chapter Ten

ARC OF THE CRAZY

Among the Democrats who had been temporarily stranded in the House gallery on the afternoon of January 6 was Tom Malinowski, a Jewish Polish émigré and former assistant secretary of state for democracy, human rights, and labor during the Obama administration. As a candidate in 2018 to represent New Jersey's Seventh Congressional District, Malinowski frequently criticized the Republican incumbent for belonging to a party that indulged right-wing violent extremists. Though Malinowski could not have predicted that a mob of the same ideological stripe would storm the Capitol, he was all too familiar with one of the factors that animated some of the rioters. It was the belief in QAnon, a conspiracy theory that was rooted in the view that Democrats like Malinowski were irredeemably evil and bent on destroying America. That opinion was rapidly becoming mainstreamed within the Republican Party.

In the spring of 2018, while Malinowski was campaigning for his seat, one of his constituents quietly launched a crowdfunded website called QMap .pub. The site dedicated itself to publishing the so-called "Q drops" that had begun springing up on the internet a few months earlier, purportedly written by a military intelligence officer who claimed that President Trump was heroically doing battle against a cabal of globalist pedophiles. As Bloomberg reporters William Turton and Joshua Brustein later reported, QMap.pub would become the most popular aggregator of Q drops on the internet, attracting up to 10 million visitors every month.

What made QMap.pub especially remarkable, however, was the website's founder: a forty-one-year-old Citigroup senior vice president named Jason Gelinas, who lived in the affluent New Jersey suburb of Berkeley Heights in Malinowski's district. According to the Bloomberg reporters, the radicalization of Gelinas occurred in the fall of 2016, as he began to burrow into the dark recesses of the internet, which at the time buzzed with rumors spurred by the recently hacked emails of Hillary Clinton's campaign chairman, John Podesta. In the warped interpretation of those leaked emails—as well as wild speculation generated by FBI Director James Comey's reopening of the Clinton email server federal investigation in late October—right-wing influencers like Mike Cernovich, Jack Posobiec, *Infowars* host Alex Jones, and incoming Trump national security adviser Michael Flynn proceeded to allege that the Democratic presidential candidate was a pedophile. Soon, a conspiracy theory began to take shape. It asserted that a Clinton fundraiser held at a popular Northwest DC pizzeria called Comet Ping Pong had, in reality, served as a front for sexual violence committed by Democrats against children imprisoned in the pizzeria's basement.

The Pizzagate conspiracy theory rested on preposterous assumptions— among them the belief that a casual mention in one Podesta email of "cheese pizza" was code for child pornography. But Pizzagate did not arise out of a vacuum. The vilification of Democrats had been the daily bread of conservative talk radio for literally decades. For just as long, the unchecked (and unproven) criminality of the Clintons had been a casually accepted fantasy in broader GOP circles. That the chant "Lock her up" would become a staple of Trump rallies in 2016—including the Republican convention in which he was formally chosen as the party's nominee—reflected Hillary Clinton's almost mythological status on the right as a demon figure. Meanwhile, the only major politician in recent times to be investigated by the Department of Justice for allegedly abusing children was a Republican, former House Speaker Dennis Hastert, who in 2016 pleaded guilty to a lesser offense and was described by the judge who sentenced him as a "serial child molester."

On December 4, 2016, a heavily armed, conspiracy-crazed twenty-eight-year-old man entered Comet Ping Pong and began frantically searching for the nonexistent torture dungeon. He was arrested on the scene before anyone was shot. Three days later, a second man phoned Besta Pizza, a few doors away from Comet, and threatened to shoot everyone inside. That man was soon arrested as well.

But the believers would not let Pizzagate die. They alleged that the various wood- and metalworking artisans who were close to Comet's owner had built elaborate tunnels leading to other torture sites in the nation's capital. They alleged that one such site was a gallery owned by the Comet restaurateur, and that the loft inside it functioned as a "kill room." They discovered that one of the artisans had posted on Instagram a photo of a small homemade table, which they alleged was in fact a child's coffin. Another artisan had a young daughter whose photograph the believers circulated, alleging that the father was abusing her. Turning their attention to a local punk band, Heavy Breathing, that sometimes performed in the pizzeria's ping-pong room, they alleged that the band's female lead vocalist was a baby killer and satan worshipper.

From the end of 2016 through nearly all of 2017—and then again in 2020, as the political cycle gave rise to new fevers—dozens of the aforementioned associates of the pizzeria were repeatedly harassed and threatened by phone and email. Their whereabouts were published online. In the case of one former Comet employee, a self-styled "citizen investigator" showed up to his new place of business with a video camera in hopes of documenting new horrors. Other pizzeria workers left the DC area for good, fearing for their safety.

And in November 2017, an aspiring Facebook influencer named Marjorie Taylor Greene called her followers' attention to a captivating new conspiracy website—one claiming, she wrote, "that John Podesta is a pedophile and pizza gate is real."

BY THE TIME THAT GREENE HAD POSTED HER SENDUP OF PIZZAGATE, CON-spirators had already begun to focus their paranoia on the first few dozen Q drops to make their appearance on the internet—tantalizingly elliptical, though replete with conservative catnip: references to sex trafficking, Antifa, George Soros, and a complicit "mockingbird" media. A year later, in October 2018, a conspiracy-crazed antisemite killed eleven worshippers in a Pittsburgh synagogue.

A month after the synagogue massacre, Tom Malinowski was elected and vowed to himself that he would do whatever a congressman could to curb violent extremism.

In the fall of 2020, the first-term New Jersey Democrat submitted a House resolution condemning the QAnon conspiracy theory. Determined that the resolution be bipartisan, Malinowski made inquiries across the aisle. He found takers in two Republicans who appreciated the threat posed by domestic terrorists: Denver Riggleman, a former air force intelligence officer, and Brian Fitzpatrick, a former FBI special agent.

Malinowski also signed on Adam Kinzinger as a cosponsor. The former air force fighter pilot had watched the spread of QAnon with worry but also a certain chagrin. Looking back on it, Kinzinger found himself wishing that he and other reality-based Republicans had pushed back more forcefully when an earlier conspiracy theory, known as Jade Helm, first reared its delusional head.

In late March 2015—four years into Kinzinger's congressional career, three months before Donald Trump had announced his candidacy for president—the internet began to throb with wild rumors about a military operation on U.S. soil. The exercise, called Operation Jade Helm, was in fact real. It was a counterinsurgency drill intended to prepare elite troops for evolving forms of adversity. Unusually broad, Jade Helm would take place between mid-July and mid-September 2015, involving four branches of the U.S. military, and would ultimately encompass seven Southwestern states because of each one's unique terrain. Though the details of such operations are of course secret, the fact that the exercises exist is not. And so when someone in the media—no one remembers who—first asked for more information about Jade Helm, U.S. Army officials nonchalantly handed over a PowerPoint presentation.

The twelve pages of slides included a map of the seven participating states, each of which was labeled either "hostile," "permissive," or "uncertain." The two designated "hostile" states happened to be the most conservative of the seven: Texas and Utah. It also happened that one of the exercises would be taking place in Bastrop County, Texas, within radio frequency range of the Austin-based conspiracy-mongering show *Infowars*, hosted by Alex Jones.

"Feds Preparing to Invade Texas, List State as 'Hostile'" screamed the

Infowars webpage headline. "I'm deep behind enemy lines, folks!" Jones yammered on his program. For weeks, he spoke about little else. Taken aback, in April the army dispatched a public affairs officer to Bastrop to quell matters.

But by then, many of the locals were already convinced that Jade Helm was a pretext for President Obama to enforce martial law in Texas, imprison dissenters, and confiscate all firearms. Egged on by Russian bots—including one internet post headlined "Jade Helm Death Squads Inserted into American Communities: Is It Just a Drill?"—the rural population descended into a kind of group madness. Ice cream trucks, it was said, were being utilized as mobile morgues. Recently closed Walmarts now served as internment camps. Military technology would engineer brutal rainstorms to weaken the state.

Adam Kinzinger understood how decent people could succumb to a conspiracy theory that, as he would say, "outperformed the brain's ability to defend against it." Two things about the Jade Helm episode greatly bothered him, however. The first was what undergirded the conservative hysteria: an unhinged loathing of a Democratic president (who happened to be Black) so bottomless that it transfigured him into a satanic dictator. Though Kinzinger often disagreed with Obama's policies, he never regarded him as a tyrant.

The other worrisome aspect of the Jade Helm saga was how the Republican governor of Texas, Greg Abbott, reacted to the delusional frenzy. Not once did Abbott state publicly, *The rumors are untrue—here are the facts.* Instead, the governor essentially legitimized the unhinged theory by dispatching the Texas State Guard to Bastrop to "monitor" the operation.

Because Operation Jade Helm was ultimately completed without further incident, one could say that Abbott's gambit was an elegant one, a matador flicking his cape as the madness barreled past. But the governor had done nothing whatsoever to disabuse his fellow Texans of their delusions. Instead, the bull lived to charge again, with deadly consequences.

THE RESISTANCE TO TOM MALINOWSKI'S RESOLUTION CONDEMNING QANON was minor but still telling. While running for reelection in his district, Malinowski learned from a constituent that she had been polled by a telephone caller and that one of the questions was "Would you be more or less likely to vote for Tom Malinowski if you learned that he had participated in a child sex trafficking ring?"

Malinowski came to believe that the poll had been commissioned by the NRCC, especially after the GOP's official fundraising group released an ad in his district claiming erroneously that while previously serving as a lobbyist for Human Rights Watch, he had personally opposed a national sex-offender registry—and, as the ad put it, "tried to make it easier for predators to hide in the shadows." Q himself linked to the NRCC ad in a Q drop. Malinowski began to receive death threats.

On October 2, 2016, the resolution condemning QAnon went to the House floor for debate. It was expected to pass easily. Republican leaders, however, pressed for a voice vote. As Malinowski would recall, "They didn't want to be put on the spot with a roll call, since unfortunately QAnon represents a portion of their base."

Democrats insisted that the vote be recorded. As anticipated, a large majority of the Republican conference sided with the resolution, but eighteen of them did not. Nearly all of those who voted no were from the conservative South, where Jade Helm anxieties had also taken root three years earlier.

As the roll call proceeded, Malinowski walked across the House floor in search of GOP congressman Tom Emmer, the NRCC chairman, whom he had never met before. Though usually placid, Malinowski could not contain his temper. To Emmer he said, loudly enough for other members to notice, "Do you know that one of your ads got picked up by QAnon, which attacked me, and I'm getting death threats as a result of it?"

Emmer reared back defensively. "I don't even know what QAnon is," he insisted.

That same day, a GOP congressional nominee to whom Emmer had donated NRCC funds, onetime QAnon believer Marjorie Taylor Greene, denounced Malinowski's resolution. On Facebook, the Georgian took dead aim at the Republican Conference she would soon be a part of.

She declared, "Our Congress, which is funded by American taxpayers' hard-earned dollars, passed a resolution today condemning QAnon and the 'conspiracy theories that it promotes'—but yet they do not pass a resolution specifically naming domestic terrorist groups Antifa and BLM. Now, I think that should give every single American serious concern. And I say this because 146 Republicans voted for this resolution today."

Tom Malinowski had endured his QAnon problem. Now the problem belonged to Tom Emmer's party.

Representative Adam Kinzinger

Chapter Eleven

INCITEMENT

I n March 2020, I attended the sentencing hearing of a fifty-five-year-old Utah resident and health-insurance salesman named Scott Brian Haven. It was a chilly late-winter afternoon in Salt Lake City. There were no other reporters or spectators in the federal courtroom, except for a few family members and church friends of the defendant and his wife.

Haven wore a shirt and tie, as well as a hooded black jacket. He was pale and his eyes were puffy. Over and over, he muttered tearfully: "This wasn't me. This wasn't me. This wasn't me."

Haven was a Mormon who served meals to the homeless in downtown Salt Lake. He had also gone through two divorces and was struggling to make ends meet, a precarious financial condition that he blamed on Obama and the Affordable Care Act.

Haven loved President Trump. More than that: as a conservative white male, he identified with Trump's sense of persecution. The conviction that the left was bent on destroying patriotic Americans such as Trump and himself was amplified on the talk-radio shows of Rush Limbaugh and Sean Hannity, both of which Haven listened to religiously. Together these elements brought out in Haven a markedly darker side, one he directed at Democrats, who he saw as the enemy.

From March 2017 until his arrest in June 2019, Haven had placed 3,950 calls to the U.S. Capitol switchboard. All of them were made to House and Senate Democrats. His three principal targets were Senator Dick Durbin, Congresswoman Maxine Waters, and House Judiciary Committee Chairman

Jerrold Nadler. The three Democrats were not randomly selected by Haven. He focused his attention on them because Limbaugh and Hannity had themselves done so—even going so far as to supply their Washington office numbers while on the air. Haven dutifully jotted them down. Then he began calling, sharing sentiments like the following:

"Tell the son of a bitch we are coming to hang the fucker!"

"I will be the first to blow their fucking heads off—that's not a threat, that's a promise."

"I am going to take up my Second Amendment right, and shoot you liberals in the head, you pussy, fuck you!"

The law-enforcement community exhibited considerable patience toward Haven. In June 2018, a female Capitol police special agent called Haven to issue a warning. After referring to the federal agent as a "cunt" several times, Haven then yelled, "Come arrest me! I would like to fucking beat the shit out of you just for trying!"

Two months later, it was an FBI special agent who called Haven. What Haven told the agent was something that he had heard repeatedly from Rush Limbaugh and other conservative influencers, such that he could recite it as gospel: "Conservatives don't commit violent acts against political opponents," Haven informed the agent. "That type of behavior is conducted by people on the left."

He then suggested that the FBI would be better off "investigating groups like Black Lives Matter instead of bothering me," and hung up.

Finally, in November 2018, a Utah-based FBI agent paid Haven a visit at home. The insurance salesman was not especially contrite at first. He said that the Democrats were unfair to President Trump, that they were also trying to steal congressional and statewide elections in Georgia and Arizona. Though Haven insisted that his calls were nothing more than "just meaningless threats that were made out of frustration," he agreed not to make them anymore.

For all of two months, Haven was true to his word. But in 2019, the dam broke. In May, the month before his arrest, Haven placed 850 calls, an average of more than 27 per day. On May 23, he said to a staffer in Jerry Nadler's office, "I'm at his office. I'm right behind him now. I'm going to shoot him in the head. I'm going to do it now. Are you ready?"

Haven was nonetheless stunned when federal agents arrived at his home on June 3, 2019, and placed him under arrest. He was charged with the federal crime of Interstate Transmissions of Threats to Injure and denied bail. Haven spent the next five months in a federal jail cell, at which point the judge decided that Haven had been brought low by the experience. Haven was granted home detention and forced to wear a GPS monitoring device on his ankle until his trial on March 4, 2020.

When U.S. District Court Judge Clark Waddoups asked the defendant if he wished to say anything before being sentenced, Haven stood and fumbled with a piece of paper. "I realized I made a mistake when I got caught up in hate that got stirred up when I listened to the radio," Haven said in a trembling voice. It had never occurred to him, he said, that there might be more to Nadler than the rancid image presented by the conservative media. During his time behind bars, Haven had learned that the Democratic congressman was in fact a father and grandfather, just like Haven was.

"There's so much more to know about people than we hear about in the news," he marveled, while apologizing to Nadler and his staff.

Though Haven did not in any way disavow his admiration for Trump and his contempt for liberalism and the media, he confessed to Judge Waddoups that such beliefs had become a toxic force in his life. He no longer listened to the news. He had disengaged from politics altogether. "I cannot live a peaceful life when I'm involved," he admitted.

Judge Waddoups sentenced the defendant to time already served, followed by three years of supervised release. He also held Haven to a rather unusual condition: he could not listen to talk radio again.

"In your case," said the judge with careful understatement, "it sets off a level of anger that's not healthy."

"THIS PARTY HAS LOST ITS DAMN MIND," ADAM KINZINGER HAD SAID DURING the February 3 Republican Conference to judge whether Liz Cheney was fit to be one of their leaders. By that, he meant not only its elected officials but also members of his family.

"Oh my God, what a *disappointment* you are to us and to *God*!" several of them jointly wrote to him on January 8, two days after Kinzinger had de-nounced Trump's incitement of the insurrection. The letter's closing senti-ment was: "Oh, and by the way, we are calling for your removal from office!"

Kinzinger shared the letter with the media and said that his conservative Christian relatives had been "misled." This spurred them to send a second let-ter, on January 19, which Kinzinger did not disseminate: "*So* you are also say-ing that 75 million people and *all* but *10* GOP Representatives are 'being misled' as well?? Seriously Adam, really! You are the one 'being misled' (brain-washed) by the Democrats and the fake news media."

The two-page handwritten letter concluded with a reference to Speaker Nancy Pelosi: "Perhaps the witch/devil holding the gavel will invite you to her house for ice cream!"

Kinzinger knew where all this was coming from. As his relatives volun-teered in one of the letters, they lived on a steady diet of Fox News, Rush Limbaugh, and First Baptist Dallas evangelical minister Robert Jeffress—the last of whom told his followers that Obama's policies were "paving the way for the Antichrist" and that Trump was the most pro-Christianity president in history. There was no point engaging with them, from their parallel universe.

Still, Adam Kinzinger's estrangement from members of his family was hardly anomalous. Rather, it represented the greater sense of exile he was ex-periencing. Among the ten Republicans who had voted to impeach Trump, only Liz Cheney was more vilified—though for reasons he could not figure out, Trump was far more bent on destroying Cheney than Kinzinger. Was it because she was a woman? Or was it because Kinzinger had served his country as an air force special operations fighter pilot, the kind of certified patriot that Trump could only pretend to be?

He and Trump used to get along quite well. "Hey, you were great on TV," the president would invariably tell Kinzinger, who had heard from Trump White House officials that the president had for a time considered nominat-ing him to be secretary of the air force. And though it was evident to Kinzinger—an avowed fiscal conservative and military hawk—that Trump "didn't have a moral center," perhaps that could be seen as a good thing. Kinz-inger would remember thinking, *Maybe he can cut deals. This country needs*

maybe about four years of just cutting through some bullshit, getting some deals done,
like immigration spending, infrastructure, all that.

But by 2020, it had become evident to Kinzinger that Trump lacked not
only a moral center but also deal-cutting expertise. That shortcoming rankled
Kinzinger, who had won his seat in 2010 on the Tea Party wave. During the
Obama administration, Kinzinger's Republicans became the Party of No. No
to Obamacare. No to deficits. No to raising the debt ceiling. Six years of that,
and then the Trump administration and . . . No replacement of Obamacare.
No infrastructure package. Only waging culture wars and claiming that the
president was a victim of a partisan witch hunt.

"The broader concern," he would lament, "is that nobody, including myself to be honest, knows any different than just being the opposition to everything. Because since I've been in politics, and I'm one of the older guys now,
that's all we've done. There's never been real deal-cutting."

But in the wake of the Capitol riot, Kinzinger's concern about the health
of his party extended well beyond its legislative failings. "The biggest danger
right now," he would say in late January 2021, "is that we've become a party
that dabbles—not just dabbles: we *traffic* in conspiracies. And we traffic
in lies."

Kinzinger had been among the ten House Republicans to vote to impeach
the president—and then, less than a month later, among the eleven in the
GOP Conference to vote to strip Marjorie Taylor Greene of her committee
assignments. She continued to present a conundrum for him and other Republicans. Do they call out Greene's lies one by one and risk giving her the
attention she craved? Or do they ignore her and run the risk that her lies might
become the kudzu that swallows up the party's soul?

Kinzinger had tried both approaches. Neither seemed entirely effective.
The committeeless Georgia freshman lived all day on social media, while
Kinzinger had professional responsibilities to attend to.

For placing him and other Republicans in this quandary, Kinzinger
blamed Kevin McCarthy. The minority leader had gone silent while Greene
and her ilk conflated the insurrection and the summer riots of 2020. Soon,
McCarthy, too, would be speaking of the two separate events in the same
breath. Kinzinger had publicly condemned the lootings and burnings that

accompanied some Black Lives Matter protests that year. Still, he said, "You could have burned down the entire city of Minneapolis and it wouldn't threaten the very foundations of democracy like this did."

Meanwhile, Kinzinger couldn't help but notice that McCarthy had defended Greene's standing in the February 3, 2021, Republican Conference with greater vigor than he had defended Liz Cheney. Of course, Trump despised Cheney and adored Greene. McCarthy in turn believed Trump's support was essential to win back the House majority.

But, Kinzinger wondered, what kind of majority would it be, with Greene and her friends in the Freedom Caucus—which Kinzinger derisively referred to as the Freedom Club—commanding all the power? This, he believed, was a problem to address *now*, while they were in a minority and frankly had nothing else constructive to do. McCarthy should be marginalizing the nuts, not indulging them. There would be no time to do so once the House Republicans became the governing party in January 2023.

Kinzinger knew he lacked any leverage. Many of his like-minded friends in the Republican Conference—Will Hurd of Texas, Martha Roby of Alabama—had seen this trend coming and headed for the exits. Others, perhaps even the majority in the conference, sympathized with Kinzinger's viewpoint but did not want to risk losing their jobs by saying so. As for McCarthy, he had left a message for Kinzinger following the minority leader's appeasement journey to Mar-a-Lago in late January.

But Kinzinger had not returned the call. He already knew where the leader stood: beside a former president who continued to say that victory had been stolen from him.

"ENOUGH LIES," PETER MEIJER WROTE ON TWITTER IN RESPONSE TO A FEBRU-ary 9 succession of tweets by Marjorie Taylor Greene suggesting that it was Antifa rather than Trump supporters who attacked the Capitol on January 6.

During freshman orientation just after the November 2020 election, the thirty-two-year-old Michigander had recorded an introductory video of himself. In it, Meijer—who had served in Iraq as an army reserve intelligence specialist, and later in Afghanistan as a conflict analyst for a nongovernmental organization—described himself as skilled in putting things back together. He was referring at the time to Washington's fractious ecosystem.

But now Meijer encountered a brokenness that he was almost certainly incapable of fixing. It was his own party, which continued to embrace Trump and to lie on the ex-president's behalf.

"I feel like I'm living in an alternate reality," Meijer told his colleagues during the February 3 conference to discuss Liz Cheney. He, Cheney, and Kinzinger—the three most vocal Republicans in the House to insist that the party's future must lead away from Trump, not toward him—were now on a kind of island, subjected to ridicule and even death threats. An anonymous caller had managed to obtain Meijer's cell phone number. The caller had said to the freshman, "We're going to have a thousand people at your home this weekend."

The former conflict analyst kept the man on the phone for twenty minutes, eventually cooling him down. Of course, the ones for Meijer to worry about were the individuals who did not telegraph their intentions.

Meijer had stepped out of the four-hour Cheney conference on February 3 because he had a Zoom town hall already on the schedule. It was the freshman's third such encounter with his constituents since being elected, and the first since he had voted to impeach Trump.

"We elected you to be loyal to Donald Trump," one of his constituents said angrily.

No, Meijer politely but firmly disagreed. He had pledged to uphold conservative values and work within the institution, in the manner of President Gerald Ford, who, before becoming Richard Nixon's vice president and then succeeding Nixon, had held Meijer's seat in Michigan's Fifth Congressional District from 1949 through 1973. Never once had Meijer promised to be Trump's unflagging ally.

By the end of the town hall, some of Meijer's constituents said that although they still disagreed with his decision, they respected his forthrightness. Whether that was enough to ensure that he wouldn't be killed, Peter Meijer had no idea.

"We need to always remember the two lies that, if they hadn't been told over and over, we wouldn't have had the insurrection," Meijer frequently told his constituents. "Lie One: November 3 was a landslide victory for Donald Trump that was stolen. And Lie Two: if November 3 was the steal, then January 6 would be the day for the steal to be stopped." He would then proceed to trot out the facts, the logic, the statutes, the Constitution.

But some of them, Meijer could plainly see, were unreachable. They would say, "Yes, but isn't it curious . . ." Or "Well, there's just things we don't know . . ." Or "But I saw on Facebook where . . ." Several of his Michigan constituents had traveled to Washington for the Trump rally on January 6. He didn't know if any of them had forced their way into the Capitol.

The freshman was more than ready to get past all this. He hadn't run for office so that he could be spending so much of his time helping fellow Republicans ferret out truth from fantasy. The Meijer family owned more than two hundred grocery stores across the Midwest. Their wealth exceeded $7 billion, according to *Forbes*. Peter Meijer didn't need this job, or any other job.

Still, he wanted to influence the national debate, particularly on foreign policy. His experiences in Iraq had caused him to regard that war as a disaster, which put him at odds with Cheney and his new friend Kinzinger, who were both far more inclined to support military action. It was the kind of debate Republicans should be having, instead of fighting over Trump and QAnon.

Meijer deeply admired Liz Cheney's fortitude. The difference between her and McCarthy was, in his view, the difference between true leadership and management. And yet Meijer did not wish to find himself painted into the corner where Cheney and Kinzinger now resided. He did not want to be defined by Trump.

But perhaps it was already too late for Peter Meijer and the other nine impeachers. As he acknowledged to his colleagues during the February 3 conference, "I'm getting raked over the coals. And I probably won't be back here in two years."

TWO WEEKS AFTER MEIJER UTTERED THOSE WORDS, RUSH LIMBAUGH DIED AT the age of seventy, after a long battle with cancer.

In the manner of a fallen president, the godfather of conservative radio was ferried from his mansion in Palm Beach to an airstrip where a private plane flew his body to St. Louis, Missouri, Limbaugh's native state. There, a horse-drawn carriage conveyed him to the chapel at Bellefontaine Cemetery, to the soundtrack of "The Battle Hymn of the Republic," a Limbaugh favorite. Rather unlike the bombastic host who called himself "El Rushbo," the affair was attended only by family and not disclosed to his admirers until several days after the fact.

News of Limbaugh's death on February 17 prompted cascades of mournful veneration from his conservative devotees. "Rush Limbaugh was a legend in the conservative movement and an American hero," Paul Gosar wrote on Twitter that afternoon. The following day, Gosar and forty-three other House Republicans cosponsored a resolution "commending Rush Limbaugh for inspiring millions of radio listeners and for his devotion to our country." H. Res. 133 was referred to the House Committee on Oversight and Reform—where, given that the committee was controlled by Democrats, the legislation instantly joined Limbaugh in death.

A week later, on February 25, Ralph Norman of South Carolina requested on the House floor "to allow a 30-second moment of silence for the passing of Rush Limbaugh, one of the greatest hosts ever." Norman's request was denied.

Limbaugh's fervent conservative admirers were hardly wrong, however. As Peter Meijer knew from interactions with his constituents, as Adam Kinzinger knew from his own family, and as Judge Clark Waddoups had noted in the Utah federal court a year before Limbaugh's death, the radio host's influence on the Brian Scott Havens of the world was impossible to overstate.

In his last months, El Rushbo—to whom President Trump had previously awarded the nation's highest civilian honor, the Presidential Medal of Freedom—had one final contribution to make to his country. On December 16, 2020, the radio host shared with his 27 million listeners a personal theory about how the upcoming January 6 certification vote could play out. Built on misguided assumptions (such as that both Georgia Senate runoff races would be won by the Republicans) and a dubious interpretation of constitutional law, Limbaugh offered up a complicated scenario in which the Senate and House separately picked a Republican president and vice president. After that occurred, Limbaugh posited, Speaker Pelosi would object, the office of the presidency would remain vacant past January 20, and ultimately the conservative Supreme Court would rule in Trump's favor and return him to power.

"A long shot," Limbaugh conceded. Still, he said, it was only fair "to take down Biden," because Biden had tried to do the same to Trump earlier, via some grand conspiracy in the Obama White House that Limbaugh had hallucinated for the purposes of this discussion.

"The American left is made up of a lot of people that hate this country," Limbaugh reminded his conservative listeners. "Hate is a very, very destructive frame of mind, it's a very destructive characteristic, and eventually it results in an implosion. You cannot survive on hatred. You cannot sustain a movement based on it."

This, he said, was why the "74 million plus and growing" Trump supporters were determined to march on Washington on January 6. "They want to take some kind of action to the left that, 'We're not buying this. You didn't win this thing fair and square. And we are not just going to be docile, like we've been in the past, and go away and wait till the next election.'"

As it turned out, Limbaugh was prescient. Hate could not sustain a movement without destructive consequences.

Still, Limbaugh did not quite see that as the lesson to be drawn from January 6. What took place at the Capitol, he told his audience the following afternoon during what would be his final month as a broadcaster, was nothing compared to the damage done to America by Black Lives Matter activists. "Republicans," he reminded listeners, for perhaps the thousandth and final time of his life, "do not join protest mobs. They do not loot and they don't riot." The "tiny minority" that did so at the Capitol, he said, were "undoubtedly including some Antifa Democrat-sponsored instigators."

But then, having just finished condemning destructive behavior as the exclusive province of the left, Limbaugh noted that "there's a lot of people calling for the end of violence. There's a lot of conservatives, social media, who say that any violence or aggression at all is unacceptable, regardless of the circumstances." He added, "I'm glad Sam Adams, Thomas Paine—the original Tea Party guys, the men at Lexington and Concord—didn't feel that way."

A day after having spoken of the Capitol riot and the American Revolution in the same breath, Rush Limbaugh on January 8 had a new thought about what had occurred two days earlier. "We got set up again," he declared. Cryptically, he added, "They knew we were coming. And they had a little surprise plan."

It was Rush Limbaugh's final tour de force of zigzagging logic. *Time to stop being docile! Only the left believes in violence! Thank God America's founding patriots believed in violence! The January 6 patriots were set up by the violent left!*

He had said it all before, and so had Brian Scott Haven, and so would others whose minds had been shaped by Rush Limbaugh's conspiratorial depiction of America. In this manner, he would live on.

"White power" gesture at Trump rally

Chapter Twelve

"A THOUSAND POUNDS OF RUBBISH"

I n the weeks after his Hail Mary attempt on January 6 to overturn the election results in Arizona failed, Paul Gosar seemed more inclined to take a victory lap.

On January 23, Gosar returned to Arizona to speak to the Arizona Republican Party's state committee—a group that until fairly recently had been composed of pragmatic, pro-business Republican grandees in the mold of Senator John McCain. But complacency had overcome the state GOP establishment, until one day they found themselves pushed aside by right-wing activists who got their news from *Infowars*. Their elected state chair, Kelli Ward, set her belief system by whatever it was that Donald Trump said recently. Ward was Paul Gosar's chief in-state ally in the Stop the Steal movement that had helped succeed in convincing most Arizona Republicans that the 2020 election had been fraudulent.

Among the activities on this day's agenda was to censure McCain's widow, Cindy, for her endorsement of Biden over Trump. The committee would also censure Arizona's former senator, Jeff Flake, for being a Trump antagonist and a "globalist." They would go on to censure Arizona's current governor, Doug Ducey, for having imposed statewide lockdowns and mask mandates at the height of the COVID pandemic.

This same group rose to shower Gosar with raucous applause as he took the stage. Manifestly among friends, the congressman then proceeded to show that he had made just the right enemies. He read aloud a letter penned by a prominent Arizona Republican, which concluded: "You are an embarrassment to Arizona. For the good of the state and the Republican Party, you should apologize to the American people, resign, and accept punishment for your acts of sedition."

After the boos died down, Gosar then reminded them of his, and their, innocence. Sedition? They hadn't advocated sedition, he said. They merely wanted "transparency in an election." Omitting any mention of his previous claims that "Biden and his thugs" were trying to steal Trump's certain victory, Gosar instead recited the familiar litany of conspiratorial puzzle pieces: corrupt Dominion machines, potentially hundreds of thousands of ballots altered, intransigent Democratic officials, a recount mysteriously abandoned. What reasonable person could deny that it all seemed "interesting"? That it warranted, as he put it, at least "a little suspicion"?

Something "interesting" was indeed happening in Arizona, something that merited concern rather than suspicion for the party. Trump had lost the state, albeit narrowly. Both Senate seats were now held by Democrats. Suburban communities in Phoenix and Tucson that were once reliably Republican were now less so. During the Trump era, the once-red state of Arizona was now, if not purple, then what state pollster Mike Noble would describe as "magenta, the lightest shade of red." And to make things worse for the state GOP, from the day of the Capitol riot to the day after the Arizona GOP issued its censures, 9,290 Arizona voters had switched their party registration from Republican to something else.

In short, the state Republican Party was hemorrhaging voters. Perhaps not in Paul Gosar's blood-red Fourth Congressional District—though even in that largely rural area, where any national GOP office-seeker would require a weighty turnout to compensate for the state's recoiling suburban electorate, there loomed a danger. As Arizona data analyst Garrett Archer would say of Gosar's district, "For a district that's so vote-rich for Republicans, to keep saying that elections are rigged could prove detrimental there."

It was not that Paul Gosar lacked the capacity for this sort of strategic awareness. It was that he went by a different calculus. Gosar was safe in his district. He was never going to run for president or governor. He had once considered running for Senate—or rather, being installed: when McCain fell ill from cancer, in December 2017, Gosar's chief of staff, Tom Van Flein, texted an associate of Governor Ducey to convey that "Gosar is interested in the Mc-Cain seat and wants to talk with your boss." (By way of reply, Ducey's team leaked Van Flein's text to the *Arizona Republic*.) But Gosar had come to recognize that the hard-right, Trump-centric rural populist brand he had built was anathema to many voters across the state.

That brand was, however, in perfect alignment with the tens of millions of American conservatives who remained faithful to Trump's MAGA creed. A politician with realistic electoral ambitions could prosper from such a base. And, as Gosar had come to learn, the best way to do so was to offend the other side—and then to be offended at their offense.

So it was that Gosar happily accepted an invitation to appear in Orlando, Florida, at the America First (AFPAC) convention on February 26, 2021. The AFPAC gathering billed itself as the far-right counterprogramming to the far more famous CPAC convention also taking place in Orlando that weekend. Outflanking CPAC to the right had become a difficult feat to accomplish, given that this year's CPAC convention featured a golden-calf bust of Trump, and of course the ex-president himself, whose kickoff address that day would reprise his perennial riffs on rapists crossing the border and windmills befouling the skyline.

Numerous Republican members of Congress had skipped a vote on the $1.9 trillion COVID relief bill to fly to Orlando for the weekend. That included Gosar, who claimed, in a letter to the House clerk requesting that another member cast a proxy vote for him, that he could not "physically attend proceedings in the House chamber due to the ongoing public health emergency."

Nearly every 2024 Republican presidential hopeful appeared at CPAC. None did so at AFPAC. The reason was simple: the organization, consisting of far-right young white men who called themselves Groypers, was unabashedly dedicated to the promotion of white supremacy. Its founder, twenty-two-year-old Nicholas Fuentes, delighted in publicly espousing racist musings, such as that Blacks were better off during the Jim Crow era than today and that "the math doesn't seem to add up" on the Jewish Holocaust death toll. Fuentes had attended the 2017 white supremacist rally in Charlottesville, proclaiming it "incredible." He was also at the Capitol on January 6, calling the insurrection "the most awe-inspiring and inspirational and incredible thing I have seen in my entire life."

All this was sufficient to repel every Republican officeholder from speaking at AFPAC, save one: Paul Gosar. He took the stage that evening just after his friend Steve King, the Iowa ex-congressman and white nationalist, explained to the crowd that the term "white nationalist" had once been an innocuous moniker until its meaning was perverted and aggressively pushed by the Jewish billionaire George Soros following a secret meeting of fellow liberals right after Trump's 2016 victory. "That tells you what they do to line up language against you," King warned his mostly white male acolytes, not needing to explain who he meant by "they."

Gosar introduced himself to the audience as "a dentist by trade but a patriot by heart." His remarks echoed King's conspiratorial utterances. "Shadowy elites and the deep state continue to collude with Big Tech and Big Media to further disenfranchise President Trump and you, the American patriots," he intoned. Domestically, he said, American voices were being canceled by "a climate of angry, violent communism." And from overseas came an additional conspiracy: "The China virus was weaponized against President Trump and against the American people—and the Americans will not forget."

As always, the congressman's oratory was unremarkable. At one point, he lost his place, finally saying, "It's kinda dark in here—as a dentist, I need bright lights." Only one thing mattered, however: Paul Gosar, a U.S. congressman, had lent the Groypers the imprimatur of his federal office by showing up.

The congressman saw absolutely nothing wrong with having done so. As he would later tell friends: *This is the new generation of conservatives. This is our future. Why not bring them into the conversation? Why exclude them? If you cancel them, then who gets canceled next?*

Still, the most radical act Paul Gosar would commit in the weeks and months after the Capitol riot was not his presence at a white-supremacist gathering. Instead, it was an act of omission—subtle but intentional, evident only to those paying close attention. Not once since Biden's inauguration on January 20 would Gosar refer to him as President Biden. Vocally and in writing, it was always Biden, Joe Biden or Mr. Biden.

When I brought this up to Tom Van Flein in July 2021, he said nothing at first. Then, with a slight smile, Gosar's chief of staff referred to a contro-versial revisiting of the Arizona electoral tally that was currently under way at the behest of the state's Trump-supporting Republicans.

Said Van Flein, "He's waiting for the Arizona audit. He has said, 'I will call him President Biden as soon as the audit confirms his Arizona victory. Until then, it's Mr. Biden.'"

OVER THE PAST CENTURY AND A HALF, THE AMERICAN POLITICAL SYSTEM had endured various versions of Paul Gosar. Until very recently, the traditional approach in Washington was to offer them a succession of opportunities to mature as legislators and constituent servants. If such opportunities provided by staffing guidance, committee assignments, foreign travel, and policy men-torship failed to domesticate them, then nature would take its course. Plum assignments would be withheld. Donations curtailed. Primary challengers supported.

The task of culling problematic members from a party's herd had become increasingly difficult by the time Gosar's designated mentee, Marjorie Taylor Greene, showed up to Washington. Shunning or even mildly disciplining a rogue with a social media following like Greene's would only entrench her status as a foe of the deep-state establishment. She could, and would, thrive without the slightest assistance from any political action committee other than the House Freedom Fund.

Gosar posed a different sort of challenge for the Republicans. He had grown somewhat as a legislator. His interest in parochial issues was made manifest in his committee work. His views were in keeping with his arch-conservative district.

Paul Gosar couldn't be reined in because Washington offered him few incentives that could compete with the approbation he received both from the state party back home and from the greater right-wing ecosystem of which Nick Fuentes and the white nationalist Groypers were a subset. Gosar was never going to be a party leader, a committee chair, or a Sunday talk-show regular.

Besides: Gosar believed the things he said, even the things that were lies.

He was not from Arizona. Then again, not many Arizonans were. The last contiguous state to be admitted into the Union, in 1912, Arizona at the time of its annexation was barely habitable, 295,000 square miles of mostly arid desert and scorching heat.

Gosar arrived in Flagstaff in 1985 at the age of twenty-seven. He was from small-town Wyoming: born in Rock Springs, where his father's Slovenian family were miners and butchers; then raised in Pinedale, where his mother's parents, from the Basque region of northern Spain, raised sheep. The closest big city was Salt Lake, four and a half hours away.

Paul Gosar was the eldest of ten children. Their father was a consulting geologist who spent a great deal of time traveling from one oil rig to the next. Their mother was a strict Catholic and devotee of the conservative antifeminist Phyllis Schlafly. When Paul, a tall and lanky star athlete in high school, indicated his desire to attend the University of Wyoming, his mother vetoed that option, saying that she disliked its party atmosphere. He instead attended Creighton University, and after that, its school of dentistry. Warned by his father that Wyoming's minerals industry was likely to undergo a crash, Paul Gosar set his sights elsewhere for starting a dental practice. He landed in Flagstaff.

The Arizona political climate that Dr. Gosar encountered in 1985 was mostly center-right, though threaded with intertwined strands of libertarianism and reactionary extremism. By way of illustrating the latter: two years after Gosar's arrival, Barry Goldwater's thirty-year career as a U.S. senator would end and Evan Mecham's governorship would begin, before terminating fifteen months later with the latter man's impeachment, following accusations that he had shifted campaign funds into his ailing car dealership. Mecham routinely made racist and homophobic comments and had canceled the state holiday honoring Martin Luther King Jr. But Mecham's bigotry, combined with his propensity for seeing malign forces organized against both him and the common man, enjoyed a stout constituency in Arizona.

After his removal from office in 1988, the Mecham subculture of aggrievement and paranoia sought out a new champion. Mecham's heir to the throne of populist demagoguery was Joe Arpaio, the Maricopa County sheriff, who achieved notoriety throughout the 1990s for his draconian penal methods, such as bringing back chain gangs and forcing inmates to sleep in tents. Later, though, Arpaio played to more nativist impulses. He repurposed himself as the state's foremost border sentinel and oversaw immigrant dragnets that bore an unmistakable whiff of racial profiling. He helped kick-start the Obama birth-certificate myth, continuing to push it even after Donald Trump abandoned it. The twenty-four-year career of "America's toughest sheriff" finally came to an end in 2017, with a federal judge's convicting Arpaio of contempt of court. Before he could be sentenced, Arpaio was pardoned by President Trump.

Meanwhile, Arizona was undergoing significant change. By 2020, the state's population had reached 7.3 million, almost exactly twice what it had been just three decades earlier. It had become one of the ten fastest-growing states in America. More than 25 percent of the new Arizonans were Californians who were drawn to the comparatively low taxes, to the Arizona State University system, and to the burgeoning aerospace and defense industries that were among John McCain's legacies. Some of the transplants took to what the resident conservatives referred to as "Arizona values."

But many of the new arrivals were seen by some as seeking to "Californicate" the red state. Arizona's population of adults aged sixty-five and older was the twelfth highest in the nation. Many of these, a longtime Arizona Republican official would say, "are retirees, folks who have traded in their suit pants for sweatpants. They're on the golf course or they're in hobby mode. They have more than enough time on their hands. They're digesting six to ten hours of Fox News a day. They're reading on Facebook. They're meeting with each other to talk about those headlines. And they're outraged that, 'Can you believe that the government is lying to us about this?'

"And," added this Arizona Republican, "they're bombarded by disinformation." By 2009, these elderly Arizonans were on the internet, growing livid over Obama's supposed government takeover of the U.S. health-care system, complete with death panels that would "pull the plug on grandma," according to what an actual Republican senator, Charles Grassley of Iowa, maintained.

Gosar himself came from this Arizona tradition of armchair conservative warriors. In the years before he decided to run for office, the Flagstaff millionaire dentist often sought to share his dim view of the federal government with his local congressman, Rick Renzi. As another Arizona Republican recalled, "Paul was the guy wearing the Hawaiian shirts and calling Renzi's office every day to complain about things."

Gosar's outspokenness had prompted the American Dental Association to elect him as their vice chairman on government affairs. It was 2008, and U.S. public health groups had begun pushing for a way to extend low-cost dental care to impoverished communities. Alaska had begun an experimental program of "dental health aide therapists," or vocationally trained health professionals who could perform rudimentary dental tasks in native villages. Dr. Gosar viewed this development (which had been successfully implemented in Australia and New Zealand) as both a threat to his profession and an affront to his conservative sensibilities. His fiery lobbying efforts caught the eye of the Alaska Dental Association's legal counsel, whose name was Tom Van Flein.

In the fall of 2009, Paul Gosar announced at a gathering of fellow dentists that he intended to run for Congress in Arizona's First Congressional District, where he resided. The ADA threw its considerable weight behind him. The "Tea Party" movement, with its overtones of fiscal alarmism and its undertones of white working-class grievance, had begun to roil the GOP establishment, making seemingly every race in 2010 up for grabs. Gosar declared himself a Tea Partier. He took to wearing a lapel pin featuring a shovel to signify the deep fiscal hole Washington had dug for all Americans. He also expressed the view that President Obama was not a U.S. citizen, to the horror of his more progressive siblings, though that belief was casually accepted among many if not most Tea Partiers. The right-wing Club for Growth deemed the millionaire dentist a lightweight and backed a different Republican.

But Gosar had an important new ally: Van Flein, who happened to be the legal counsel to Alaska governor Sarah Palin. In the 2010 election cycle, no Republican's endorsement mattered as much as Palin's. Since losing on the ticket with McCain to Obama and Biden in 2008, Palin had perfected the performance art of cultural vendetta, drawing crowds that no other conservative could eclipse.

Van Flein brokered a meeting between her and the Flagstaff dentist. Palin expressed admiration of Gosar's shovel lapel pin. She then blessed him with an endorsement—the only Arizona Republican to receive Palin's seal of approval. Gosar proceeded to swamp the GOP field. The Tea Party wave then carried him to Washington.

Even among a 2010 freshman class replete with amateur politicians, Gosar cut an awkward, untutored figure. He spoke in rambling, know-it-all sentences. Those who attempted to befriend him found him a bit odd. He worked out alone in the House gym at 10:30 in the evening, when the place was quiet. Then he took a quick shower, followed by four hours of sleep on a cot in his office on the tomb-like fifth floor of the Cannon Building. Mornings he sat at his desk munching on gluten-free waffles from the office toaster oven while poring over the voting recommendations of conservative groups like the Heritage Foundation.

The former dentist seemed fated for a short, forgettable second career. But political trajectories invariably have their fortuitous moments, and Paul Gosar benefited from two of them. The first occurred a month after his election, with the disclosure of Operation Fast and Furious. The botched operation, carried out by Arizona-based undercover agents with the Bureau of Alcohol, Tobacco, and Firearms, had intended to disseminate illegally purchased assault weapons among drug-runners in hopes of tracking their whereabouts to the Mexican cartels. Fast and Furious became public only after December 2010, when one of the straw purchases was used by a thief and Mexican national to kill a Border Patrol agent named Brian Terry. The assault rifle fired by the killer was one of hundreds that the ATF had lost track of.

To most observers, Fast and Furious was a tragic episode highlighting bureaucratic incompetence. In Gosar's eyes, however, something more mendacious than bungling was afoot. He befriended Terry's family, who lived in his district. The Arizona freshman began to frame Fast and Furious as Obama's Watergate, though perhaps worse. How far up did this scandal go? What was being covered up? Were the wayward straw purchases and the ensuing tragedy all a planned pretext for passing harsh gun-control legislation? Gosar darkly hinted that Obama administration officials were accessories to murder. He maintained that Attorney General Eric Holder had lied in his testimony to Congress and therefore should be impeached. Meanwhile, Gosar became a go-to source for conservative journalists for whom Fast and Furious resembled a Defcon-1 scandal.

None of this, however, was of political benefit to Gosar back home, in Arizona's First Congressional District, which had become notably less conservative after the new maps had been redrawn following the 2010 census. He therefore decided to try his luck in the newly created Fourth District, which was a right-winger's dreamscape. The only problem, besides the fact that Gosar did not live there, was that numerous other Republican hopefuls had the same idea—among them Paul Babeu, a telegenic conservative local sheriff and outspoken critic of undocumented immigrants. Babeu drew crowds everywhere he campaigned. Gosar watched with envy, lacking anything approaching his opponent's level of star power.

Then Gosar caught his second lucky break. It was disclosed that Sheriff Babeu had a gay lover who was an undocumented immigrant and whom Babeu had threatened to deport if he did not keep their relationship a secret. The frontrunner subsequently withdrew from the race. Paul Gosar won in a walk.

In subsequent elections, one GOP opponent after the next attempted to run to Gosar's right in AZ-4. The incumbent made that task impossible, particularly when it came to what had been Paul Babeu's pet issue and was now Gosar's: border security. "Our Southwest border with Mexico is becoming more dangerous by the day," he told Arizonans in 2011. Never thereafter did he relent from that alarmist viewpoint. The irony seemed lost on him, if not others in the Gosar family, that the Arizona congressman was the grandson of Slovenian and Basque immigrants, the latter of whom were not welcomed with open arms in Wyoming. Those Basque immigrants in turn employed illegal immigrants from South and Central America to herd their sheep, and they were also viewed with some hostility.

But that was somehow a different world for Paul Gosar. He drew his lessons selectively, much as his designated House GOP protégée Marjorie Taylor Greene would. He did not view the new generation of undocumented immigrants as bearing any relationship to the ones that his own family once employed. This later crop seemed to Gosar more in confederacy with a permissive radical Democratic socialist experiment.

To Gosar, they were "illegals." Criminals, by definition.

———————————

ON MAY 5, 2021, PAUL GOSAR AND A COUPLE OF STAFFERS VISITED THE SMALL Arizona border town of San Luis in Yuma County. The town was not in the congressman's district, but it nonetheless drew his interest because of a parcel of federal land in San Luis that might be available to transfer for a pet project of Gosar's. Before coming, the congressman's team contacted local officials in San Luis. They learned that because of the city's impoverished budget, San Luis had to rely on volunteers to clean up the trash on its downtown streets.

Gosar's congressional website that day in May included several photos, accompanied by this statement: "I was just at the border again this past week filling countless bags of trash from all the litter, drugs and crack-pipes dumped on our ground by illegal aliens when they cross our southern border. In addition to the health, humanitarian and national security crisis there also exists a growing environmental crisis caused by the open border policies of the Biden Administration. We picked up over a thousand pounds of rubbish and literally filled countless trash bags."

Three weeks later, I paid a visit to San Luis. Because of the town's small size, it didn't take long to find the vacant concrete lot that appeared in the photos on Gosar's official website. Several empty beer and soft drink bottles and fast-food wrappings were strewn along the lot's perimeter, but I found nothing that suggested drug use. When I asked the attendant at the adjacent automotive repair shop if he had ever seen undocumented immigrants congregating there, he laughed and shook his head.

I managed to contact two of the city officials who accompanied Gosar and his team that day. Yes, they said, there had been lots of garbage to clean up, because the pandemic had kept volunteer teams away for the entirety of the past year. Neither of them recalled seeing "drugs and crack pipes," however, or hearing Gosar say anything about it at the time.

Furthermore, I was told, undocumented immigrants did not cross into San Luis. There was, after all, a segment of Trump's border wall there.

Then who was it that left all the litter? I asked them.

Day laborers, I was told. They arrived legally, on foot, across the pedestrian bridge early each morning to work in the nearby lettuce fields. Yuma

County, it turns out, supplies close to 90 percent of the green leaves purchased in the United States. The industry, and the county's economy, rely on the Mexican day laborers, who apparently congregate in that vacant lot, waiting for buses to arrive that transport them to the farms.

Later, I saw the buses for myself, full of day laborers returning from their agricultural work, and then heading back on foot to the port of entry. It was a tableau of everyday border life, entirely aboveboard, there for anyone to see and know.

But that was only if the facts mattered.

Sign outside Representative Marjorie Taylor Greene's office

Chapter Thirteen

"I'M LITERALLY YOU"

M r. Speaker," declared Marjorie Taylor Greene from behind the podium on the House floor, "I move that the House do now adjourn."

A few audible groans ensued. House Majority Leader Steny Hoyer turned to Minority Leader Kevin McCarthy and asked, "Can't you do something to control her?"

McCarthy offered an exaggerated shrug and said, "I mean, if she had something else to do with her time, like be on a committee . . ."

Ever since the House Democrats had voted on February 4, 2021, to strip the Georgia freshman of her committee assignments, Greene had made the most of her free time. She was on Twitter and right-wing talk shows constantly. She was raising unheard-of sums of money online. She was filing bill after bill that stood no chance of being considered by the Democratic majority. And just after her committee removal, Trump's chief of staff, Mark Meadows, had suggested that she take advantage of her light schedule. "You know, there's a lot you can do with floor procedure," Greene would recall Meadows telling her. "You need to learn some floor procedure. You can ask for recorded votes."

"He gave me all these ideas," Greene said. "And I was like, 'Okay.'"

Today was March 10, and the House was due to vote on Biden's $1.9 trillion stimulus package, known as the American Rescue Plan. Owing to the Democratic majority, its passage in the House was a foregone conclusion. (It did so on partisan lines, 220–211.) But Greene was not about wins and losses, much less about legislating. She wanted conservative voters to see her fighting. The performance was what mattered.

Greene's motion to adjourn would force every member of Congress, Democratic and Republican alike, to leave their government offices and trudge through the tunnels to the House chamber, where they would then have to vote on whether to keep Congress in session that day. There were side benefits to the gambit. Besides the virtue of annoying her colleagues, it also forced Republicans to side with Greene—because if a GOP member was to vote to keep the House in session, then they would be on record essentially saying they were fine with the radical socialist Democrats passing a swampy "Pelosi payoff" bill.

It also had the effect of underscoring who was really in charge of House Republican strategy. (Hint: not Kevin McCarthy.)

The freshman from Georgia was waging her skirmishes on multiple fronts. On February 18, the committeeless congresswoman filed the Gun Owner Privacy Act, which would prevent the federal government from monitoring lawful gun owners—an aggressive solution to a problem that did not exist.

Six days later on the twenty-fourth, Greene took to the House floor to oppose the Equality Act, a bill submitted by the Democrats to offer additional protections to the LGBTQ community. Evoking an Equality Act hellscape in which biological male predators would be lying low in girls' locker rooms and battered women's shelters, she noted the plaque in the Capitol that said IN GOD WE TRUST and observed, "Well, it says in Genesis, God created us male and female. In His image, He created us."

A day later, the freshman submitted an "amendment" to the Equality Act that would in fact replace the bill with hers: the Protection of Women and Girls in Sports Act, forbidding "biological males" from participating in women's sports.

It happened that Greene's office on the ground floor of the Longworth Building was directly across from the office of a House Democrat, Marie Newman, whose daughter Evie is transgender. The day Greene submitted her Protection of Women and Girls in Sports Act, the Illinois congresswoman planted a pink, white, and blue transgender flag outside her door. Newman posted the video of her doing so on Twitter, adding that she had placed it there so that Greene "can look at it every time she opens her door."

As a top Democratic staffer would later lament, "You bring a knife to an alley fight, and she brings a bazooka." To absolutely no one's surprise, Greene retaliated the next day with a Twitter video of her placing a large sign next to her office: THERE ARE TWO GENDERS: MALE & FEMALE. "TRUST THE SCIENCE!"

The ensuing "liberal tears" were of course delicious to her. It was the second time in two months that the Georgia freshman had taken her bazooka to a Democratic House member. A few weeks earlier, her refusal to wear a mask in the Capitol tunnels had infuriated another Longworth neighbor, Cori Bush of Missouri, who while crossing paths with Greene yelled, "Follow the rules and put on a mask!" Greene then posted a video snippet of the exchange, falsely adding that Bush, a former Black Lives Matter activist, had been part of "a terrorist mob who trespassed into a gated neighborhood to threaten the lives" of residents there. At Bush's request, Speaker Nancy Pelosi subsequently moved the Missouri congresswoman's office to a different location.

"We got a Spartan here—we got a fighter," Steve Bannon gushed while welcoming Greene to his *Bannon's War Room* podcast on March 11, the day after Greene's motion to adjourn failed to prevent passage of the American Rescue Plan. To Trump's former senior adviser, the freshman recounted her early days in Congress, when members regarded her warily because "the media had made me this horned, scary lady." But, she added, "The more my colleagues have gotten to know me, they've gone, 'Oh wait, they've lied about her.'"

"Is leadership—is McCarthy or Cheney—lending any support, even behind the scenes?" Bannon asked.

"No, I don't feel like I have support from leadership," Greene said. "If I did, they wouldn't have removed me from my committees."

Rather than point out that it was the House Democrats who had exercised their majority to strip Greene's assignments, Bannon simply asked, "Did they betray you?"

"I don't know," she said. "I think they stood back and said, 'Let it happen.'"

Greene then added, "Because they don't want to be connected to me, because they know the Democrats in 2022 are going to use me as the face of the Republican Party, just like they used Trump, and they're going to use me and the crazy image they've created of me and try to tear down other Republicans."

Her prediction was politically astute but not entirely sympathetic. A part of Greene seemed to relish giving her GOP colleagues heartburn. She described them to Bannon as "lazy" for not wanting "to walk to the floor and go vote for a motion to adjourn because it might mess up their schedule." What those members failed to recognize, she told the former Trump consigliere, was that "the people back at home, the regular people, which is what this country's made of—they're pissed off." The freshman then recited the litany of egregious Democratic bills to make their way to the House floor, from Biden's stimulus plan to the Equality Act, which she described as the "biggest attack on God, attack on God's creation; it's absolutely immoral and disgusting."

"I've done nothing wrong," she insisted on Bannon's podcast a few days later. Referring to her earlier online posts—the ones in which citizen Greene described mass shootings as fake, characterized the Clintons as murderers, insisted that Obama was a secret Muslim, and called for Pelosi's execution—Greene went on, "They're going to sit in outrage over tiny little pieces of video. . . . If they had shown the whole videos of where those teeny tiny pieces had come from, the American people would love me."

She was, she said, an ordinary person, not a politician. She had run for office as a mother of three who was "terrified for their future, because we are truly living in a Communist revolution."

To her fellow regular people, Greene said, "We're all the same. I'm literally you—in Congress."

Then she asked for their donations.

GREENE HAD BEEN ON STEVE BANNON'S PODCAST THAT SECOND TIME TO DIScuss her Protect America First Act. More radical even than President Trump's border restrictions, her bill would place a four-year moratorium on *all* immigration, including medical specialists and the kinds of workers on whom Trump properties like Mar-a-Lago depended. "We have to completely close immigration and fix all our problems before we can reopen to the world," the freshman explained to Bannon.

In a sense, Greene's challenge as a committeeless freshman wasn't much different from the one faced by the GOP House minority. They were powerless and had nothing of much substance to do, other than attempt to make the Democrats look bad.

But there was in fact a different approach available. It was the one pursued by both parties in the recent past when they were out of power. In addition to attacking the reigning party, the minority would attempt to demonstrate to voters what they would do if they were in the majority. They would put forward bills and policy agendas and in essence say to voters, *This is what you'll get if you vote for us.*

That was not what Greene was up to with the Protect America First Act. Her bill stood no chance of passage, or even of making it out of committee for consideration—now, or two years later under a possible GOP majority. One measure of its futility was the fact that her own leaders in the Republican House did not support Greene's extremist measure.

In fact, four days after she introduced her immigration bill on March 12, only one other Republican was willing to be a cosponsor. That House Republican was her appointed mentor, Paul Gosar of Arizona.

Then again, no one in the GOP leadership was stopping Greene either. Kevin McCarthy was not warning her that she was hurting her party's chances of retaking the majority by making them look shrill and coldhearted.

McCarthy's refusal to lecture the Georgia freshman bespoke more than his leadership style. There was in fact little he could do to discipline her. She had no committee seats to take away. She didn't need the party's money. She didn't need McCarthy's support back home. She had Trump, after all.

But Greene was also not out of step with her party, when it came down to it. Hers was not a data-driven remedy to the recent surge in undocumented immigrants—many of whom would likely wind up working in the peach orchards or tobacco fields or poultry processing plants in Georgia, a state whose leading revenue producer was agribusiness. As with Gosar, Greene was not viewing immigration through the lens of Georgia's economy.

Rather, this was, to them, about Democrats willfully destroying the American way of life—a message of hysteria that was thoroughly congruent with the greater Republican Party's incantations of "radical socialism." As Greene would describe it, those crossing the border were "invading our country because they want our jobs and our American lives. And that's the truth. You don't have to read; you don't have to know anything to see the truth that's happening every single day at the southern border. These are the facts."

Greene uttered these rather alarming words at a press event in the Capitol Visitors Center one spring afternoon to discuss a resolution promoted by the Freedom Caucus to censure President Biden for his dereliction at the border. The organizer of the event was Greene's Colorado colleague and fellow freshman Lauren Boebert. Nine Republicans each delivered a short condemnation of Biden's supposed inaction at the border, replete with specious statistics: that under Biden, the number of illegal crossings had increased by 944 percent; that 25 percent of the women crossing the border were raped; that 90 percent of the asylum claims were fraudulent; that a 300 percent jump in fentanyl use by Americans was directly attributable to illegal immigration.

Greene arrived late and was the last to speak. Several of those preceding her had made a show of concern for the young children and vulnerable women who had crossed the border. The Georgia freshman did not exhibit any such pretenses. Instead, she spoke of "the Americans that have been killed by illegal crime and murder committed by people that come into our country illegally." And she suggested that Vice President Kamala Harris's upcoming visit to the border was a dress rehearsal for 2024, with Harris's running against Trump, because "everyone knows that Joe Biden is failing and can't do the job as president of the United States."

The Republicans then began to leave. But a reporter called out to them that according to the protocol of Capitol Visitor Center press events, "The rule is, you have to take questions."

That was indeed the rule, one that presented a quandary for the Freedom Caucus members. It was their habit to ignore interview requests from the mainstream media and then pillory the same outlets for refusing to give equal airing to conservative viewpoints. In this case, however, there was no easy exit. The TV cameras were watching. Greene and Boebert gamely stuck around to take a handful of questions while their colleagues inched away.

Up until this point, I had never been given the opportunity to speak to Greene—other than to volunteer to take a picture of her and Boebert with GOP back-bencher Tom Tiffany. ("Very kind of you," Greene had said to me, somewhat reluctantly.) My interview requests, sent to her communications director, Nick Dyer, might as well have been letters addressed to Santa Claus, care of the North Pole. I was happy, then, to seize the moment:

"A question for both of you all: We just heard from Congressman Gohmert that he believes that what's happened at the border, the border crisis, is basically the result of President Biden's incompetence, his cluelessness, his lack of mental acuity. But we heard from a couple of your other colleagues who've already left, that in fact this is quite intentional, deliberate, and willful policy. I'd love y'all's thoughts on this—and if you think it's the latter, what is the actual motive, then, that underlies President Biden's deliberate policy, if that's what you think it is."

Boebert responded first. She decided to have it both ways, saying, "I do believe that this is deliberate. I also believe that President Biden should have a cognitive test."

I asked Greene if she would speak to the matter. The freshman looked directly at me. "Yes," she said. "I think to me, I see it as a means to the end goal. You see, it's not just Joe Biden's policy. It's the entire Democrat Party policy. Because the end goal is socialism. It's not about being an American party that cares about our country, cares about our borders, cares about our laws, cares about our businesses, cares about our children and our country's future. They have a different outlook on policy, and it's quite the opposite of half of our country—the patriots, people who love our country."

What Biden's Democrats wanted, Greene went on, was "systematic destruction." And, she observed, they were succeeding: an economy shut down, an enforcement of useless pandemic masks, the coddling of Antifa and Black Lives Matter rioters . . . "So this is systematic destruction to our country. And it's also American tax dollars that are being used to pay for these people once they get here.

"Because let's be real," Greene continued—her "tell" that something unreal and conspiratorial was about to take wing—"They don't just cross over and stay in the town where they come in. They get shipped, they get sent, they get flown to cities all over, all over America. So you see, it's a completely different outlook on what America's supposed to be—and that's the Democrats' view. It's socialism. And socialism, we all know, is a bridge to communism.

"And," she concluded, "we have many members in the Democrat Party that you could definitely look at, read their bills, listen to what they say, and you could call them Communists."

With that McCarthyesque flourish, Marjorie Taylor Greene had spoken her piece. She moved quickly out the door with her entire senior staff trailing behind her.

Representative Liz Cheney after her removal as conference chairperson

Chapter Fourteen

THE FALL OF THE HOUSE OF CHENEY

The day before Marjorie Taylor Greene introduced her Protect America First Act, Liz Cheney convened a news conference on the section of the eastern lawn of the Capitol complex known as the Triangle. She and about thirty other House Republicans, including Kevin McCarthy and Steve Scalise, were there to discuss what a cardboard prop called BIDEN'S BORDER CRISIS.

Cheney was fulfilling her duty as conference chair by organizing an event that featured a subject all Republicans could agree on. Given the popularity of Biden's $1.9 trillion COVID stimulus bill and the continued progress of the vaccine rollouts, her party was eager to change the subject. It was also an opportunity to turn the page from the unpleasantness within the party that had lingered since January 6. Two of Cheney's fellow impeachers, Peter Meijer of Michigan and John Katko of New York, were among those in attendance.

Like most Triangle events, Cheney's border gathering was an exercise in making news, but not the bad kind of news. What made this one peculiar was that a nearly identical news conference had been staged on this same spot the day beforehand, March 10, featuring not only the same BIDEN'S BORDER CRISIS placard but also some of the same speakers. The only material difference was that Cheney had not been at the first gathering. Apparently that first event had been convened for the benefit of certain Republicans who wanted to talk about the border but didn't wish to be in the same camera frame as Liz Cheney.

There was something else notable about the event organized by Cheney:

it was the last public event in which she and Kevin McCarthy would stand together. Unknown to all but a few was that the two Republican leaders had stopped speaking to each other. More specifically, they had not spoken since February 24, the day that they and Scalise were concluding a routine press conference when a reporter asked McCarthy if he believed that former President Trump should speak at the upcoming CPAC event.

"Yes, he should," the minority leader had replied briskly. The reporter then asked the same question to the conference chairwoman.

"That's up to CPAC," said Cheney. "I've been clear about my views of President Trump and the extent to which, following January 6, I don't think he should be playing a role in the future of the party."

McCarthy seemed dumbstruck for a moment. Then, with forced cheeriness, he said, "On that high note, thank you all very much!" and moved swiftly out of the conference room.

Even among the two-thirds of the House Republican Conference that had voted to keep Cheney on as conference chair, a kind of buyer's remorse had begun to settle in. The belief held by many of them was that the overwhelming message of the four-hour conference on February 3—that Cheney had made their lives profoundly uncomfortable by her impeachment statement and vote—was somehow lost on her. Rather than move on from that episode and commit to stifling her misgivings about Trump going forward, Cheney seemed incapable of shutting up about the subject. Why did the conference chair, above all, continue to go off message, continue to rise to the bait?

"It was a mistake," Cheney acknowledged a couple of days after the February 24 press conference. She was sitting on the House floor talking with Patrick McHenry and agreeing with the North Carolinian that she could and should have simply taken a pass on the reporter's question.

McHenry happened to agree with Cheney that McCarthy should not have been so unequivocal in his "yes, he should" answer to whether Trump should attend CPAC. Still, he expressed concern to her that she was reopening the wound every time she took a shot at Trump.

"The trick here is going to be getting you through this term without another vote taking you out," he said to her as they sat together.

Cheney respected McHenry but did not see things quite as he did. Yes,

she probably should have avoided openly contradicting McCarthy's sentiments. But how, exactly, did McHenry propose that the party move on from
Trump if they refused to say aloud why moving on was necessary? Were they
supposed to pretend *not* to believe that Trump was a threat to the Republic?
Was silence on the subject really the answer? If Cheney, Kinzinger, and others
stayed quiet while right-wing mouthpieces like Sean Hannity and Tucker
Carlson of Fox News continued to insist over and over that President Trump
was a victim of something other than his own unpopularity, would Republican voters ever see the light on their own?

To paraphrase the ex-president: would Trumpism one day simply go away,
"like a miracle?"

THE BREAK BECAME A COMPOUND FRACTURE DURING THE REPUBLICAN CON-
ference retreat in Orlando, during the last week in April. An interview was
published in the *New York Post* in which Cheney said that for any 2024 Republican presidential hopefuls like senators Ted Cruz of Texas and Josh Hawley
of Missouri "who led the unconstitutional charge, not to certify the election,
you know, in my view that's disqualifying." When the *Post* reporter asked
Cheney if she herself might be running in 2024, her answer was, "I'm not ruling anything in or out."

To several Republicans at the conference who were already carping about
Liz Cheney's fawning press coverage and snickering about how the gift bags
the conference chairwoman was handing out included items labeled "Made in
China," the interview was all too revelatory. Here again, Cheney was bringing
up January 6, unsolicited. And here for the first time, it seemed evident why:
Liz Cheney was positioning herself to run in 2024 as the post-Trump Republican presidential candidate.

Cheney had also differentiated herself from the view espoused by Kevin
McCarthy and most other Republicans that a select committee should not
focus solely on the January 6 insurrection but should also investigate the summer 2020 riots. "What happened on January 6 is unprecedented in our history," she said to the media at the retreat. "And I think that it's very important
that the commission be able to focus on that."

McCarthy, meanwhile, no longer bothered to conceal his irritation with her. When asked during a press conference at the same retreat whether Cheney was still a good fit for the House GOP leadership, he replied, "That's a question for the conference." Pressed to offer his own opinion, the minority leader thought for a moment before saying, "I think from a perspective if you're sitting here at a retreat that's focused on policy, focused on making America in the next century, and you're talking about something else, you're not being productive."

To *Politico* reporter Melanie Zanona, McCarthy went a step further. Asked by Zanona about Cheney's behavior, the minority leader responded as he often did on a variety of matters. He quoted the title of a book from Simon Sinek, a leadership expert whom McCarthy admired (though Sinek was also a noted Trump critic who had spoken at past Democratic retreats): "Leaders eat last."

A week later, on May 4, McCarthy was on a fundraising trip in Atlanta when he sat down for an interview with a Fox News reporter. Off camera, but with the microphone on, the minority leader said about Cheney, "I've had it with her. It's—you know, I've lost confidence in her." When asked by the reporter whether Cheney likely faced removal, he replied, "Well, someone just has to make a motion. But I assume that will probably take place."

It was not simply that McCarthy had been hearing from other House Republicans that Cheney was becoming a major distraction and a problem for their voters back home. He was also hearing from Trump, who had been greatly upset that the Republicans had failed to dump Cheney at the special conference on February 3. The ex-president had his own opinion as to who would make a far better conference chair: Marjorie Taylor Greene.

But it had gotten personal for McCarthy as well. In the minority leader's view, it was he who had saved the chairwoman on February 3 with his speeches preaching unity before and after the discussion. For this, he had not received a word of thanks from Cheney.

In fact, there was a reason why Cheney had not thanked McCarthy, and it wasn't because she tended toward stoicism—or, as McCarthy had put it in the February 3 conference, "I'm not going to ask Liz to help me with my Valentine's Day card for Judy, all right?" Rather, she had not thanked him because there was nothing to thank him for. Her whip count, going into the February 3 conference, had been almost identical to the final 145–61 vote. There was perhaps a single individual McCarthy had flipped: John Rutherford, a former Florida sheriff, who had told the minority leader that he had been disinclined to vote for Cheney but ultimately had done so because as sheriff he had learned the importance of picking one's own team and therefore believed McCarthy should have that privilege as well.

But Cheney was additionally of the view that McCarthy in many ways bore some responsibility for her predicament with the Republican Conference. The phrase "leaders eat last" was a military concept, where commanding officers showed appreciation to their troops by letting them line up first in the mess hall. Still: They led. Did McCarthy? *Ever?* The man who on January 6 had yelled to Trump on the phone that the rioters were "trying to fucking kill me" was now carrying on as if Trump had done nothing wrong that day. Rather than help Cheney move the party away from Trump, McCarthy had wrapped himself around the ex-president like a tourniquet. He was in fact *encouraging* Trump to play a role in the 2022 elections. For all intents and purposes, Kevin McCarthy had ceded his leadership role to a twice-impeached former president and his most radical followers, like Marjorie Taylor Greene and Paul Gosar.

Just after the House Republican Retreat in Orlando, Cheney flew to Sea Island, Georgia, to take part in the off-the-record annual World Forum of the American Enterprise Institute, a conservative think tank whose trustees included her father. To those in attendance, the chairwoman seemed unflappably defiant but also reflective. She read to one friend an excerpt of Abraham Lincoln's famous address before the Young Men's Lyceum in 1838. The speech, which the twenty-eight-year-old Springfield lawyer had written following the lynching in St. Louis of a freed Black man named Francis McIntosh, spoke to the dangers of "mob law." One of Cheney's staffers had texted the speech to her during the afternoon of January 6.

"She was really thinking about all this," the friend who heard her read the Lyceum speech would recall. "And of course, Lincoln was only a one-term congressman because he'd put forward a hugely unpopular resolution opposing the Mexican–American War. I think her strategy before all this was to one day become Speaker. That strategy got interrupted. And so she was probably thinking, 'I'm doomed anyway, because I voted for impeachment, and sooner or later it'll come and get me.'

"But now it's, 'If I can get through this, survive a primary next August where five MAGA weirdos run against me, and I come back here—then I stood up to all of them, and I lived. I'm unbreakable.'"

THE REMOVAL CONFERENCE AT NINE IN THE MORNING ON MAY 12 PROVED TO be as quick and clinical as a lethal injection. Minority Leader Kevin McCarthy did not even waste a phone call to let Liz Cheney know it was coming. She had already read about it in the media.

Accompanying Cheney from her office in the Cannon Building to the conference room in the Capitol Visitors Center that morning was her communications director Jeremy Adler and two plainclothes security officials. Having recently received a credible threat on her life, the chairwoman had contacted the office of Speaker Nancy Pelosi, who had granted her request for security.

Virginia Foxx of North Carolina, who had not been among those agitating for Cheney's removal, stood and read the resolution. Cheney gave a short speech on her behalf. After reiterating her belief that the GOP could not let Trump "drag us backward," she pointedly added, "If you want leaders who will enable and spread his destructive lies, I'm not your person. You have plenty of others to choose from."

No one else stood to offer their thoughts. As her final act as chairwoman, she called for a voice vote on the resolution to remove her. The yeas had it, overwhelmingly.

Fifteen minutes after it had begun, Liz Cheney in her striking periwinkle dress strolled down the aisle of the conference room, out the door, and into a sea of microphones. She fielded two questions with her usual casual efficiency. No, she said, she wasn't bitter about the vote to remove her. "I think it's an indication of where the party is," she said. "And I think the party's in a place that we've got to bring it back from."

She also vowed, "I will do everything I can to ensure that the former president never again gets anywhere near the Oval Office."

Thanking the reporters, she then moved away and stepped into an elevator with Adler and her security detail. Even without the pandemic mask pulled over her nose and mouth, the bespectacled Wyoming congresswoman betrayed no emotions as she waited for the doors to close. Once they did, another Republican member in the elevator, her friend Jackie Walorski, gave her a hug.

"It's just politics," Walorski said.

THE NEXT DAY, CHENEY'S REPUBLICAN COLLEAGUES VOTED TO REPLACE HER with Elise Stefanik. The thirty-six-year-old upstate New York congresswoman had moved aggressively to get the job, not waiting for an assist from Kevin McCarthy, who had been more inclined to elevate one of the female freshmen like Kat Cammack or Stephanie Bice. A few hours after Cheney was ousted from leadership, Stefanik showed up to the conservative Republican Study Committee meeting. She dined that evening with the House Freedom Caucus. Both groups naturally preferred a true conservative—which, as everyone knew, Elise Stefanik was not.

But they also knew that Stefanik had spent the past one and a half years doing a fine impression of a conservative. Her transformation was easily dated: November 13, 2019. Prior to then, she had been a Washington-based Republican aide and then, in 2014, the youngest-ever female congresswoman at age thirty. A self-described "moderate conservative," she was well liked by Democrats and had much in common with Liz Cheney, both in their service together on the House Armed Services Committee and in their issue-by-issue regard of President Trump.

Then, on that November morning in 2019, the House Intelligence Committee began its public hearings on whether to impeach President Trump for abuse of power in pressuring Ukraine's president to dig up dirt on Joe Biden. Stefanik's sharp and undisguisedly Trump-defending interrogation made the once-obscure congresswoman an overnight darling among conservatives.

More than that, however, during that week of testimony in the impeachment hearings, Stefanik spent her free hours in a war room in the headquarters of the Republican National Committee on Capitol Hill. There she came to see how much money her performances could accrue to her campaign war chest through the digital fundraising tool WinRed. She became adept at feeding the technology's algorithms with overheated language to conform with the apocalyptic, warlike rhetoric of right-wing activists.

"Those first four days of news cycles," an associate who spent time with her during that period would recall, "Stefanik went from 'WinRed is a conspiracy to steal my data' to its most fervent user. As a result of that whole experience, Elise speaks to the internet audience now, not the DC audience.'"

With Stefanik's arrival, the House Republican leadership now spoke with one unambiguously pro-Trump voice. Now it was only Liz Cheney and Adam Kinzinger protesting from the sidelines about January 6 and quaint notions of truth.

Representative Alexandria Ocasio-Cortez

Chapter Fifteen

BÊTE NOIRE

Before Marjorie Taylor Greene decided to run for Congress, the Fourteenth Congressional District of northwest Georgia had been represented by Tom Graves. The former self-described "north Georgia country boy from a single-wide trailer," high school football star, landscaping entrepreneur, and state legislator from the town of Ranger had first been elected to the Ninth District, arriving as a forty-year-old firebrand in 2010 on the Tea Party wave. When Ranger was drawn into Georgia's newly created Fourteenth District in time for the 2012 midterms, Graves campaigned for the open seat and won.

Like many of his 2010 class, Graves was animated by opposition to the Affordable Care Act. His first piece of legislation called for the defunding of Obamacare. He introduced it every year, watching it pass in the House and then fail in the Democratically controlled Senate. Graves achieved momentary infamy for his role in the 2013 government shutdown, when he worked with Senator Ted Cruz to tie a government funding resolution to the defunding of Obama's health-care act. The sixteen-day shutdown caused the Republican Party's approval ratings to plummet. But Graves achieved folk hero status back home for standing up to Obama and the "big-spending" Democrats.

Though the Speaker at the time, John Boehner, was not pleased that Graves had confederated with the much-despised Cruz to shut the government down, he saw something in the northwest Georgian. Graves was made a cardinal, or subcommittee chair, on the House Appropriations Committee. He came to be known on K Street as a substantive legislator who preferred obscure but important committee work over TV appearances. In 2014, Graves became a key conservative ally in Kevin McCarthy's quest to succeed the recently defeated House Majority Leader Eric Cantor, delivering a nominating speech on McCarthy's behalf against Graves's 2010 classmate Raul Labrador. (The conservative Georgia-based writer Erick Erickson called Graves a "Judas goat" for backing the establishment candidate, McCarthy.) Back home, meanwhile, Graves held his seat with little effort. In what would prove to be his final race in 2018, Graves clobbered a Democrat who spent much of the campaign behind bars for a DUI conviction.

Graves's decision at the end of 2019 to retire from Congress, thus paving the way for Marjorie Taylor Greene's ascendancy, stunned political observers both in Georgia and in Washington. The banal reasons he offered—kids out of the house, "a new season in life" beckoning—masked unspoken discontents. His friend McCarthy had not thrown his weight behind Graves's campaign to be the top Republican on the Appropriations Committee, an effort Graves lost by a single vote.

But in recent years, a more disconcerting reality had become apparent in the district Graves represented. It was not simply that the Republican voters there overwhelmingly supported Donald Trump, a man whom Graves found to be morally lacking. It was also that they were looking for Graves to *be* Trump-like.

Over the Christmas holidays in 2015, Graves the appropriator had been tasked with protecting Georgia's interests in the ongoing water wars with Alabama and its senior senator, Richard Shelby. Graves spent much of the holidays fighting to strip language Shelby had inserted in an omnibus bill that would have affected water allocation in the Alabama-Coosa-Tallapoosa basin. When Graves at last succeeded and was able to head back to Georgia for the tail end of the holidays, the congressman stopped into a General Dollar store to chat with constituents and hear what was on their minds.

What was on their minds was not water rights. Instead, they told him, "I wish you were on Fox News more."

A close observer to Tom Graves's final years representing the Fourteenth District would recall the congressman's diligent work on the water wars, mediating a dispute over the Paulding Airport, seeking to boost tourism for the region's sixty-two-mile-long Silver Comet Trail, and in general working with local business leaders to improve the district's economic conditions. "The thing fundamentally to understand about this district," the observer would say, "was: *that stuff didn't matter.* Being a fighter. Being on talk radio and Fox. That's what mattered."

THE DISTRICT MARJORIE TAYLOR GREENE WAS ELECTED TO REPRESENT IS both sprawling and remote, encompassing eleven counties, nearly all of them decidedly rural. At the time of her election in 2020, just over 75 percent of its population was white, a group roughly eight times the size of either its Latino or Black population. Its median household income, $56,150, was approximately half that of Georgia's Sixth District, where Marjorie Taylor Greene originally ran and lived. Its poverty rate of 14.2 percent exceeded the national average. By far, the racial group with the greatest share of impoverished individuals was Caucasian. In short, Georgia's Fourteenth District was overwhelmingly white and economically downtrodden, before state legislators redrew the congressional map at the end of 2021 and moved some of Democrat Lucy McBath's racially diverse suburban constituents in Cobb County into the Fourteenth, knowing that the addition would politically imperil McBath but not endanger Greene.

In the district's second-biggest city, Dalton (population 33,571), once the American hub of tufted textiles, the local economy has tied its future to globalism. Two of its biggest employers are the Canadian-owned artificial turf manufacturer SYNLawn and Hanwha Q Cells, a South Korean maker of solar panels whose Dalton factory is the biggest solar plant in America. A Chinese vinyl flooring company, Novalis, recently opened a $30 million plant in Dalton as well.

Elsewhere in the district, however, change is less readily embraced. Its history is bound up in an agrarian lifestyle that clung to slavery for its viability, and bound up as well in the humiliating forfeiture of the same. In the months leading up to the Civil War, when abolitionists from the North received a beating for trying to appeal to the consciences of the locals, a columnist for the Rome, Georgia, newspaper wrote on February 9, 1860: "It is a most astonishing thing to us that a Northern man at this juncture will permit an anti-slavery opinion to escape his lips in the South. They must be most stupid folks if they cannot learn under the experience of such teachings as they have had."

After war began, Rome's strategic importance as a transportation hub made it a frequent target of Union attacks. The city's valiant defender in 1863 was Confederate general Nathan Bedford Forrest, but only for a time. The beginning of the end for Dixie came with General William Tecumseh Sherman's Georgia campaign in November of 1864. Sherman's Union troops razed Rome, four days before doing the same to Atlanta.

Nearly a half century after Forrest's defense of Rome—and, as well, decades after the Confederate general was made the first grand wizard of the Ku Klux Klan—the United Daughters of the Confederacy erected a statue of him in the city's most prominent cemetery. That same year, 1908, the UDC also funded a statue of another defender against Sherman's troops, Confederate general Joseph E. Johnston, in downtown Dalton. These monuments did not reflect an innocuous spasm of nostalgia for a region's defeated warriors. Rather, their placement coincided with the rise of Jim Crow, after the Election Compromise of 1877 brought an end to Reconstruction. Lynchings and whippings of innocent Blacks at the hands of the Klan took place in both Dalton and Rome during the last decade of the nineteenth century and first decade of the twentieth.

Only in June 2020 did the two Confederate statues face the prospect of removal, following the murder in Minneapolis of George Floyd, a Black man who was suffocated to death by a white police officer. Animated but civil discussions ensued in both Rome and Dalton. Defenders of the statues argued that Forrest was a brilliant military tactician who also had renounced the Klan and advocated for equal treatment of Black people before his death in 1877 at the age of fifty-six. They pointed out that Johnston had opposed both slavery and secession and claimed he was merely defending his native Virginia.

Other arguments were less nuanced, however. At a Dalton city council meeting on June 15, 2020, a nonresident showed up: Republican congressional candidate Marjorie Taylor Greene. "It seems to be an effort to take down history," she said of the move to take down General Johnston's likeness. "Whether

I see a statue that may be something that I fully disagree with, like Adolf Hitler, maybe it's a statue of Satan himself, I would not want to say, 'Take it down.' But again, so that I can tell my children and teach others about who these people are and what they did and what they may be about."

Greene was perhaps unaware of William Faulkner's observation that the past not only is not dead, it is not even past. Four years earlier in the spring of 2016, a Klan group of about eighty black-garbed individuals held a "white pride" march through Rome. And during the same month of Greene's comments at the June 2020 Dalton city council meeting, Georgia Bureau of Investigation agents raided a militia camp just outside of Rome in Silver Creek. Three residents, members of a white supremacist group called the Base, were hosting fellow militia members from out of state and planning "accelerationist" acts of murder and assorted violence with the hopes of instigating a race war.

The three white supremacists were still being held without bail in the Floyd County jail when I visited Marjorie Taylor Greene's district for the first time, during the spring of 2021.

GREENE WAS ALSO IN GEORGIA DURING THAT TIME, UNDER SOMBER CIRCUM-stances. On April 12, her father, the construction firm founder and "Taylor Effect" author Bob Taylor, died at the age of seventy-four. The Georgia freshman sat beside her father as hospice employees aided his passage after a multi-year battle with melanoma cancer.

Bob Taylor's demise occurred as the first-quarter FEC fundraising reports were being disclosed. Greene's quarterly haul was $3.2 million, a staggering amount for any member of Congress, much less a freshman who had not even been a candidate two years earlier. The vast majority of Greene's contributions came from small-dollar donors, raised online through the GOP digital fundraising firms WinRed and Anedot. "These are absolutely incredible numbers," she texted one of her associates as Greene tended to her father's final days.

She added: "We'll keep doing what we're doing." By which she meant: her beloved father's death would not slow the Greene machine. So it was that on the morning of April 14, hours before the final visitation of her father's body at a Georgia funeral home, the freshman found time to tweet this, at liberal Congresswoman Alexandria Ocasio-Cortez:

"I'd like to challenge you to a debate on the Green New Deal economic policy. Since you sponsored the Green New Deal and have a degree in Economics, I'm sure you are more than qualified. I just have a degree in Business Admin and have owned a construction company for 20 years. A debate between AOC and I on the Green New Deal economic policy would be informative to the American people. They deserve to hear the two sides with pros and cons."

Greene proposed that the debate be televised and that each of them could choose a moderator. Then, about two hours before her father's visitation, the freshman left no doubt that this debate was intended to leverage more online donations. She tweeted the hashtag "#MTGvsAOC."

For some time now, the second-term New York congresswoman had been a hero of the left and an object of unhinged vitriol from the right—but also an object of palpable envy, given her prodigious social media platform. No doubt it was true that, as Marjorie Taylor Greene often said, the Georgian reserved a special contempt for pro-choice, anti-gun, Muslim-sympathizing liberals like AOC. Such women, in her view, made America less safe, free, and Godly.

Yet AOC's celebrity also seemed galling to Greene on a psychological level. The offense she took had manifested itself in the way she taunted Ocasio-Cortez's staff in early 2019 through the slat of the congresswoman's office door, rearranging her Post-it notes, and later revisiting the tableau with lurid sentimentality in YouTube discussions, declaring more than once that she and her right-wing buddies should go back and do it again. Later, she had inaugurated her Fourteenth District campaign with a campaign ad targeting the New Yorker as someone who "wants to plunge us into Communism," and then posted the notorious ad of Greene's proclaiming herself as the "worst nightmare" of AOC and her Squad cohort while firing rounds from her AR-15.

Her request for a debate went ignored by Ocasio-Cortez. A week later, however, several of the Georgia freshman's Republican colleagues broke House rules and photographed her approaching the Democrat on the floor. Greene posted a photo of their encounter on Twitter, along with the false claim that Ocasio-Cortez had agreed to a debate once Greene had read her fourteen-page Green New Deal summary that would form the basis of any such discussion.

The next morning, Greene tweeted: "I read your 14-page Communist manifesto, @AOC. Looking forward to debating you. #MTGvsAOC."

Again, her challenge fell on deaf ears. On the afternoon of Wednesday, May 12, the House voted on a bill to federally fund a suicide-prevention life-line. The bill passed overwhelmingly, with 349 votes—including those of Kevin McCarthy, Steve Scalise, Elise Stefanik, and Liz Cheney, while 74 opposed it, including Marjorie Taylor Greene, Paul Gosar, and other stalwarts of the House Freedom Caucus. At around 4:45, Alexandria Ocasio-Cortez departed the chamber and was walking toward the Rotunda when a voice called out:

"Alexandria! Alexandria! Why won't you debate me?"

Greene was running from the chamber's main entrance toward the Demo-crat, who began to pick up speed as the Georgia freshman yelled out, in the presence of numerous witnesses: *"Why won't you debate me? You don't care about the American people! Why do you support terrorists and Antifa?"*

AOC and her staff hustled across the Rotunda and down a flight of stairs adjacent to the Speaker's office suite. Fuming, Greene wheeled back around. "She's a chicken," the freshman snarled.

Reporters and staffers stared agape. The Capitol police stationed nearby seemed unsure of what to do. Not since January 6 had any of them seen a per-son inside the Capitol behave with such outdoor-voice derangement.

Or was it derangement? Greene then gravitated toward the reporters nearby. As one witness, Marianna Sotomayor of the *Washington Post,* would record it, the freshman declared, "These members are cowards. They need to defend their legislation to the people. It's pathetic."

As a different witness would recall, "There definitely seemed to be a per-formative aspect to it."

Two days later, on Friday, May 14, Ocasio-Cortez told reporters that Greene was "deeply unwell and clearly needs help." And that was before the afternoon, when CNN's Andrew Kaczynski published the early 2019 videos of citizen Marjorie Taylor Greene harassing the staffers of Alexandria Ocasio-Cortez. She had not yet seen the videos when her Democratic colleague Eric

Swalwell told her on the House floor that afternoon, "Just so you know, we've got your back."

Another California Democrat, Jimmy Gomez, burst through the doors of the chamber. "She's coming onto the floor!" he warned.

Swalwell walked out of the chamber and was striding down the marble steps outside when he ran into Greene. He sidestepped her. Then he heard a loud male voice: "Take your mask off, Congressman! Biden says you can take off your mask!"

One day earlier, the Centers for Disease Control had declared that COVID masks indoors were no longer necessary for those who had been vaccinated. Swalwell still had his on and had forgotten to take it off.

Incensed, the Democrat headed back inside. Just outside the metal detector by the front entrance to the chamber, he caught up to the male staffer accompanying Greene. "Hey man, what's your name?" he demanded.

Nick Dyer, Greene's press aide, backed up. "Look," Swalwell said to him, "you don't ever tell me what to fucking do."

Seeing reporters nearby, Greene pointed at Swalwell and hollered, "He's abusing him!"

Determined not to be goaded into the cage fight, Eric Swalwell turned and exited the Capitol.

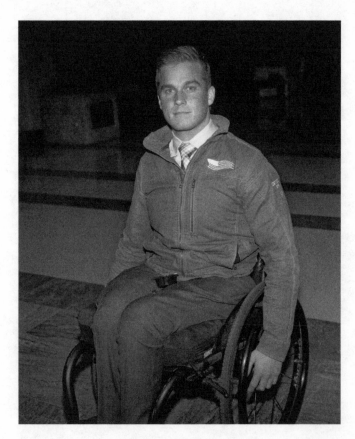

Representative Madison Cawthorn

Chapter Sixteen

BAD COMPANY

I'd really like to find a way to get on Ways and Means," Madison Cawthorn was telling Patrick McHenry on the House floor in May 2021.

McHenry regarded his fellow North Carolinian with a neutral expression that masked deep exasperation. "It's a very difficult committee to get on," he said to the freshman. Plus, McHenry added, there was already a member of the North Carolina Republican delegation in line for the next available Ways and Means Committee seat: Greg Murphy, who had two years' more experience in Congress than Cawthorn, and who previously had served four years in the state legislature.

Cawthorn, by contrast, was a handsome twenty-five-year-old self-described "motivational speaker" with no lengthy history of motivational speeches, whose supposed "real estate investment company," SPQR Holdings, consisted of a single six-acre plot of vacant land in rural Georgia that had generated no income. That was Cawthorn's résumé. It did not include the fact that at his tender age and only four months into his first term in the House, Madison Cawthorn was already developing a reputation as one of the most dishonest elected officials on Capitol Hill.

"So," Cawthorn continued carefully, "if there are two people going for a committee in the same state, could one person get ahead of the other person?"

No, McHenry responded flatly. "If you have two people going from the state, Greg is the next person. He's already in line. He's met the threshold. He will get on the committee when there's an opening."

"Are there things I could do to get ahead of him?" the freshman pressed.

"At this point, no. No. That's just not possible."

"Even if I gave $1.5 million to that NRCC?"

McHenry managed to conceal his astonishment. That was not how things worked, he explained to Cawthorn. What you donated to the House GOP's fundraising organization had no bearing on your committee assignments. They were not for sale to the highest bidder.

Of course, McHenry could see where this was coming from. After all, when House Republicans expressed dismay over Marjorie Taylor Greene's incendiary past writings about Jewish space lasers and Nancy Pelosi being eligible for the death penalty, the Georgia freshman had promptly cut the NRCC a check for $175,000. Greene had gone unpunished thereafter. A Madison Cawthorn could infer from that episode that everything on the Hill had its price, presumably including committee assignments.

Still, the senior North Carolinian explained, "Here's what you have to figure out. If this is sincerely what you want, then you have to be content to spend the next two or three terms focusing on what you need to do in order to be on Ways and Means." Or, of course, Cawthorn could make the most of his current positions on Veterans Affairs and Education and Labor. After all, those were two more assignments than Marjorie Taylor Greene currently had. (McHenry did not mention to Cawthorn that, as the latter's representative on the House Steering Committee, he had already gone to bat for Cawthorn, whose obnoxious comments during the 2020 campaign—vowing to clean house in the GOP leadership chain and to support primaries against insufficiently Trumpian Republicans—had not been forgotten. But for McHenry's entreaties, Cawthorn might have spent his first term without *any* assignment.)

The North Carolina freshman considered McHenry's advice about putting in the time to make himself worthy of a Ways and Means slot down the line. Then he said, "Well, what about Appropriations?"

Jesus, McHenry thought. The House Appropriations Committee was the most prestigious committee in the lower chamber. The prospects of Cawthorn's landing a seat on it as a freshman were subzero. "You can't just say 'I'd like to either be on Appropriations or Ways and Means,'" he said. "People will look at you like you just want the nicest dinner possible. You've got to decide: which one do you want to be on? Decide that this year, and then focus next year on getting that assignment, knowing that it may take you a term, or two, or three, to get on that committee."

"Well, I may not be here that long," Cawthorn explained. "I'm a term-limits guy. There are other things I'm going to do next. So I really need to get on one of those committees now."

It was then that McHenry noticed the card in Cawthorn's hand. Written on it were three discussion topics:

1. Ways and Means
2. Appropriations
3. Firefighter bill

McHenry knew exactly what the third matter was about. The firefighter bill, proposed by the North Carolina chapter of the International Association of Firefighters, would permit full-time volunteer firefighters to be eligible for state or local retirement benefits. The reason that McHenry knew about it was that it was *his bill.* Cawthorn, however, had attempted to file the very same bill before McHenry had gotten the chance. The latter's office had contacted the former's staff to say, in effect: *You do not want to do this. You are pissing off a senior member in your delegation.*

Cawthorn sought to assure McHenry that he had not meant anything underhanded. At this point, however, the senior North Carolinian was looking for a way to wrap up the conversation. There was an entire spiel the nine-term congressman had been prepared to give about how a freshman like Madison Cawthorn found one's way in the House. *Don't shit on the leaders in the media when you're also asking them for favors. Don't think that you're going to get away with saying one thing at home and a different thing here in DC, because that stuff gets out quickly. Don't be an asshole to your colleagues. Don't spread conspiracies.*

McHenry decided to save his breath. Such wisdom would be lost on Cawthorn, who, it was now evident, was seeking the shortest, straightest, and least labor-intensive pathway to political celebrity available. Of course, the twenty-five-year-old had telegraphed his disinterest in governance during his first month on the job. According to an email from the freshman to his GOP colleagues on January 19 that *Time* had managed to obtain, Cawthorn boasted, "I have built my staff around comms rather than legislation."

One could, perhaps, chalk up at least a portion of Cawthorn's smug bravado to youth. By way of declaring victory over his Democratic opponent on November 3, he had simply tweeted: "Cry more lib." At the House GOP retreat in Orlando in May, he was seen sitting out by the hotel pool one early afternoon, shirtless in his wheelchair, while a fellow freshman, Lisa McClain of Michigan, poured liquor down his throat. And just after Liz Cheney was removed from her leadership post on May 12, Cawthorn tauntingly tweeted: "Na na na na, na na na na, hey hey, goodbye Liz Cheney."

Patrick McHenry had never sneeringly celebrated the humiliation of a fellow Republican as Madison Cawthorn had Cheney. Still, he well recalled how he, too, had been something of a jerk when he arrived on the Hill in January 2005 as a twenty-nine-year-old upwardly mobile conservative who did not display the humility one might expect after having just defeated his Republican primary opponent by all of 85 votes. McHenry proceeded to fashion himself as a pugilistic conservative, the better to clear out opposition back home. The day came when Steny Hoyer's Democrats teamed up with other Republicans to deny McHenry an earmark he had submitted. It occurred to him that he was making more enemies than friends, in both parties. Running for his third term in 2008, in the general election McHenry found himself pitted against Daniel Johnson, a navy veteran who had lost both legs saving the life of another serviceman. The biggest newspaper in North Carolina's Tenth Congressional District endorsed Johnson. McHenry knew that he had won only because he had an *R* next to his name.

He decided, then, to quit being aggressively dumb and instead become a serious legislator. He hired superior staff. He put in the hours understanding the issues. He sought out the guidance of more experienced legislators like Eric Cantor and Tom Reynolds. By 2011, it was Patrick McHenry offering mentorship to Tea Party freshmen like Todd Rokita and Martha Roby. It became his practice to do so. He thus had every intention of assisting Madison Cawthorn, but for two formidable obstacles.

The first was that Cawthorn appeared to be a compulsive liar. He had lied during his 2020 candidacy by claiming that his plans to attend the U.S. Naval Academy "were derailed that year after he nearly died in a tragic automobile accident," as he put it on his campaign website. (In truth, the academy had already rejected him before the accident.) He had lied about being left for dead in the car accident. He had lied in claiming that his job working for Congressman Mark Meadows was full-time. He had lied about training for the 2020 Paralympics before running for Congress. He had lied in insisting that his 2020 Republican opponent was a Never Trumper. So profuse a liar was Madison Cawthorn that one Republican colleague had theorized to McHenry that perhaps the North Carolina freshman had a brain impairment stemming from his leg injuries.

In any event, Cawthorn's tenuous association with the truth was one obstacle to Patrick McHenry's taking him under his wing. The second obstacle was related to the first: Cawthorn endorsed lies. Or more to the point: Cawthorn had vigorously promoted the dangerous lie that Trump's election had been stolen from him. A couple of days after the Capitol riot, McHenry asked a staffer to provide him with a list of the Republicans who had spoken at Trump's Stop the Steal Rally on the morning of January 6, 2021.

Sure enough, there was Madison Cawthorn's name. To the thousands of Trump supporters gathered at the Ellipse, he had called out fellow Republicans who refused to challenge the election results "cowards."

PATRICK McHENRY WAS ONE OF THOSE 64 REPUBLICAN MEMBERS WHO HAD voted to certify the 2020 electoral tally. Roughly half of the 147 who had objected did so not out of sincere belief that the election was fraudulent but out of fear that they would be jobless. They, along with the 64 certifiers like McHenry, were endeavoring to ride out the craziness that had overtaken their party—hopeful that it would implode of its own madness or migrate to some nutty new party, all while struggling to work on behalf of their districts and to convince themselves that they were not enablers of the insanity.

It had become a custom of McHenry's to begin his meetings back home with a proactive explanation of why he voted on January 6 to acknowledge

Trump's electoral defeat. It was a dry and legalistic monologue that his North Carolina constituents seemed to appreciate, even if it did not alter their belief that Trump had gotten the shaft.

McHenry recognized that his vote to certify the 2020 election results did not qualify him for a Medal of Honor. He had not voted to impeach Trump after the Capitol riot. He avoided any public discussion about what, if any, role Trump should play in the party going forward.

McHenry was not confident that this storm of delusion within his party would ever pass. He was, however, supremely confident that he would not be around to toast its passing if he made it his life's mission to constantly lecture his conservative North Carolina constituents about how awful their favorite president really was.

His party had historically accommodated Rockefeller coastal elites, John Birchers, Goldwater libertarians, small-government Reaganites, Newt Gingrich's revolutionaries, the Bushes. None succeeded in purging the other. Rather, they layered themselves atop each other like mountain stratigraphy. Trumpism was just another layer. It would not rupture the mountain altogether.

That, at least, was what history convinced Patrick McHenry to tell himself.

"Stop the Steal" rally

Chapter Seventeen

THE BIG LIE, IN PERPETUITY

For decades, it had been accepted wisdom among Republicans that Democrats habitually cheated in elections. The cities, it was said, were controlled by party "machines." Corrupt politicians colluded with precinct captains. Black ministers participated in furtive exchanges of moneybags and ballots. Pickup trucks and buses rolled in and out of polling stations, ferrying voters of dubious legitimacy.

Vote-rigging on this score did indeed take place during the Jim Crow era, when white Southern conservatives—most if not all of them Democrats—served as gatekeepers for who could or could not participate in elections. The most notorious case of fraud, painstakingly reconstructed by author Robert Caro, involved the 1948 U.S. Senate race in Texas between Democrats Coke Stevenson and the victor, Lyndon Johnson, who outcheated his opponent in the primary runoff by 87 votes.

But since the passage of President Johnson's 1965 Voting Rights Act, and the subsequent migration of Southern conservatives to the GOP, a different dynamic has occurred. Even as Republicans have cited instances of Democratic voter fraud where none exists, they have sought to limit the franchise of Black voters, who overwhelmingly skew Democratic.

So it was that in the pivotal state of Florida, in the lead-up to the 2000 presidential election, Republican officials undertook to aggressively scrub the voting rolls. The rationale for doing so was the 1997 mayoral election in Miami, in which five thousand absentee ballots had heavily favored the independent candidate, Xavier Suarez. Despite the fact that the ballots in question were mainly cast by Cuban American voters, who as a demographic tend to be relatively conservative, the subsequent voter-roll purges overwhelmingly affected that segment of the Florida electorate who happened to be Black. The nonpartisan U.S. Commission on Civil Rights investigated the matter and, in its report, "found a strong basis for concluding that violations of Section 2 of the Voting Rights Act (VRA) occurred in Florida." The disenfranchisement that had occurred in 2000, the commission added, "fell most harshly on the shoulders of Black voters." Though the commission did not "find that the highest officials of the state conspired to disenfranchise voters," it did say that those "highest officials"—the highest of whom, Governor Jeb Bush, was the brother of Republican candidate George W. Bush—"failed to fulfill their responsibilities and were subsequently unwilling to take responsibility."

Candidate Bush, of course, won the 2000 presidential election by a scant 537 votes in Florida (while losing the overall popular vote by a half million) in a race that was ultimately settled by the U.S. Supreme Court. In a refrain that would be echoed sixteen years later, Bush's supporters would cast the Democrats objecting to the Florida results as "whiners" who needed to "get over it." But four years later, when incumbent Bush triumphed over John Kerry by 2.4 percentage points, it was the Bush campaign claiming that their narrow loss in Wisconsin by just over 11,000 votes was due to fraud. In Milwaukee alone, it was alleged, 8,300 more ballots were cast than there were voters.

After a six-month investigation, a task force revised the over-vote from 8,300 to 4,609, nearly all of which were found to be a result of administrative error. The U.S. attorney in Milwaukee ultimately determined that two hundred felons had voted improperly and upward of one hundred instances of double voting had occurred in the city during the 2004 election—but all cases were isolated rather than suggestive of any kind of conspiracy. Only seven cases, all involving ex-felons, could be substantiated where someone had deliberately cast an invalid ballot.

It was a fact that Democratic machine politics in Milwaukee had, in decades past, conspired to defraud elections. But the victims weren't Republicans. They were Black voters whose power the party bosses—often of white European origin—sought to dilute. By 2004, those dynamics had changed. Still, Republicans persisted in their claims that systematic fraud had occurred in Wisconsin, necessitating restrictive measures such as photo IDs. (As a Brennan Center for Justice report observed, none of the violations would have been prevented by requiring the ex-felons to present a photo ID.)

In particular, Bush senior adviser Karl Rove remained convinced that voter fraud had taken place throughout the United States and had not been thoroughly investigated. Eight U.S. attorneys were ultimately fired by Bush White House officials for their lack of vigilance on the matter. Bush's Department of Justice undertook a multiyear investigation, resulting in eighty-six convictions nationwide. (Nearly all the offenders were immigrants and ex-convicts who were confused about their eligibility.) In speeches, Rove continued to evoke the malevolent specter of elections being decided by "who can stuff it the best and most."

In the years to follow, a few cases of voter fraud did emerge. They had one thing in common: nearly all involved Republicans rather than Democrats. (A notable exception was former Democratic Congressman Ozzie Myers of Philadelphia, who was found guilty of bribing an election judge to stuff ballot boxes in the 2014, 2015, and 2016 primary elections. Just as notable was the fact that the mass-voting scheme conducted by a single judge in a voting booth could not have occurred through mail-in ballots, which are tied to specific names and addresses.) In 2010, for example, an Indiana GOP county chairman named Charlie White was elected to be secretary of state, Indiana's top election official. White was forced out of office fifteen months into his term after a jury had found that the secretary of state had deliberately voted from the wrong precinct and then lied about it.

In 2016, a Republican Baptist minister named Mark Harris sought to challenge the GOP House incumbent in the heavily rural Ninth Congressional District of North Carolina. Harris lost by fewer than 200 votes, and he believed he knew why: his primary opponent had somehow managed to win 98 percent of the mail-in ballots. State election officials shared Harris's concern. The state election board's chief investigator determined that the culprit was a Bladen County Republican political consultant named Leslie McCrae Dowless Jr. The operative had a team of workers who would show up on the doorsteps of Bladen County households where absentee ballots had been mailed. They would then show the residents—most of them low-income whites—how to fill out the ballots, offer to turn the ballots in, and, when necessary, forge the required witness signatures.

The election board's director, Kim Strach, forwarded the hefty file on Dowless to Raleigh-based U.S. attorney Bobby Higdon, a Trump appointee, believing the matter to be worthy of federal prosecution. Higdon elected to do nothing with the matter. His office was instead focused on determining how many noncitizens in North Carolina had voted in the 2016 election. (Ultimately, two North Carolina immigrants were charged with illegally voting in 2016.)

Meanwhile, Mark Harris decided that he would run again in 2018. Among his first campaign hires was Leslie McCrae Dowless Jr., whose antics in 2016 at Harris's expense had gone unpunished and who therefore was more than happy to continue his balloting scheme for his new client. It paid off: in November 2018, Harris defeated his general election opponent, a Democrat named Dan McCready, by 905 votes, out of 282,717 cast. The balance was tipped in Bladen County, where Harris somehow managed to win 61 percent of the absentee ballots, despite the fact that only 19 percent of those ballots were submitted by Republican voters.

Now wise to Dowless's methods, state officials ordered a do-over election. Harris dropped out; Dowless was arrested. (He died in April 2022 before his case could go to trial.) Far from chastened, however, Republicans throughout 2019 and much of 2020 continued to insist that Democratic concerns about election integrity were thinly disguised attempts to undermine President Trump's legitimacy. In October 2019, not a single House Republican voted for the SHIELD Act, intended to combat foreign involvement in U.S. elections. (The measure died in the Republican-controlled Senate.) In January 2020, House Democrats convened a hearing with the CEOs of America's three major voting machine companies, including Dominion. The Republican questioners were low-key and not exactly probing.

Eleven months later, the fevered hysteria over fraudulent mail-in ballots and corrupt Dominion machines would spawn a thousand conspiracy theories, with no corresponding arrests. However, six known cases of voter fraud did emerge from the 2020 election. Three occurred in the conservative central

Florida retirement community known as the Villages. Each of the residents voted both in Florida and out of state.

The other three alleged fraudsters lived in Pennsylvania. One seventy-one-year-old man was arrested for attempting to vote twice—the second time in disguise, pretending to be his son. The other two men, aged sixty-seven and seventy, were each caught attempting to cast a ballot for their deceased mothers.

All six of them were registered Republicans—as was a seventh: Trump's chief of staff, Mark Meadows, who registered to vote in 2020 using the address of a mobile home in Scaly Mountain, North Carolina, that he apparently never once stayed in.

TWO HOURS AHEAD OF THE MAY 21, 2021, AMERICA FIRST RALLY FEATURING Paul Gosar, Marjorie Taylor Greene, Matt Gaetz, and Andy Biggs, a line of several hundred conservatives stretched outside the Marriott hotel convention hall in Mesa, Arizona. Many of those in line seemed to know one another, a nomadic tribe that had gathered together yet again to celebrate an undying movement. MAGA regalia predominated: campaign flags, the trademark red caps, a T-shirt worn by a young woman proclaiming TRUMP IS MY SUGAR DADDY. But a single theme, more acutely focused than the all-encompassing Trump-love, pervaded the gathering.

That theme was that the 2020 election had been stolen and the audit currently in process would prove it.

"No *way* this state flipped," said the young man behind me in line—pudgy, bespectacled, appropriately red-capped and MAGA-shirted. By way of evidence, he cited Trump's rally-size superiority and the fact that he, a former Obama supporter, had never met a Biden voter other than his parents, whom he no longer spoke with owing to the manner in which MAGA politics had thoroughly overtaken his life. (His new family, he said, was the Facebook group he had started, with 1,500 followers from all over the world.)

I asked him if he had any ideas as to how the election had been rigged. The young man ticked off the usual suspects—Biden, Dominion, secretaries of state of both parties—but then added, "And the intelligence community had to be in there too." He'd done his own research, much of which was confirmed by his most trusted news sources: Breitbart, *Infowars* ("Alex Jones has been proven right about a lot of stuff"), and One America Network ("Chanel Rion is smoking hot"). He assured me that he tended to steer clear of conspiracy theories such as QAnon—though, he reflected, "Democrats very well *could* be brain-eating pedophiles for all I know."

We filed into the convention room, which quickly reached its capacity of roughly a thousand. (Matt Gaetz would later falsely claim that two thousand had been turned away by the fire marshal. The more accurate number hovered around one hundred.) A riser in the back held several media crews, which the crowd viewed with scorn. In this and in all other ways, the prevailing ethos was unambiguously MAGA nostalgia, right down to the golden-oldies Trump rally soundtrack. Men bellowed out *WE LOVE TRUMP!*, while a young woman loudly spat out the Pledge of Allegiance as if it were a call to arms: *with LIBERTY and JUSTICE for ALL!*

The overwhelming if not unanimous consensus in this thousand-strong crowd was that Trump had rightfully won Arizona. It was a remarkable thing to witness, given that two days earlier I had met with the former chairman of the Maricopa County Board of Supervisors who oversaw the 2020 election in that pivotal county. His name was Clint Hickman, and the well-heeled poultry entrepreneur was not simply a Republican: he was the only board supervisor who had endorsed Trump in the 2020 elections. Hickman had counted as one of the highlights of his life the October 27, 2020, Trump rally in Goodyear, Arizona, one week before the election, when the president had called him out by name, in the presence of Hickman's sons: "Thank you, Clint, for all your help."

But a little over two months later, on January 1, 2021, at thirty minutes before midnight Eastern time, with the Arizona election results already certified, Hickman received a call on his cell phone from the White House switchboard, requesting that he call President Trump. Leery of the legal implications, Hickman decided not to respond.

Late on the evening of Sunday, January 3, the White House switchboard again left a message on Hickman's cell phone: "If you could please give him a call back soon, that would be great. You have a good evening." By that point, however, Clint Hickman had more than an inkling about what Trump wanted. For the news had broken that very day about a call the president had placed to Georgia's secretary of state Brad Raffensperger, imploring him to "find" 11,780 votes.

That call had taken place on January 2, one day after Trump's first call to Hickman and a day before his second. Hickman strongly suspected that what Trump wanted was for him to find 11,000 votes in Maricopa County.

Hickman contacted his attorney, Tom Liddy—the son of former Watergate felon G. Gordon Liddy—who advised him, "This is an American president already on tape going outside his power to sweat someone. I think it's a total overreach of power by the president of the United States."

Hickman never called Trump back. Republican though he was, the board chairman was thoroughly convinced that the Maricopa County election tally was accurate and free of tampering. For having publicly issued his stamp of approval, Hickman received threats and protesters outside his residence. The right-wing conspiracy website *Gateway Pundit* had alleged that a fire at Hickman's poultry plant that had destroyed 160,000 chickens had been caused by Hickman's burning ballots.

And now Clint Hickman watched with weary chagrin as the Arizona audit was under way. Conducting the audit was an outfit calling itself the Cyber Ninjas, a Florida-based cybersecurity firm that did not advertise itself as having any election expertise. What Cyber Ninjas did have going for it, besides its bargain-basement $150,000 fee, was the belief publicly expressed by its CEO that Biden had stolen Arizona from Trump. The Republican-controlled Arizona senate commissioned the group to conduct a "full forensic audit" of the election.

And as state party chair Kelli Ward, the first speaker of the May 21 America First Rally, declared onstage, "This audit is going to give other states the courage, the passion, the wisdom to follow in our footsteps."

Paul Gosar followed Ward. "There was fraud in this election," he told the audience without equivocation. The Arizona congressman leaned into his roll call of Stop the Steal lies—that "China owns Dominion outright," that up to 700,00 ballots were altered.

But neither Gosar nor the next speaker, Freedom Caucus chairman Andy Biggs, nor the final act Matt Gaetz, could hope to measure up to the penultimate speaker. In her bright blue dress, Marjorie Taylor Greene mounted the stage to adoring applause. "So let me just check and make sure with all of you," she began after the clapping ceased. "Who do you think won Arizona on November 3?"

The crowd exploded: *TRUMP! TRUMP! TRUMP! TRUMP!*

"That's how we feel in Georgia too." She grinned. "As a matter of fact, that's how Michigan feels. Pennsylvania. Wisconsin. I think that's how at least seventy-four-plus million people feel. As a matter of fact, *no one* went out for Biden! Did you see the rallies Trump had?"

Standing out in front of the podium, pacing without notes, the Georgia freshman proceeded to make sport of Congress. She referred to Nancy Pelosi as Speaker Maskhole, snickering at "the woke COVID religion" that had everyone imprisoned behind masks. Riffing off a famous refrain by Southern comedian Jeff Foxworthy, Greene said, "You know you might be a Democrat if your name is Liz Cheney. You know you might be a Democrat if your name is Adam Kinzinger." And she added with venomous glee, "You might be a Democrat if you're one of the eleven Republicans that voted to kick Marjorie Taylor Greene off her committees."

"Vengeance is sweet!" someone near me hollered.

Greene recited with pride the fines she had accrued for refusing to wear a mask on the House floor: $500 for the first offense, $2,500 for the second. She described her tête-à-tête with Alexandria Ocasio-Cortez, alternately saying that AOC had agreed to debate her and that the New York congresswoman had responded with a juvenile "Like, whatever." And though the media "tattle-told" on her for harassing the Democrat just off the House floor, Greene pledged to the audience, "Well, I will continue to tell her she needs to debate me."

Taken only by its verbiage, Greene's speech was little more than a compilation of well-worn conservative jabs: Hunter Biden's laptop, Barack Hussein Obama, Sleepy Joe Biden in the basement, "the little swamp creatures up in the DC bubble," rampant abortion, CNN sucking, gas lines at home, and chaos abroad . . . But the words were secondary. Ebullient with the knowledge that the crowd was thoroughly with her, Marjorie Taylor Greene turned in a performance that no American conservative since Sarah Palin could replicate—not even her idol, Trump, the "greatest president of [her] lifetime." By turns impish and tart, indignant and gossipy, the freshman slowed and stopped and resumed her monologue as if time were entirely of her ownership—which in this hall, it was. No one remembered Ward, Gosar, and Biggs before her. No one wanted to hear Gaetz after she was done. Her grievances, her enemies, her champion were theirs. The synchronicity was total. The air she expelled was the oxygen they breathed.

"But let me tell you what's happening," she said near the end. "President Trump is not giving up. You want to know why? He loves this country. He loves the American people. He loves everything we stand for. And," Greene vowed, "you'll see him. He's coming back."

Just before exiting the stage, Marjorie Taylor Greene had another conspiracy theory to float. "Let me tell you," she said, "none of us agree with the violence on January 6. No one's arguing that."

But, she suggested, something nefarious was at work. Numerous rioters under arrest "are being held twenty-three hours in solitary confinement, and they haven't seen a court day yet." And she added, "There are questions that need to be answered from that day. Who killed Ashli Babbitt? Her family deserves justice. There's more questions that need to be answered. There was intel ahead of time that there was going to be violence on January 6. President Trump requested 10,000 National Guard to be at the Capitol on January 6. The question that needs to be answered is: Who turned that request down?"

It did not matter that the claim about Trump's requesting National Guard troops was simply a parroting of what the ex-president later insisted, without evidence. Nor did it matter that accused Capitol rioters being confined away from the general prison population was for their own protection. It also did not matter that Babbitt, in leading a brigade of insurrectionists through a window of the Capitol in an effort to halt the activities of Congress by force, had invited deadly force in return.

What mattered was that Marjorie Taylor Greene had seized upon an exquisite new formulation in the factually parallel universe of the right wing. The Democrats were obsessed with the Capitol riot, she said, because "they need Witch Hunt 2.0. They want Witch Hunt 2.0 so the media can talk about it and talk about it and talk about it until everybody wants to vomit about this. Right? So they can cover up exactly the horrible things that Joe Biden is doing to this country."

Now it all made sense. And of course, the questions posed by Greene—*Who killed Ashli Babbitt, and who turned down Trump's request for National Guard troops?*—were entirely rhetorical, requiring no fact-based answer. In a sense, so was the question of what the Cyber Ninjas "audit" might uncover.

Simply asking the questions, over and over, QAnon-style, was tantamount to saying that the truth was not known—that the truth was whatever anyone wanted it to be.

National guardsman at the Capitol

Chapter Eighteen

THE LEVIATHAN LIE

arjorie Taylor Greene's insinuation at the Mesa rally that Trump's patriotic Americans could not possibly have been responsible for the Capitol riot was hardly an original thought. Within weeks of the insurrection, the chain of lies had come to form a perfect circle. The first lie—the Big Lie—was that the election was stolen. The second lie was that the "steal" could be unstolen on January 6, whether through legal or extralegal means. The third and final lie was that those who attempted to unsteal it were in fact not Trump supporters.

These were the lies that encircled the recent life of Capitol rioter Alan Hostetter like a noose.

Hostetter had been in law enforcement for twenty-three years, rising to the rank of police chief in the small city of La Habra, situated in Orange County, California. After just four months on the job, he went on medical leave. The psychological stresses had been taking a toll on his spine, and his marriage of twenty years was disintegrating. Three months later, in August 2011, the police chief quit the profession altogether.

He underwent two spinal surgeries, took up Yin yoga, and began looking for a new life partner on Match.com. By 2018, Hostetter was a yoga and meditation instructor, enhancing his training in China while cruising the Li River with his new wife, Krissie. The Southern California community of spirituality and wellness was one that would over time become entangled with QAnon and other conspiracy theories. Still, Alan Hostetter seemed to drift contentedly above politics, until the pandemic hit.

On March 10, 2020, at the very start of the coronavirus lockdowns, Hostetter's Instagram page—hitherto apolitical, a wallpaper of yoga poses and family photos—now dedicated itself to dismissing the outbreak of COVID-19 as "fear mongering" on the part of the media. He wrote, "Do yourself, and those you love, a favor . . . turn off the TV, take a deep breath, wash your hands, hug those you love and go on with your life. By summer, we'll all be wondering why so many of us lost our minds over a less deadly virus than the common flu."

By Election Day, Hostetter was a full-blown Trump cheerleader, organizing rallies in Orange County while issuing Q-inflected declarations on his American Phoenix Project Instagram page like "#thestormishere." On November 5, when it had become evident that the electoral results were going south for Trump, Hostetter organized a Trump Motorcade from Mission Viejo to Beverly Hills to "protest this massive, nation-wide voting scandal." A week later, the yoga instructor was in Washington participating in the Million MAGA March—in which, he vowed in a video shortly before the rally, "some people at the highest levels need to be made an example of, with an execution, or two, or three."

"The time has come," he posted on December 16, alongside a photo of his wielding an axe, "when good people may have to act badly . . . but not wrongly." Hostetter awaited a plan of action. Two nights later, it came. As Hostetter wrote the next day, "Late last night President Trump tweeted that all patriots should descend on Washington DC on Wednesday, 1/6/2021. This is the date of the Joint Session of Congress in which they will either accept or reject the fake/phony/stolen electoral college votes. I will be there, bullhorns on fire, to let the swamp dwellers know we will not let them steal our country from us. I hope you will join me!!"

Hostetter booked a room at the George Hotel a few blocks from the Capitol. At a rally in Orange County on December 20, Hostetter took the microphone and said of January 6, "Those people sitting inside the House are going to be listening to us chanting inside those walls. They're gonna hear millions of patriots in a rage over what has happened to our country and what's happened to these elected whores that we sent to Washington, DC. And they're gonna realize: 'We have one choice. We either fix this mess, and keep America America—or we become traitors, and those five million people outside the walls are gonna drag us out by our rear and tie us to a fucking lamppost. That's our option.' Not to sound violent or anything, but this is it, folks. This is for all the marbles."

He began his four-day journey to the swamp accompanied by his wife in his car on the early morning of New Year's Eve 2020. "Things are going to come to a head in the U.S. in the next several days," Hostetter vowed on Instagram. More furtively, Hostetter had set up a private Telegram account through which he communicated plans with six other comrades who had formed the California Patriots–DC Brigade. One of them, Russ Taylor, wrote, "I personally want to be on the front steps and be one of the first ones to breach the doors!"

On the morning of January 6, Alan Hostetter attempted to attend Trump's rally on the Ellipse but was turned away by Secret Service agents because he was wearing paramilitary gear. He and Taylor marched to the Capitol. Eyeing the nearby police officers, Taylor said in a selfie video: "We'll see who these guys end up working for."

By 2:30 that afternoon, Hostetter and Taylor were on the upper West Terrace of the Capitol, plowing through a phalanx of outmanned Capitol police. "Hundreds of thousands of patriots showed up today to take back their government!" Hostetter exulted in a selfie video.

FOUR MONTHS AFTER THE JANUARY 6 INSURRECTION, ALAN HOSTETTER— now a subject of inquiry by a federal grand jury, facing an indictment any day now—launched a new podcast series. It was entitled "The Root Cause of the Capitol Riot."

Hostetter's new message—entirely of a piece with his previous musings and at the same time completely contradictory of them—was that the insurrection, the one Hostetter himself promoted and participated in, was an elaborate hoax. Speaking now as a veteran expert on law enforcement, the podcaster listed his data points. "We *know* that legitimate Trump supporters love cops." The scaffolding on the West Terrace, ostensibly set up for the upcoming Inauguration, was deliberately left there to serve as "a ladder," just as the bicycle racks surrounding the Capitol served no tactical purpose except perhaps to be used as battering rams by rioters.

So who were the actual rioters, and who were the actual masterminds? Time would tell, Hostetter predicted. The "fakesurrection," he went on, was "obviously staged and faked," just as COVID was a Chinese bioweapon and the Black Lives Matter protests were hardly organic but instead "funded, recruited for, trained for and years in the making." Biden, he said, was "a Marxist imposter president completely controlled by the transnational criminal syndicate, also known as the Chinese Communist Party, along with the globalist deep state." At the same time, Hostetter observed, evidently thinking out loud, Obama clearly had a hand in all this, because some called it "the JoeBama administration with good reason" and "we know who's really calling the shots."

In a more detailed description of Marjorie Taylor Greene's pronouncement at Mesa that Trump would be "coming back," Hostetter explained to his podcast audience that the ex-president had deliberately walked away from the White House after exhausting his legal options, "letting us watch and experience the horror of it all, until a maximum number of Americans could be awakened to what their future might actually look like under a Marxist government. His move will go down in world history as one of the most brilliant and strategic moves ever made to defeat an enemy force during a time of war, which is what this is."

Amid this hyperventilative whirlwind, the former police chief and yoga instructor—who in early June would face four counts of federal charges relating to the January 6 insurrection—neglected to address a single nettlesome curiosity, a riddle to his own life that perhaps he simply could not answer:

If the January 6 riot was in fact a "fakesurrection," then why had Alan Hostetter been enthusing about it and the necessity of violence for weeks, all the way up until he stood on the West Terrace of the Capitol with thousands of other patriots to "take back their government"?

ALAN HOSTETTER RECORDED HIS FINAL PODCAST ON MEMORIAL DAY, MAY 31. That same day, Democratic congressman Emanuel Cleaver delivered his annual Memorial Day address at the National World War I Museum and

Memorial in Kansas City. Cleaver, a former pastor and mayor of Kansas City, had represented Missouri's Fifth District for the past fifteen years. His freshman class included Republican Patrick McHenry of North Carolina. The two served together on the Financial Services Committee. Though McHenry was a great deal more conservative than Cleaver, the two men got along well.

Reverend Cleaver got along with most members of Congress. But January 6 had begun to change that. After spending much of that tumultuous day in his House office with the blinds closed while rioters pounded on his door and the TV screen flickered images that to Cleaver would have made more sense in Guatemala or Southeast Asia, the Missouri congressman watched with astonishment late that same evening as most of his Republican colleagues voted to overturn the election results. It was what Reverend Cleaver termed a "Leviathan lie," monstrous and all-devouring. Eventually, his own fury died down, and Cleaver figured that Congress would return to some sense of normalcy.

It had not happened yet. Most days were bad days. For the crimes of speaking out against Trump and cheekily ending a prayer on the House floor with the words "Amen—and A-women," Cleaver had received multiple death threats. The open hostility pouring out of this new group of House Republicans from members like Marjorie Taylor Greene was something he was at pains to understand. And in the meantime, more level-headed Republicans held their tongues, justifying their own complicity, as one GOP congresswoman did to Cleaver, by saying, "I'm doing this so I can come back. And believe me: you *want* me to come back. Because if I don't come back, the person coming here in my place will be fifty times worse." Because Cleaver knew this Republican to be a decent, God-fearing human being, he wanted to give her the benefit of the doubt.

What prevented Emanuel Cleaver from ultimately doing so was that in the face of such meek acquiescence, the Leviathan lie was growing ever larger. This became evident during Cleaver's annual Memorial Day speech at the World War I Museum and Memorial. At one point, the Missouri congressman deviated from his prepared text. He looked up at the audience and said, "Look, I cannot finish this day of remembering those who have sacrificed for us and not include the Capitol police who were engaged in medieval hand-to-hand combat as they sought to protect our democracy."

After finishing his speech, Cleaver prepared to leave the gathering until he saw a woman approach him. The woman unleashed a string of profanities. "You politicized this!" she hollered. "My husband's a veteran—you made him cry!"

A couple of security officers pulled Cleaver away, though not before he said to her: "Ma'am? I was there. *I was there!* Do you understand that?"

As Cleaver retreated, he could hear her shouting: "*IT DIDN'T HAPPEN!!!!*"

PART FOUR

TOO MUCH TRUTH

Senate Minority Leader Mitch McConnell

Chapter Nineteen

McCONNELL

I n Kevin McCarthy's view, the Republican Party could prosper only if it wedded itself to Donald Trump, lest the former president turn on the GOP and spoil McCarthy's last chance to be House Speaker. From Liz Cheney's perspective, the party would suffer continued losses and all moral standing if it did not break decisively from Trump, make clear to the American public that it had done so, and return to its pre-Trump status as a party based on truth and reason.

Senate Minority Leader Mitch McConnell had a somewhat different viewpoint from either Cheney or McCarthy. His approach first became apparent on February 14, at the conclusion of the impeachment trial. "Former president Trump's actions preceding the riot were a disgraceful dereliction of duty," he intoned. McConnell decried "the entire manufactured atmosphere of looming catastrophe; the increasingly wild myths about a reverse landslide election that was being stolen in some secret coup by our now-president." He denounced the Trump-induced "intensifying crescendo of conspiracy theories, orchestrated by an outgoing president who seemed determined to either overturn the voters' decision or else torch our institutions on the way out." And of the January 6 insurrection, McConnell made clear his view that it was "one person," Trump, who undertook to "engineer the campaign of disinformation and rage that provoked it." In short, the Republican minority leader of the Senate offered the best case imaginable for convicting Donald Trump of impeachable offenses.

But McConnell did not vote to convict Trump. Referring to the Senate, the minority leader's conclusion was that "we have no power to convict and disqualify a former officeholder who is now a private citizen." He was saying that a president can be impeached and tried only before the expiration of his or her term on January 20. For an offense committed on January 6, such a trial was not practically possible—particularly when McConnell succeeded in persuading Senate Majority Leader Chuck Schumer and Speaker Nancy Pelosi that Trump's lawyers deserved a full week after the House impeachment hearing on January 13 to prepare an adequate defense. This was exactly the loophole—"the January exception"—that the House impeachment managers warned against during the Senate trial. A defeated and spiteful president like Trump could spend his last weeks in office breaking laws, punishing enemies, rewarding friends, and subverting democratic norms with impunity—and then, as a final act, issue a pardon to himself.

As Democratic impeachment manager Joe Neguse put it, with his attention noticeably fixed on McConnell: "Presidents can't inflame insurrection in their final weeks and then walk away like nothing happened. If Congress were just to stand aside in the face of such an extraordinary crime against the republic, it would invite future presidents to use their power without any fear of accountability."

McConnell did not address Neguse's concern—not in his February 14 speech, and not anytime thereafter. Beyond issuing the reminder that any ex-president was subject to future criminal investigation, he had spoken his piece on the matter. When asked to elaborate, McConnell would refer to his public statements on the subject and refuse to say more.

And in this way, the minority leader distinguished himself from Liz Cheney. Without question, Mitch McConnell wanted Donald Trump in the GOP's rearview mirror. But he did not believe the way to accomplish that objective was to keep denouncing or otherwise picking fights with the ex-president.

By May 2021, momentum was gathering for an independent commission to examine the events of January 6, modeled after the commission that had been established to investigate the failures to anticipate the 9/11 attacks. On May 19, McConnell announced his opposition to a January 6 commission, saying that it would be unavoidably partisan and duplicative of existing investigations. Discreetly, the minority leader reached out to individual Republican senators, asking them to withdraw their support for such a commission.

What McConnell said to others was different from what he was saying publicly. Yes, January 6 was a travesty. But, he believed, it was also a bad subject for Republicans. To pick at the scab of the Capitol insurrection would be to focus a harsh spotlight on Republican malfeasance: Republican rioters, elected Republican agitators like Congressman Paul Gosar and Senator Josh Hawley, Republican enablers like House Minority Leader Kevin McCarthy...

How was critiquing Republicans a way for Republicans to win in 2022? That was Mitch McConnell's question. He believed it answered itself.

WINNING WAS NOT THE ONLY THING THAT MCCONNELL CARED ABOUT. SCIENtific truth, for example, mattered to him. McConnell had been crippled by polio as a child. Ultimately, he was able to walk again, thanks to two vaccines that had taken seventy years to be developed. In less than a year's time, three coronavirus vaccines had been produced. It alarmed McConnell to see so many Americans resist them. He knew, of course, that Trump's dismissiveness of the virus accounted for some if not most of the aversion. McConnell had made it a point to advocate wearing a mask and to defend Trump's top COVID scientist, Dr. Anthony Fauci, publicly describing his confidence in Fauci as "total."

Truth in a broader sense also mattered to McConnell. The Senate minority leader did not bother to contact his counterpart in the House, McCarthy, before publicly condemning a Republican on the other side of the building, Marjorie Taylor Greene, for her "loony lies and conspiracy theories" three days before Greene was stripped of her committee assignments by the House Democrats. But here McConnell acknowledged his predominant concern. An unhinged ranter like the Georgia freshman posed a reputational risk for McConnell's party. She was bad for business—"a cancer," as he put it in a statement.

Greene, of course, responded on Twitter: "The real cancer for the Republican party is weak Republicans who only know how to lose gracefully."

McConnell ignored her goading. Twitter kabuki was not his thing. Scoring points on social media was not his idea of winning.

McConnell did not come across as a natural-born winner. Oratorically limited, vaguely amphibious in appearance, the eighty-year-old drawling Kentucky politician did not radiate charisma or in any way personify Hollywood's rendering of a leader. He led because he won, and he won through a combination of discernment, ruthlessness, and Olympian-level self-discipline. McConnell's capacity to focus only on things that he could control was perhaps his most formidable trait. Marjorie Taylor Greene was Kevin McCarthy's responsibility. McCarthy had a tough assignment, and it was not up to McConnell to tell the House minority leader how to pull it off. McConnell's quest to win back the Senate majority in 2022 involved different calculations, because the Senate and the House were different bodies.

Unlike McCarthy, Mitch McConnell did not intend to solicit Trump's help. Nor, however, did he intend to rebuke Trump at every turn, as had become Liz Cheney's habit.

"WHY DO YOU FEEL THE NEED TO ANSWER ALL THE CRITICS?" MCCONNELL asked then-candidate Donald Trump, during one of their earliest meetings in 2016.

Trump seemed flummoxed by the question. "I *have* to answer," he sputtered. "I *have* to respond."

"Why?" asked McConnell, equally puzzled. Over time, he came to understand that what animated Trump most of all was grievance. It caused the president to lose focus. McConnell did, however, come to admire Trump's feral survival skills. It surprised him when Trump, at the dawn of his candidacy, lashed out at the senator and Vietnam POW, McConnell's friend and colleague John McCain: "He's a war hero because he was captured. I like people that weren't captured, OK?" Somehow, this seeming unforced error did not finish Trump off. Nor, apparently, had his conduct before and during January 6.

McConnell had been a U.S. senator for three decades before Trump was elected president. By Trump's inauguration in January 2017, the Republicans controlled every branch of government. That would remain the case for two years, while McConnell would preside over a Republican Senate majority for all but the final two weeks of Trump's presidency. His two-track mission was therefore to accomplish as much as he could during Trump's term in office while not allowing the president to define Mitch McConnell's career.

And though McConnell chalked up win after win, it was his conclusion that President Trump made everything harder. That included Trump's two most lasting accomplishments: the confirmation of three conservative Supreme Court justices, and a $1.5 trillion tax-cut bill.

From the start, McConnell did not pretend to like Trump. It was the Senate majority leader, after all, who directed Senate Intelligence Committee chairman Richard Burr to investigate the Trump campaign's dealings with Russia. (The new president frequently called McConnell to complain about Burr, whose only offense was that he had not instantly declared Trump's innocence and immediately shutter the inquiry.) In meetings with the president at the White House, the majority leader did not join in on the unctuous laughter as the back-slapping House Majority Leader Kevin McCarthy did. He did not publicly gush, as Speaker Paul Ryan had, that a Trump speech was "a home run." He thought that Trump's self-described "perfect phone call" to Ukraine's president was at minimum inappropriate and arguably impeachable. And though McConnell did not vote to convict Trump, and in fact led the backstage effort in the Senate to exonerate him, he also made a point of assuring the one Republican who did vote to convict, Mitt Romney of Utah, that his standing in the GOP Senate caucus had in no way changed as a result of his vote.

In any event, Donald Trump was the Republican leader whom the voters had installed in the White House, and McConnell preferred a Republican over a Democratic president. He awaited a legal or evidence-based rationale for Trump's claim that fraud had swung the 2020 election to Biden. When no such rationale was produced and the Electoral College formally declared on December 14 that Joe Biden had prevailed in the electoral tally, McConnell called the winner the next day and congratulated him. Trump then called the Senate majority leader and yelled at him. It was the last conversation the two men would have. McConnell later told others that even if Trump expressed interest in a rapprochement, he was done with the man.

At the time, however, the 2020 election season was far from over in

McConnell's eyes. The two Senate run-offs on January 5, both in Georgia, would determine whether he would stay on as majority leader of the Senate. McConnell feared that Trump's incessant and fact-free claims that the presidential election had been fraudulent would cause Georgia Republicans to stay home. Those worries were confirmed by a young Senate staffer McConnell dispatched to northern Georgia immediately after Election Night. The field team coordinated by McConnell's staffer went door to door. What they repeatedly heard from Georgia residents was: "My vote's not going to count."

Having learned that Donald Trump had likely cost him his majority leader post (a belief that was later validated by a voter analysis published in the *Atlanta Journal-Constitution*), Mitch McConnell was not in the jauntiest of moods in the early afternoon of January 6. His spirits worsened when he, Pelosi, Hoyer, and McCarthy were evacuated to Fort McNair, and when he subsequently received frantic phone calls from his senior staff as they crouched behind doors barricaded with office furniture while rioters pounded against the windows. Those same staffers were calling colleagues who worked for the GOP senators who had intended to object to the election results, telling them, *We need to bring this to a close.*

McConnell, according to a witness at Fort McNair, was visibly the most infuriated of the House and Senate leaders sequestered there. While the others concurred with him that Congress should resume its business that evening, McConnell's focus was characteristically strategic and pointed: he wanted Congress back in session by prime time, when a nationwide audience could see the plain evidence that democracy had held firm in America.

After that, he believed he could get back to the business of winning.

"THINGS CHANGE IN A HURRY IN POLITICS," MCCONNELL WOULD REMIND HIS associates. Obama had gotten elected on the Iraq war and the financial meltdown. Two years later, the only things that mattered were Obamacare and America's soaring debt. Six years after the Tea Party wave, Trump's "America First" populism amounted to the sum total of the GOP platform. Yes, Trump remained the dominant force in Republican politics—for the time being. Already, however, the ex-president's approval rating among Republicans was starting to lose altitude. The way to speed Trump's decline, McConnell believed, was to leave him in the dust in 2022.

The minority leader relished few things more in life than the opportunity to shape the composition of the GOP Senate during the primaries. In 2010 and 2012, McConnell had stood by helplessly as Republican Tea Party candidates he viewed as clowns—Sharron Angle, Christine O'Donnell, Richard Mourdock—were clobbered in winnable general elections, allowing the Democrats to hang on to the Senate majority. That passivity would soon change. "I think we're going to crush them everywhere," McConnell vowed in 2014 to *New York Times* senior congressional journalist Carl Hulse as McConnell's chief of staff sat nearby, the blood draining from his cheeks. McConnell succeeded that year with more mainstream candidates like Cory Gardner of Colorado. At long last, Mitch McConnell was running the Senate, with a majority consisting of fifty-four Republicans.

By 2021, his caucus had dwindled to fifty. Though he required the barest of net gains—a single Senate seat—to win the majority in 2022, exactly how he would do so required a fair amount of wishful thinking on McConnell's part. He believed, not without cause, that Trump's paramount consideration was his win-loss record, which the ex-president would be loath to jeopardize if McConnell recruited a strong Republican candidate in states like Pennsylvania and Ohio. But the GOP nominees in both states would turn out to be Trump endorsees who parroted the claim that there had been widespread fraud in the 2020 election. They were far from McConnell acolytes.

Meanwhile in Arizona, McConnell's ideal recruit, Governor Doug Ducey, had declined to run, all too aware that he remained a hated figure in Trump World for certifying the election results. In Alaska, McConnell fully intended to support incumbent Lisa Murkowski, whose vote to impeach Trump meant that she was already facing a well-funded primary opponent. In Georgia, for that matter, Trump had succeeded in urging Herschel Walker—a Black conservative and former football superstar who faced allegations of violent behavior toward the women in his life—to enter the ring against Democratic incumbent Raphael Warnock, a Black minister. A political novice like Walker in so high-profile a race was far from McConnell's ideal choice. He endorsed the Trump favorite anyway.

McConnell had a fallback rationale for acquiescing to Herschel Walker. It was the same reason why he did not contest the Senate candidacy of Ted Budd, a North Carolina congressman and favorite of Trump. What McConnell told others was that Budd and Walker were Trump acolytes only for the moment. As Trump's influence waned, so would these men shed their MAGA skin and adapt to the more even-tempered ways of the Senate. McConnell would see to it—though his handiwork in this regard had yet to be made manifest in the behavior of Trump-adjacent senators like Josh Hawley, Ted Cruz, Ron Johnson, and Tommy Tuberville.

What McConnell believed most of all, however, was that he understood the Senate better than any living soul and that he possessed the power to flip a single seat to give the Republicans fifty-one senators. If he did so with a Trump wannabe, so what? The most important thing, McConnell would cheekily point out, was the first vote that the newly minted U.S. senator would cast for majority leader: Chuck Schumer or Mitch McConnell?

He would rule the Senate again, rendering unto Trump what was Trump's.

DC police officer Michael Fanone

Chapter Twenty

THE BLUE

Aweek after Senate Minority Leader Mitch McConnell announced in late May that he would oppose an independent commission to investigate the January 6 attack on the Capitol, Gladys Sicknick—the mother of Brian Sicknick, the forty-two-year-old Capitol police officer who died the day after he fought the rioters—visited her son's former workplace to meet with some of McConnell's fellow Republican senators.

With Ms. Sicknick were her son's girlfriend, Sandra Garza; a colleague of her son, Officer Harry Dunn, who had defended the West Terrace of the Capitol that day; and Metro police officer Michael Fanone, who had been beaten unconscious by the rioters on the West Terrace. Accompanying them was a former Republican congresswoman, Barbara Comstock, whose friend Liz Cheney had asked her to help set up meetings between Sicknick's mother and GOP senators, in hopes that a few of them might defy McConnell and support a January 6 commission.

The first meeting, with Senator Mitt Romney, went well. The group expressed appreciation for his vote to convict President Trump and for his general supportiveness of the law enforcement officers who had defended the Capitol. The Utah senator modestly assured them that he had done nothing heroic. He sat next to Fanone and together they watched the officer's body-cam footage of his being dragged down the steps of the West Terrace and repeatedly shocked with his own Taser. Romney pledged that he would vote to support a commission, against the wishes of McConnell.

Their meetings with Lisa Murkowski and Susan Collins were similarly encouraging. Everything afterward amounted to a letdown, however. Lindsey Graham of South Carolina (who had brought along three other senators, including fellow South Carolinian Tim Scott) was inattentive to Fanone's body-cam video and kept looking out the window until Sandra Garza snapped, "Brian loved you guys! And this is how you're reacting? This is how you're treating Officer Fanone?"

"No, no, I'm just upset about it," Graham insisted.

"That's just how Lindsey acts," Scott interjected.

"I'm a licensed clinical social worker," Sicknick's partner shot back. "I know what I saw."

"You're wrong," Graham said testily to her. Taking the temperature down, Graham then offered to put Fanone and Dunn in touch with Senator Roy Blunt, who along with Democratic senator Amy Klobuchar was amassing information for a Senate Rules Committee report on security failures during the riot.

"Have they arrested the guys who did this to you?" he asked Fanone.

"Yes," said Fanone. He added that the assailants were all avowed Trump supporters.

"Why didn't you shoot them?" Graham asked. "I would have."

Fanone and Dunn attempted to explain the myriad ways in which firing off a few rounds into a crowd of rioters would have been ineffective at best and a prelude to a bloodbath at worst. The meeting broke up without any of the four senators so much as hinting at a willingness to support a January 6 commission. Shortly after that, Ted Cruz of Texas canceled their scheduled meeting after the group notified his staff that they were running slightly behind.

Then came the meeting with Ron Johnson. The sixty-six-year-old, two-term Wisconsin senator, who had made a fortune off his in-laws' plastics business, served as a notable exception to Mitch McConnell's stated belief that the institution of the Senate had a tempering effect on a member's untamed impulses. Johnson entered the upper chamber "somewhat starry-eyed," recalled a top Republican Senate staffer. "But then he surrounded himself very quickly with extremely cynical Heritage Foundation types whose entire goal was to convince members that their wildest dreams would all come true if only the Republicans stopped being sellouts. And it affected his staffing. And over time he just kind of became dark."

In Johnson's dark view of things, the Democrats were not a party so much as a corrupt and sinister force that was determined to subvert American values. As chairman of the Senate Homeland Security Committee in 2020, he zealously investigated Biden's son's activities in Ukraine, proclaiming that his findings would disqualify the Democratic nominee. (Johnson had been a reliable advocate for Ukraine, until 2019, when he began to parrot Trump's insistence that it was Ukraine rather than Russia that interfered in the 2016 election. Johnson also refused to accept the possibility raised by U.S. intelligence officials that he had been fed disinformation by Russian intelligence operatives. As Trump's expert on Russia in the National Security Council, Fiona Hill, would tell me, "It was like something out of *Invasion of the Body Snatchers*. Was that the same guy I was just talking to a week ago?") A Democrat who sat on the Homeland Security Committee, Chris Murphy, came to view Johnson as "one of those Republicans that does believe that there is a deep state of Democratic loyalists inside government that worked for four years to frustrate the Trump agenda."

In the weeks following the Capitol riot, Johnson's allegiances to Trump led him into the same briar patch of tangled theories. The Wisconsin senator first maintained in a Senate hearing that the rioters might well have been "fake" Trump supporters and entered into the record a depiction of the mob as having fallen under the sway of left-wing agitators. Not long after that, Johnson told a conservative radio talk-show host that the insurrectionists were "people that love this country, that truly respect law enforcement, would never do anything to break the law, and so I wasn't concerned."

Barbara Comstock had warned Gladys Sicknick and the others that Johnson was a lost cause. They wanted to meet him anyway. The Wisconsin senator genially received them and led them into his office. A framed copy of Johnson's legislation granting terminally ill patients access to experimental drugs, passed by Congress in 2018 and bearing President Trump's distinct signature, hung prominently on a wall in front of them. He began by assuring them he was not what the media had made him out to be. "They've taken my statements out of context," he said.

"But," said Ms. Sicknick, "we've seen and heard you on TV."

Johnson continued his harangue against the media for several minutes.

Then he abruptly reversed course. "You know, I've been to several Trump rallies," the senator told them. "These are God-fearing, peace-loving people."

The air went out of the room. Because they were already there, Fanone went ahead and showed the senator his body-cam footage—thinking nonetheless, *Ron Johnson couldn't give any less of a fuck about what happened that day. He just doesn't care.*

IF KEVIN MCCARTHY CARED, HE CARED ABOUT OTHER THINGS A GREAT DEAL more. Like McConnell, the House minority leader viewed a January 6 commission as a golden opportunity for Democrats to trot out Republican misconduct at a lavishly slow pace. McCarthy also knew that the very existence of such a commission would enrage Trump. That mattered to McCarthy, even if it didn't matter to McConnell.

In the spring, the House minority leader had deputized John Katko, the New York congressman who had voted to impeach Trump, to negotiate the details of a commission with Democrats who served within the bipartisan House Problem Solvers Caucus. McCarthy had every reason to believe that the Democrats would not make meaningful concessions. The Democrats would insist on choosing the staff, controlling the witness-subpoena process, and dragging out the investigation indefinitely.

But McCarthy turned out to be wrong. Katko succeeded in winning every key negotiating point. He was also successful in convincing other Republicans on the Problem Solvers Caucus that such an independent commission would be far preferable to a Benghazi-style partisan inquiry in which Pelosi called all the shots. Over 75 percent of the caucus's twenty-nine members backed the legislation for a commission that Katko had helped to craft. The draft was presented to the House Rules Committee as a bipartisan product.

McCarthy was now in a jam. The minority leader protested to other Republicans that Katko had ironed out the final details of the bipartisan legislation without first sharing the specifics with McCarthy. Those specifics, however, had already been discussed when John Katko originally agreed to act as the minority leader's designated negotiator. Katko's effectiveness at striking a deal was something McCarthy apparently had not counted on.

The minority leader chose to whip his members to vote against the very bill he purportedly sought out. Katko, a former hockey player and federal prosecutor who had incurred death threats throughout his career, was not easily ruffled. Nonetheless, he angrily declared to more than one Republican colleague, "Kevin threw me under the bus."

The alternative to an independent January 6 commission was a select House committee composed of seven Democrats and five Republicans. McCarthy could pick his five members, though they were subject to Speaker Pelosi's final approval. The process was inherently more partisan, and thus its work could serve as a far more inviting target for McCarthy to criticize. He pronounced himself noncommittal, holding his cards close.

On June 25, during a House Oversight Committee hearing relating to the attack on the Capitol, two of McCarthy's Republican colleagues cast the events that day in a breathtakingly fantastical light. One of them, Georgia freshman Andrew Clyde—who on the early afternoon of January 6 could be seen panic-stricken, hollering on the House floor as the mob tried to force their way in—declared that the TV footage of that day showed "people in an orderly fashion" walking through the Capitol, such that "you would actually think it was a normal tourist visit."

The other Republican to make light of the insurrection at the hearing, Paul Gosar, lamented that the slain rioter Ashli Babbitt had been "executed," while saying of the ongoing federal investigation, "The DOJ is harassing peaceful patriots across the country."

EARLIER THAT SAME MORNING, MICHAEL FANONE, HARRY DUNN, AND GLADYS Sicknick had visited Kevin McCarthy's spacious office. Fanone had been adamant about such a meeting since May 12, the day House Republicans had voted to remove Liz Cheney from her leadership post. The only other guest was an unusual one: a young woman who did not identify herself but who Mike Fanone later learned from contacts on the Hill was McCarthy's general counsel, Machalagh Carr.

McCarthy began by offering his condolences to Brian Sicknick's mother— the first time he had expressed this to her. (Since her son's death, Gladys

Sicknick had frequently received calls from Pelosi, Cheney, and Kinzinger.) Then, seeking to establish a lighter mood, he said to the two police officers, "You guys like to hunt?"

Seeing that the officers were in no mood for pleasantries, McCarthy offered a show of empathy. "Tell me what happened to you that day," the minority leader said.

Fanone guessed that McCarthy was going to try to run out the clock. He ran through a brief synopsis of how he had nearly lost his life defending the Capitol. Then the police officer arrived at the specific points he wanted the minority leader to commit to. On June 19, Fanone noted, twenty-one House Republicans—including Marjorie Taylor Greene and Paul Gosar— had voted against awarding medals to those who had defended the Capitol on January 6. He wanted McCarthy to denounce them.

"Or at least get them all in the same room," suggested Ms. Sicknick, "and tell them, 'You can't be doing and saying these things.'"

"The way I lead my members," the minority leader replied, "is by conducting those conversations in private."

"Your definition of leadership and mine could not be more different," Fanone said. "This is a moment that calls for a public airing. Because it's not just about what those twenty-one Republicans did with their vote. It's also about how they and the whole party have sworn allegiance to Donald Trump."

At minimum, Fanone said, McCarthy should call out Gosar and Andrew Clyde for their outrageous recent comments. "I'll conduct these conversations in private," the minority leader reiterated.

"And I'd like to see you go on TV and denounce this crazy theory"—and here Fanone mentioned the latest of Gosar's conspiratorial notions—"that the FBI incited the insurrection."

With a helpless smile, McCarthy said, "Look, I don't have control over who the voters send up here."

"No, but you have the biggest voice," said Harry Dunn. "You're the leader. And, you know, on January 13 you said the same thing about Trump being responsible for the riot as Liz Cheney did. So why did she become the scapegoat, and not you?"

McCarthy seemed dumbfounded for a moment. Then the minority leader picked up on a tack he often retreated to when it came to January 6. There were gross security errors, he told them sympathetically. The upper levels of police management had failed to heed the intelligence, failed to send proper reinforcements. They had failed Officers Sicknick, Fanone, and Dunn.

"We get that management sucks," Dunn said. But that was a side matter. At issue here was whether the Republicans in Congress intended to show their support for their defenders. Pointing to a member of McCarthy's Capitol security detail stationed just outside the office door, Dunn said, "That man spends more time with you than he does his own family."

"Oh, we love you guys," McCarthy assured him.

"But we're asking for a little more here than just bringing us doughnuts and sandwiches," said Dunn.

"Look," cut in Fanone, "the chance for supporting the independent commission has obviously come and gone. Now we've got the select committee coming up. We're just asking that you take it seriously and make serious appointments to the committee. No obstructionists. Obviously, no Marjorie Taylor Greene or Paul Gosar."

"Or Lauren Boebert," Dunn added.

"I'll be very upset if you select five Jim Jordans," Fanone said. "To be honest with you, I think I'd be pretty damn upset if you select *one* Jim Jordan."

"I will commit to taking the special committee seriously," McCarthy said with solemn finality.

What the fuck does that even mean? Fanone wondered.

"We love you guys," said McCarthy as he shook their hands. Dunn noticed that McCarthy's counsel Carr, who had said nothing during the meeting but had often nodded while taking notes throughout, gave the officer's hand an extra squeeze.

"If there's another insurrection," Gladys Sicknick warned Kevin McCarthy, "you might not be so lucky next time."

The grieving mother elected to slip out the back door and down the elevator, thus avoiding the press. The next day, she saw the photograph of Mike Fanone exiting through the front, rubbing his forehead in anguish.

That's exactly how I felt, Gladys Sicknick thought.

FIVE DAYS LATER, ON THE AFTERNOON OF JUNE 30, THE HOUSE CONVENED TO
vote on House Resolution 503, which would establish a select committee to
investigate the events that had transpired less than six months earlier. The
debate preceding it had been sparsely attended, as the arguments were now
well known. Repeatedly, Democrats stood on their side of the aisle to insist
that this was a quest for truth and to wonder aloud why Republicans were
afraid of the truth. Just as repeatedly, the House Republicans said that the
events of January 6 had already been fully investigated and that this proposed
select committee was nothing more than a partisan witch hunt to distract
from President Biden's myriad failings.

The only mystery to the matter of H.R. 503 was whether any of the 211
Republicans would defect and vote for it. In languid waves, the members arrived, cast their votes, and then in most cases took their seats. On the front
row by the center aisle, two Michiganders sat together and talked with easy
familiarity: Republican Fred Upton and Democrat Debbie Dingell, Hill veterans in their late sixties reenacting a lost era of civility. Dingell had succeeded
her now-deceased husband, John Dingell, the legendary dean of the House
who had held his seat for just shy of sixty years, just as his father had held it
for two decades. Upton, an easygoing moderate who had been among the ten
Republicans to impeach Trump, had himself been a House member for thirty-
four years. Politically imperiled like the other nine impeachers, Upton had not
yet told his friend Debbie Dingell whether he intended to run again.

Marjorie Taylor Greene bustled into the chamber, in head-to-toe black
and carrying a white binder. Plopping down in the vacant seat next to the new
GOP conference chair, Elise Stefanik, Greene pulled out a slip of paper and
handed it to her. Its headline read: WE MUST DEFEAT THE RULE (H. RES. 508).

With a somewhat pained expression, Stefanik listened as the Georgia
freshman spoke with alarm about an upcoming vote that would extend the
COVID-19 national emergency declared by Trump on March 13, 2020, until
the end of the 117th Congress in early January 2023. Greene viewed this as an
act of tyranny by the Democrats. After she finished talking to Stefanik, she

marched up to Kevin McCarthy with an additional copy of her memo. Mc-Carthy shoved it into his pocket without looking at it.

As the roll call on the January 6 select committee continued, a woman wearing a white pantsuit entered the chamber. It was Liz Cheney. Without speaking to anyone, she touched her voting card against the scanner at the rear of the chamber. Then, having cast the first of two Republican "yeas" for H.R. 503—Adam Kinzinger would supply the second vote a few minutes later—she turned and walked out.

Cheney then took an elevator up to the third floor of the Capitol. Stepping into the gallery, she greeted the visitors sitting there: Gladys Sicknick, Sandra Garza, Mike Fanone, and Harry Dunn. They had been there all afternoon, listening to the debate—which included Democratic Rules Committee chairman Jim McGovern looking up at them at one point and apologizing, saying, "You deserve better"—and then waiting to see how many Republicans would vote to investigate what had happened on the most fateful day of their lives.

For close to a half hour, Cheney spoke to the police officers, Ms. Sicknick, and the friends they had brought along—knowing that there was no comfort she could offer, other than to say that with or without Republican support, a Democratic majority had now seen to it that a committee would dig for the truth. What Liz Cheney did not tell them was that she had already made up her mind: if the Democrats wanted her to serve on the committee, she would do so. And indeed, the following morning, July 1, Speaker Pelosi would ask that very thing, and receive that very answer.

Finally, Cheney had to excuse herself, because there was another matter she had not mentioned to the visitors in the House gallery. On her way up to see them, her communications director, Jeremy Adler, had intercepted her with some unexpected news. Dick Cheney's mentor, the former secretary of defense Donald Rumsfeld, had died at the age of eighty-eight. She had known Rumsfeld her entire life; he was in many ways her mentor as well, perhaps the man she most admired after her father.

Still, she had not shared any of this with anyone in the House gallery. Instead, she listened to their thoughts, letting the moment remain theirs. Finally, she said goodbye and walked to her office, to write a statement about Rumsfeld.

Representative Kevin McCarthy

Chapter Twenty-One

===========

THE BOWL

K evin McCarthy had never seen the HBO series *The Wire,* so Patrick McHenry felt the need to send him a YouTube link to a particular scene from the show that seemed applicable to McCarthy's quest to be Speaker.

In one episode, the precocious new mayor of Baltimore, seething with ambition, has coffee with a former mayor from years past. The new mayor wishes to know why the old mayor left his job after only one term. Reflectively, the old mayor answers in the form of a parable. He describes his first day on the job, when his chief of staff walked in with a gorgeous silver bowl. It was a gift from the local unions. The mayor smiled with delight, until he smelled what was inside the bowl.

"What the hell am I supposed to do with that?" he demanded to his chief of staff, gesturing to the pile of fresh manure inside the bowl.

"You're supposed to eat it," said his chief of staff.

Reluctantly, the mayor did so. A few minutes later, the chief of staff walked back in, bearing another bowl. This one was from the local ministers. The mayor was supposed to eat what was inside that bowl too.

Other bowls came from other groups, each one heaped with a fresh meal. "That's what it is," concludes the old mayor to the new one with a mournful shrug. "You're eating shit day after day, year after year."

McCarthy was amused by the tableau but not the least bit deterred. McHenry continued to send the link to him throughout the year, typically accompanied by a single sentence: "How's your day going?" Or: "Get used to it."

MCHENRY WAS SITTING ON THE HOUSE FLOOR ONE DAY DURING THE LAST
week of June 2021 when Madison Cawthorn wheeled up to him.

"I'm going to the border this week," the North Carolina freshman
announced.

"Good for you," said McHenry. He had already read about the upcoming
trip to the Texas border, which was being led by Trump and Governor Greg
Abbott. It would mean that Cawthorn would miss the June 30 vote on the
January 6 select committee and would therefore have to find someone to cast a
proxy vote on his behalf. This would be the second time, after attending CPAC,
that Cawthorn had voted by proxy after having sneered that the procedure was
for "cowards." But hypocrisy was a small price to pay for the chance to be in the
company of Trump, who on June 30 at the border would tell the crowd that the
twenty-five-year-old congressman "has got the best face in the business."

Changing the subject, McHenry asked Cawthorn, "Are you going to Israel in August?" He was referring to the trip organized for Republican freshmen by the American Israel Public Affairs Committee (AIPAC), and led
by McCarthy and Michael McCaul, the ranking member of the House Foreign Affairs Committee. The AIPAC junkets were informative and featured
lavish amenities that spouses were also invited to enjoy.

"No," Cawthorn muttered. "The wife and I aren't going."

"Why?" McHenry asked.

"Because of the vax policy," he said. Cawthorn was referring to Israel's
requirement that all foreign visitors first be completely vaccinated against the
coronavirus.

Taken aback, McHenry then managed to say, "Well, that's a shame. It's
the single best trip I've ever been on in my life. I'm sorry you're going to miss
out on it."

Shrugging, the freshman said, "My constituents won't have it. They don't
like the vaccination stuff and mandates and everything else. I'm not doing it."

"Do people ask you if you've been vaccinated?"

"Oh, yeah, all the time."

No one in his district had ever asked McHenry if he had been vaccinated against COVID-19. "It's nobody's business," he told the freshman. "Why should anyone lecture you about your health-care decisions, Madison?"

Cawthorn nodded thoughtfully. "That's a good point," he said.

"I mean, just a thought," McHenry persisted. "You can get vaccinated and go on this amazing trip and you don't have to tell anyone you've been vaccinated."

Cawthorn looked at McHenry. "I'll think about that," he assured him.

Ultimately, the issue would become moot: the raging Delta variant of COVID-19 would cause AIPAC to reschedule the trip for early 2022. Still, McHenry's conversation with Madison Cawthorn was yet another reminder of what life would be like if the Republicans retook the House the following November.

All signs pointed to the likelihood of this. Kevin McCarthy's GOP needed to gain only five seats to assume the House majority. Of course, Trump's influence remained an X-factor: he would inevitably seek to make the 2022 midterms all about him, a scenario that would be a gift for the Democrats. No doubt the Democrats would also seek to elevate Marjorie Taylor Greene, Paul Gosar, Lauren Boebert, Matt Gaetz, and Madison Cawthorn as the Mad Hatter poster children of the GOP.

Already, Kevin McCarthy was anticipating the moment of victory. The minority leader had organized several task forces—on energy, Big Tech, national security, freedom, China accountability—which would develop policy papers that might then become the basis for legislation in 2023. McCarthy had appointed Patrick McHenry the lead member for the task force on jobs and the economy. Though he had made clear his desire for McHenry to run for majority whip, it did not take much imagination for McHenry to envision what life would be like rounding up the votes of Greene, Gosar, Gaetz, and the others. The mayor in *The Wire* had it easy by comparison.

In late June, McHenry procured a silver bowl. It had once been the property of the British Army in the 1950s and came with a spoon and a lid. He bought it online with his own money and had it shipped from the UK to his home address.

McHenry then presented it to Kevin McCarthy, who searched its exterior to see if McHenry had engraved it, which he had not. McCarthy had missed the point anyway.

It was what was inside the bowl that counted.

Ashli Babbitt, killed during the Capitol riot

Chapter Twenty-Two

TO BE UNSERIOUS

H ey, are you having a fundraiser Friday night?" Kevin McCarthy asked Paul Gosar in his office on June 30.

Gosar was expecting the question, which referred to a campaign fundraising event for the Arizona congressman that had been posted on the far-right social media platform Telegram. Sponsoring the fundraiser was Nicholas Fuentes, the twenty-two-year-old founder of the white nationalist America First movement whose convention Gosar had spoken at in late February. Staffers for Fuentes had reached out to Gosar's chief of staff, Tom Van Flein. They had begun to iron out details when word became public that Paul Gosar was yet again consorting with dangerous bigots.

"No," replied Gosar to McCarthy.

This was true, strictly speaking: the date for the America First fundraiser had not yet been formalized. Moreover, because Gosar had yet to give his formal blessing to the event his longtime consigliere had been planning with Fuentes, the congressman had plausible deniability regarding the matter.

"Good," said the House minority leader with a grin, and flashed a thumbs-up as he showed Gosar the door.

The Arizona congressman had been prepared for a lengthier dialogue about whether he shared Fuentes's antisemitic views. He had brought with him a thick folder of material assembled by Gosar's legislative director, demonstrating his long-standing support for Israel. But McCarthy apparently had no interest in probing Gosar's sympathies.

FOR THAT MATTER, KEVIN MCCARTHY DID NOT BRING UP WITH GOSAR THE
latter's recent remarks that the Capitol rioter Ashli Babbitt had been "executed" on January 6, despite the minority leader's pledge five days earlier to
Gladys Sicknick, Mike Fanone, and Harry Dunn that he would do so. Mc-
Carthy apparently hoped that Gosar's comment would be forgotten.

But Paul Gosar had no such intentions. In the days and weeks to come, he
would bring up his revisionist view of January 6 again and again, because it
mirrored his deep hostility toward the federal government. He would also do
so because his role in the post-election Stop the Steal rallies had awakened in
the once-obscure dentist-turned-politician a yearning for attention.

During Gosar's freshman term in 2011, the gun-walking fiasco of Operation Fast and Furious and the tragic security meltdown at the U.S. embassy in
Benghazi had provided the Arizona congressman with early glimpses of federal incompetence. But Gosar saw something uglier at work. From his viewpoint, officials in the U.S. government compulsively lied to, and in all other
ways harbored contempt for, ordinary Americans. This malevolence particularly hit home for Paul Gosar following the Yarnell wildfire.

After departing his more precarious perch in Arizona's center-right First
District in 2012 to run successfully in the newly created deep-red Fourth District, Gosar was only five months into his maiden term there when a bolt of
lightning sparked a blaze that quickly became a galloping inferno outside the
small town of Yarnell in his new district. Nineteen young firefighters from
Prescott, ranging in age from twenty-one to forty-three, were fatally trapped
in the wildfire. One-third of the town's 650 residents lost their homes. Shell-
shocked by the news, Gosar canceled a town hall that had been on the schedule the day after the wildfire was extinguished and instead attended a memorial
service in Prescott. Over a thousand residents of the district showed up for the
July 9 event, along with six other Arizona members of Congress, Governor
Jan Brewer, Senators Jeff Flake and John McCain, two Obama cabinet members, and Vice President Joe Biden.

Soon, however, Gosar's grief turned to suspicion, which hardened into
conspiratorial outrage. His belief was that the tragedy was entirely preventable.

Had the community been permitted to conduct prescribed burnings and other methods of forest thinning, the blaze would have been more easily contained. Environmental groups had resisted such practices, saying that they enriched timber companies while imperiling forest ecosystems. This, then, was the problem, in Gosar's view: the federal government had taken the side of environmentalists who, he said, were, above all else, "motivated to save species and forest." By his reckoning, the nineteen Prescott firefighters had been deemed expendable by the left.

Gosar did not seek proof for these unswerving beliefs. He did not urge an investigation into the cause of the swift-spreading wildfire. It seemed to escape his notice that the Arizona State Forestry Division, rather than the U.S. Department of the Interior, bore responsibility for the restrictions on forest thinning. Nor had Gosar considered the fact that Yarnell's bone-dry surroundings had not been subjected to fire in fully half a century, making it a literal tinderbox that the community had done nothing to buffer itself from, despite having received a grant from the state for that very purpose.

Had such a natural tragedy occurred in, say, New York and New Jersey—as Hurricane Sandy had the previous year—a conservative like Paul Gosar might have lamented this act of God but otherwise urged bootstrapping personal responsibility rather than a demand for federal redress. Indeed, just five months earlier on January 13, 2013, Gosar had voted against the Hurricane Sandy Relief Bill, asserting that it was "stuffed with pork" without citing any specifics.

Notwithstanding these facts, the Yarnell fire became a touchstone in Paul Gosar's war on the feds. "Listen, you're the ones causing this," he said of federal bureaucrats and their role in forest fires, as he recounted to residents of Kingman during a town hall in 2014. He added, with characteristic rhetorical maladroitness, "Bureaucrats are held to a different realm than the rest of us."

Such bad actors in the federal government extended well beyond forestry officials, of course. "*Everybody* ought to be scared of the IRS," he told the same audience—and, indeed, Gosar had accused IRS official Lois Lerner to her face during a committee hearing of engaging in "the worst form of authoritarianism" in targeting Tea Party nonprofit groups for audits. (A 2017 investigation launched by President Trump's Department of the Treasury determined that liberal groups had been scrutinized by the IRS as well.) Similarly, in a different House hearing, Gosar suggested to Dr. Jonathan Gruber, one of the chief consultants on the Affordable Care Act, that he was guilty of "outright lies." He accused Cecile Richards, the president of Planned Parenthood, which was a recipient of federal funding, of "profiting off death." And Gosar lectured EPA administrator Gina McCarthy, saying that she had fostered a culture "that is built of fraud, denial, incompetence, and bureaucratic nepotism," thereupon demanding that McCarthy resign or face impeachment.

Of course, the "deep state" in the federal government could not do their dirty work alone, Gosar believed. The Democrats, he maintained, were hopelessly corrupt—starting with Hillary Clinton, who, he said in a town hall, had managed to "get away with everything under the sun." Even as the bipartisan Senate Intelligence Committee was amassing evidence that key members of the 2016 Trump campaign had been in contact with Russian intelligence sources, Paul Gosar was insisting on conservative shows that "the real collusion was with Hillary Clinton and the Democratic side." The media, he lamented, was nothing more than "a propaganda machine for the other side—there's no impartiality anymore. . . . The only way you can get that is listening to Fox and Breitbart and some of the others where you're starting to hear some of the facts."

Gosar's beliefs were thoroughly in step with many in his district. But for its swath of Latino voters in the farmlands of Yuma County near the border, Arizona's Fourth Congressional District, like Marjorie Taylor Greene's, was overwhelmingly white, with a median household income significantly below that of the nation at large, easily the most conservative district in the state. Gosar would describe his constituents as "fairly old," and he enjoyed hearing their blunt views, telling them, "I like to come to rural America. You teach me more than I teach you."

That last statement was significant. Gosar gave out his personal cell phone number to literally thousands of his constituents and heard from them frequently. He came to rely on them as trusted sources of information, just as they trusted what they heard and read on conservative media. Gosar spoke for these Arizonans when he mused, to Arizona's PBS news division Cronkite News just before the 2020 election, that race relations would be far better in America if people stopped using the word "racist" and instead took "a chill pill."

Above all, he channeled their belief that the federal government was at best a nuisance in their lives, and at worst a force of malevolence. Such tension is hardly unique among congressional districts where a significant percentage of the land is under federal control.

But the persona embraced by Gosar and his constituents—that of rugged self-reliance—was belied by the Fourth District's historic dependence on government largesse. The mountain highway connecting Prescott (which lay in Gosar's district until the latter was reconfigured in late 2021) to urban Arizona, State Road 69, was made possible not by hardy pioneers but instead by federal funding as well as revenue from state gasoline taxes. At the western border of the district, Lake Havasu City owes its tourist-based economy to the federal damming project that created the lake in the 1930s. And in 2014, Congressman Gosar fought tooth and nail to prevent the Fish and Wildlife Service from closing a rainbow-trout stocking program that the same federal agency created in 1962, arguing without irony that the federal program had created almost 1,700 jobs and close to a billion dollars in annual revenue for his district.

"We've seen a lot of that," one of Gosar's constituents, Jim Arroyo, said when I asked him if he had detected signs of federal corruption in the Fourth District. Until the 2020 election, Arroyo said, such corruption principally consisted of the way federal lands and natural resources were used to the detriment of ordinary Arizonans such as himself and his wife, Janet, who was also sitting with us in a restaurant in Prescott one Wednesday evening.

Arroyo, a compactly built middle-aged man who owned a local gun shop, wore a military vest as well as a hat and T-shirt on which were emblazoned the words OATH KEEPERS. Arroyo happened to be the founder of the Yavapai County chapter of the organization, which he preferred not to describe as a militia group but instead as a kind of volunteer security force. He explained that a prime illustration of how Arroyo's chapter conducted its affairs took place in September 2020, when roughly seventy progressives staged a Black Lives Matter demonstration in downtown Prescott. About a hundred of Arroyo's Oath Keepers arrived, heavily armed, in preparation for what he had heard would be a busload of Antifa agitators from Phoenix. Arroyo told me that the Antifa group must have learned about the armed resistance they would be facing, because no such bus showed up in Prescott that day.

He said that his Oath Keepers chapter was Arizona's biggest, with about eight hundred members, and that they often held their meetings at First Baptist Church in Chino Valley. Gosar, he said, "has come to our meetings. He's spoken to us. We have a very good relationship with him."

Arroyo and his wife were well aware that the Oath Keepers were seen in a negative light after sixteen of its self-described members were indicted for their role in the Capitol riot—eleven of whom would later be charged with seditious conspiracy. The Arroyos could not speak to the conduct of those individuals (some of whom were in the process of striking plea deals with the federal government). That said, the Arroyos doubted seriously that the events of January 6 had been accurately described—except, they said, by MyPillow CEO Mike Lindell, Newsmax, One America News, and in the research shared by friends on Facebook.

"What we've seen," Jim Arroyo said, "is that often anywhere when there is any kind of a patriotic rally by the right, the left shows up with the intent to disrupt and hurt people."

"You think that's what happened on January 6?" I asked.

Said Arroyo, "We know for a fact that all the intelligence is pointing, including videotaped evidence, to Antifa getting off the buses and starting to don Trump MAGA hats and carrying Trump banners and everything. A lot of what you saw there was not as it seemed."

I then informed the Arroyos that I had been there that day. And yes, I had seen buses parked at Union Station, and people getting off the buses wearing MAGA caps and carrying Trump banners. But those buses were later found to have been funded by conservative groups. And yes, there were many outside the Capitol who did not seem violent, and others still who went inside but urged their friends to conduct themselves peacefully. And there was also a great deal of nervous chatter about Antifa's possible presence on the Capitol grounds. But the vast majority of those who would later be indicted had bragged about storming the Capitol on Parler and Telegram. They had incriminated themselves. Those same rioters, I told the Arroyos, had social-media feeds that indicated a long-standing allegiance to Trump.

"This was not an Antifa thing," I said in conclusion.

Neither of them said anything. Janet Arroyo's gaze at me was one of welling pity.

ONE AFTERNOON IN EARLY JULY 2021, I DROPPED BY PAUL GOSAR'S OFFICE IN the Rayburn Building. Befitting the status of a six-term congressman, the office suite was large but otherwise unremarkable, except that Gosar had seen fit to enlarge and hang on his wall a tweet he had posted on his official account in 2019, during the Ukraine impeachment hearings. It read: "The only reason Adam Schiff is conducting these unclassified interviews in a SCIF [a secure room where classified information is discussed] is to allow Democrats to control the narrative getting to the press. We are watching a coup happen right in front of us. It's time to fight back."

I was there to visit with Gosar's chief of staff, Tom Van Flein. I had first met him in Anchorage in 2010, when Van Flein was serving as Sarah Palin's general counsel. After deciding to quit his practice and move to Washington in early 2011 to work for Gosar, Van Flein offered to introduce me to his boss.

I walked away from that introductory interview in March 2011 doubting that Paul Gosar would ever be newsworthy. What I did not know was that Gosar intended to do something about his lack of newsworthiness and that Tom Van Flein would be instrumental to achieving that goal.

Seldom does a congressional staffer stick around in one office for a decade, unless the boss is on track for a leadership position or higher office. Neither scenario applied to Gosar. And yet Van Flein had remained by his side, literally. From meetings with Brian Terry's widow after the Fast and Furious debacle to the Yarnell memorial service to driving across the state line into Nevada to observe the standoff at Bundy Ranch to the first Stop the Steal rallies, their inseparability over the years had resulted in a mind-meld. The low-key and lawyerly chief of staff had authored many of Gosar's most incendiary social media posts. Like his boss, Tom Van Flein believed that the election had been stolen from Trump. He believed that a deep state, a political party filled with radical socialists, and a left-wing media had conspired to strip away traditional American values. He believed, like Gosar, that the FBI had played some sort of unacknowledged role in the Capitol riot on January 6—because, as he told me, "We have, like, sixty solid years of them infiltrating groups like the Black Panthers and Students for Democratic Society. If they didn't infiltrate the Proud Boys and Oath Keepers, then they weren't doing their job."

But he seemed to believe most of all in the importance of his boss's getting attention. Unprompted by me, Tom Van Flein kept returning to that subject in the course of our two-hour conversation. By way of underscoring the credentials of a Gosar ally, right-wing commentator Raheem Kassam of the *National Pulse,* Van Flein mentioned that Kassam appeared regularly on Steve Bannon's podcast, "which has good numbers." Referring to Gosar's designated mentee, Marjorie Taylor Greene, and to Lauren Boebert, Van Flein marveled, "If you have the right social-media profile, then you can fundraise and become a mini national superstar. Which they are. In political circles, they're stars. And they just got on the scene. Marjorie, Lauren. It's like AOC too. She's on the left. She has millions of Twitter followers. She was pouring drinks four years ago."

I asked Van Flein about Gosar's fervent support for Ashli Babbitt, the rioter who, Gosar claimed publicly, had been "executed" at the Capitol. Gosar had met with the Babbitt family's lawyer, who had started a social-media account, Justice for Ashli Babbitt, in hopes of receiving donations for legal fees. Gosar—or more likely Van Flein—had tweeted a paraphrased lyric from a song about Martin Luther King by the Irish band U2: "They took her life. They could not take her pride." In Paul Gosar's eyes, the QAnon-believing rioter was now a martyr.

"'Executed' is a pretty charged word," I said to Van Flein.

"It's a charged word," he agreed. "But it broke the dam open. Right? I mean, even Trump has started talking about her. It changed the whole tenor of the discussion. Now people are asking, 'What is up with that?'"

People are asking. All Paul Gosar was doing was asking innocent questions, Tom Van Flein insisted. Like the 2020 election: "We've never, never once said that fraud was in fact committed," he maintained.

I reminded the chief of staff that on November 4, Gosar had declared, "We're not going to let Biden and his thugs steal this election."

"That's hyperbole," he said. "But generally speaking, the position we've taken consistently is we just need to double-check."

It was much like Gosar associating with Nick Fuentes, the avowed white nationalist. Fuentes and his Groypers were merely young conservatives who were disaffected and whose traditionalist sentiments aligned with Gosar's. "They may not all share *every* view together," Van Flein said, adding that Fuentes himself was simply "an entertainer" and sometimes lacking in maturity: "I'm pretty certain *I* said some stupid shit when I was twenty-two. Probably when I was thirty-two."

OR, IN PAUL GOSAR'S CASE, SIXTY-TWO. BUT THERE WAS A PRICE TO BE PAID for suggesting, with feigned innocence, that Barack Obama was not an American citizen, that federal bureaucrats were more interested in protecting the spotted owl than the lives of firefighters, that it was Hillary Clinton who had tried to rig the election in 2016, that the white-supremacist riot at Charlottesville had been plotted by the Jewish billionaire George Soros, that the 2020 election was stolen, that patriots needed to take back their country, that "Mr. Biden" was not a legitimate president, that a rioter breaking into the Capitol was an "executed" martyr, and that the insurrection may well have been staged by the FBI as a pretext for locking up Trump supporters.

For all the attention that such baseless claims may have brought him, for all the praise they elicited from Trump and the right-wing commentariat, the price was that Gosar was widely viewed on Capitol Hill as an unserious nut job. His own leader in the House, Kevin McCarthy, had not seen fit to assign Gosar to any of the 120 posts on the seven task forces intended to formulate future GOP policy. Even new members Marjorie Taylor Greene and Lauren Boebert had been given assignments.

Among the far right, of course, being snubbed in this manner by the Republican establishment constituted a badge of honor. The problem was that Paul Gosar's time as a public servant was on the wane. His unspecified neurological disorder was advancing. Gosar had begun to speak to Tom Van Flein and others of a "legacy" project, a lasting mark on Arizona for which the congressman would be remembered.

Gosar had a specific project in mind. For the past couple of years, the Arizona congressman had been imagining a desalination plant that would bring more water to the state's residents, thereby relieving pressure from the Colorado River. Rather than source the water from the West Coast—which would require negotiating with California's environmentalists—Gosar conceived of a federally authorized pipeline that would travel from the Sea of Cortez, coordinated by a joint U.S.–Mexico commission and likely with the cooperation of neighboring states. (Later, fretful that the Mexican government might be rife with corruption, Gosar modified his plan to connect the pipeline from the Mississippi Valley.)

In effect, it would be Paul Gosar's version of the Central Arizona Project, the landmark legislation signed into law by President Lyndon Johnson in 1968 that enabled water from the Colorado River to flow into the Phoenix metropolitan area. The passage of CAP had been made possible by the efforts of Arizona's two senators, Democrat Carl Hayden and Republican Barry Goldwater, working together with Democratic congressman Mo Udall. All of them were experienced at the craft of governance and working across the aisle. All of them were serious.

When I considered whether Paul Gosar, with all his performative maneuvers, had it within himself to bring something so monumental to passage, I recalled a conversation I'd had a few weeks earlier with Brad Schneider, a Democratic congressman from Illinois. Schneider was a member of the Problem Solvers Caucus, for whom it was a point of pride to forge consensus among members from both parties.

But Schneider had also been among the Democrats who had been stranded in the House gallery after the Capitol riot had compelled an evacuation. Subsequent to the late-night vote to certify the election results, the Democrat had developed his "Schneider Standard" in which he would do business only with Republicans who had acknowledged the validity of the 2020 election results.

Schneider had worked with Paul Gosar on what he considered to be "a noble bill"—one that would extend family leave to parents who had lost a child. Gosar had been a co-lead on the legislation—surprising, given that most Republicans opposed the idea, even though it did not cost a cent of the taxpayers' money. Gosar saw it as a pro-family bill. He was eager to work on the issue with the help of Democrats and however many Republican votes he could scrounge up. But that was in the previous session of Congress, before the 2020 election.

Now, Brad Schneider told me, "I'm not doing it with him. We'll either do it without a Republican co-sponsor or someone else will come on and we'll go forward with that member."

It was not that the Illinois Democrat had second thoughts about extending family leave to parents who had lost a child. Rather, it was that he saw little chance of its passage with heavy reliance on Democratic votes so long as the Republican cosponsor was a man who refused even to say the words "President Biden."

Paul Gosar was not seen as serious. That was an unfortunate reality for Gosar and for Arizonans, of course. But it also carried implications for the entire U.S. legislative branch, given that Brad Schneider's list of governance-minded Republicans was becoming shorter with each term. This invited the question: Would *any* "legacy project" sponsored by any member of Congress henceforth become the law of the land as long as Republicans viewed Democrats as enemies of America while the latter regarded the former as delusional and dangerous?

Later in the year, President Biden would seek passage of just such a legacy project. Entitled the Infrastructure Investment and Jobs Act, the $1 trillion package included funding for high-speed internet expansion and the rebuilding of roads and bridges across America. In November 2021, the Senate passed the infrastructure bill by a remarkably bipartisan vote of 69 to 30 that included the support of Republican leader Mitch McConnell. The bill then went to the House, where a number of progressive Democrats had spent the past two months vowing to vote against the measure unless the Senate also passed the $3.5 trillion social-spending and climate-change bill known as the Build Back Better Act. It therefore appeared likely that Pelosi would need several offsetting votes from the other side of the aisle.

Paul Gosar was among the House Republicans who responded to the infrastructure bill with derision—this despite the fact that Trump during his presidency had championed an even larger, $2 trillion infrastructure package that featured many of the same components. At the time, Gosar and his fellow Republicans said as little as possible about their party leader's mammoth scheme, hoping that it would go away, which it eventually did. No such reticence greeted the Democratic bill, which, claimed Gosar, "only serves to advance the America Last's socialist agenda."

Gosar's leader in the House, Kevin McCarthy, knew that passage of the bill would count as a win for the Democrats and thus undermine his chances to be Speaker. His staffers prepared a video montage in which various Democrats had said, on camera, that the $1 trillion infrastructure bill and the $3.5 trillion Build Back Better Act were inextricably linked. McCarthy's message to his Republican members was: *If you vote for this smaller bill, your constituents back home are going to hammer you for helping to pass the bigger bill.*

After McCarthy had played the video montage and spoken his piece to the House Republican Conference, a number of Freedom Caucus members chimed in, declaring Biden's bill to be the very embodiment of radical socialism. Throughout it all, a moderate Republican, Fred Upton, somberly assessed the situation. Upton had furtively promised House Democratic leaders that he would try to recruit as many as a dozen Republicans to vote for the bill. Now, the veteran legislator could see, he would be lucky to recruit five GOP colleagues.

Just after the conference, Upton offered his gloomy prediction to a top Democrat, who said, in a voice of genuine lament, "It's so sad what's happened to your party."

"I know," said Upton.

But in the end, Fred Upton was happily wrong. Despite the vigorous whipping efforts of McCarthy and Steve Scalise, twelve other Republicans had joined Upton in support of the infrastructure bill, with only six progressive Democrats opposing it. President Biden signed it into law on November 15, 2021.

Paul Gosar issued a statement declaring that he had proudly voted "against the Democrats' phony infrastructure legislation." He made no mention of one obscure element in the 1,039-page legislative package: authority given to conduct a feasibility study for mitigating sediment in the reservoir of Arizona's Verde River. The study would be the latest in the decades-long effort to supply residents in Central Arizona with potable water—an effort to which serious Arizona lawmakers from both parties had made small but significant contributions over the years, even as naysayers on the sidelines hollered about high taxes and socialism.

It was the same effort that Gosar envisioned as the key to his legacy. He stood on the sidelines, shaking his fist at it.

PART FIVE

TOO MANY LIES

Representatives Matt Gaetz and Marjorie Taylor Greene

Chapter Twenty-Three

A TWITTER HOLIDAY

A s probably most of you know," said Marjorie Taylor Greene to the eight journalists who were gathered in her office on the late afternoon of July 20, 2021, "I was suspended, or I guess banned, on Twitter for twelve hours last night after—they said it was two tweets that I had tweeted, tweeting information that anyone can have access to on the internet, looking up and reading."

It was a day of committee work on Capitol Hill, and thus a day when the Georgia freshman had little to do. Owing to her suspension from Twitter that morning—her third such time-out to date, though not to be her last—she had even less on her plate. And so just before 1:30 that Tuesday afternoon, an aide sent out an email saying that the congresswoman would be having a press availability in about three hours at her office in the Longworth Building.

She sat behind a large desk in a mostly vacant room, next to a placard showing an enlarged email by Dr. Anthony Fauci dated February 5, 2020, in which he at the time counseled against wearing masks—proof, Greene had taken to saying on social media, that "Fauci lied, people died." (Fauci and the CDC revised their mask guidance less than two months after the email.)

Twitter had suspended Greene for tweeting: "Thousands of people are reporting very serious life changing vaccine side effects from taking covid vaccines. 5,946 deaths are reported on the CDC website. Social media is censoring their stories & the media is silent. Biden is going to homes to push shots. Just say NO!"

The tweet was overloaded with misleading and false claims. While it was true that 5,946 people had died after receiving a COVID vaccine, nothing in the way of a causal relationship had been established. The same number of people likely used toothpaste and drank tap water before their death. The vaccine's fatality rate was 0.0018 percent.

"I think it's important to investigate it," Greene said of the deaths, though at least up until that point the committeeless congresswoman had elected to devote her energies to fearmongering rather than investigating. Meanwhile, if media outlets were exercising caution about publishing random tales of vaccine dangers, that was likely because Russian trolls and bots had been spreading disinformation on the subject since the first domestic outbreak of COVID in early 2020. And though President Biden had recently advocated a door-to-door vaccine information campaign, the door-knockers would be community leaders and clergy, not federal bureaucrats.

(At least Greene had not claimed, as Lauren Boebert had, that these door-knockers were "Needle Nazis"; or that the next federal door-knocker would be at the expense of gun owners, according to Jim Jordan, or to confiscate Bibles, as Madison Cawthorn warned.)

Greene had also retweeted a claim by her Republican colleague Thomas Massie that many members of the military would quit rather than be forced to take the vaccine. She and Massie apparently did not know that U.S. military personnel were already required to take numerous vaccines as a condition of their employment—or that they were not permitted to quit simply because they disagreed with a policy.

"But here's the problem, everyone," she informed the handful of us who were gathered in her office. "I get banned for twelve hours for sharing this information and being willing to talk about things, because they're calling it misinformation. But yet, we have Dr. Fauci who has spread misinformation for a long time now." And, she observed, Twitter hadn't ever suspended Fauci as far she knew—though this was perhaps because the National Institute of Allergy and Infectious Diseases director did not have a Twitter account.

For the next hour, the Georgia freshman treated the eight of us to a kaleidoscopic array of untruths. She said flatly of COVID-19, "It's a man-made virus, and the proof is coming out more and more." (No such proof existed, and the consensus opinion within the scientific community continued to be that the coronavirus was likely of natural origin.) She claimed that Fauci had approved funding for a "gain of function" research project that resulted in the creation of the coronavirus. (The project in question was *not* gain of function, which involves increasing the transmissibility of a virus.) She insisted that COVID-19 was a "bioweapon," which she incorrectly defined as "a virus that can be spread from human to human."

She said that Fauci had "lied to us over and over and over and over," apparently confusing lies with revisions of opinion in accordance with updated scientific findings. She said that Fauci had claimed early in 2020 that "millions of Americans" would die from COVID-19, when what he actually said was that it was *highly unlikely* that the death toll would be in the millions. (Though, alas, the death toll would reach seven figures in 2022.)

She said that Twitter was suppressing her the way communist China would "silence" someone "when they don't like what they're saying"—in effect equating a twelve-hour suspension from a single social media platform with decades languishing in a forced-labor camp. She said that "conservatives are banned, censored, and kicked off of social media every single day," which was a gross exaggeration that presumably included not-exactly-conservative entertainment celebrities like Rose McGowan and Courtney Love as well as Islamic extremists and Russian bots. She said that she had recently been "sued by a Communist PAC"—referring to the anti-Trump PAC MeidasTouch, founded in Los Angeles by three brothers (a lawyer, a marketing director, and a video director for Ellen DeGeneres's TV show)—"for banning them from my page because of the horrible, nasty things they were saying to me on my Twitter page." Because Greene was a federal officeholder who had blocked them from her official account, the lawsuit was successful. Still, Greene seemed to believe that because MeidasTouch could say mean things about her even as she was prevented from merely sharing misleading information, that amounted to "a hypocrisy" on Twitter's part.

She defended her preposterous and lethal claim on Twitter that COVID-19 was "not dangerous for non-obese people and those under 65." Said the Georgia freshman inaccurately, "I was talking about the highest amount of deaths. The highest risk factor is for the older people and the people that fall into obesity. And those are the facts that you can simply look up." (Greene had it wrong: while an obese person was 48 percent likelier to die of COVID than a non-obese person, a pregnant woman was 70 percent more likely to die of COVID than a woman who was not pregnant.)

She claimed that the COVID vaccines were "experimental," which they were not. When asked by a reporter if she herself had received the vaccine, Greene replied that the question itself constituted "a violation of my HIPAA rights," which of course it did not. She asserted that children in particular should not be forced to wear masks because they "need to see each other's faces. This is what helps them learn emotion and expression. It's how they play and talk with one another. It helps them phonetically. It helps them with their speech." If there was evidence to support these claims, she did not offer any.

When Greene said that America needed "to ask China a lot of questions," I asked her, "Do you think they'll tell us?" In reply, Greene said that she "would handle China a lot different. I certainly would not allow anyone involved with the CCP in our colleges and universities. I would not give student visas to any students that are loyal to the CCP. I certainly would not allow Chinese businesses to function inside of our country if they're loyal to the CCP. And I would demand for China to tell us what is the protocol that you've developed when it comes down to COVID-19? And then secondly, China, how many other bioweapons do you have, what are they, and what are you planning to do with them? See, I think these are the questions all of us should be asking because China really is our common enemy."

"But given that," I said, "you don't expect they'd level with you, do you? I mean, even if we prevented CCP members from going to our colleges, do you think they'd say, 'Oh, okay. Yeah. All right, now we'll tell you?'"

Greene's lengthy reply was an evocation of China's ruthless obsession with dominating the world. She warned that if the United States enacted the Green New Deal with the intent of reducing our carbon emissions to a net zero, "they're saying they're going to *increase* their carbon emissions." (In fact, China had not said any such thing and instead was publicly negotiating a European Green Deal that would net-zero the country's carbon emissions by 2060.) Observing that "they care about money and business," Greene espoused the belief that tariffs "are a great way to deal with China," adding that America should "send these people back out of our colleges."

I strained to imagine how the U.S. educational community would react to a forced expulsion of America's 373,000 Chinese students (including 886 students from Greene's alma mater, the University of Georgia) unless they could demonstrate their disloyalty to their own government. Presumably the roughly 12,000 Americans studying in China would find themselves expelled in return, just as any ban on Chinese investment in the United States (like the Industrial and Commercial Bank of China's multimillion-dollar leasing agreement with Trump Tower) would result in the immediate removal of American businesses in China. Any number of things could take place in a soft war between the United States and China. Rising consumer costs, dwindling exports, unquantifiable losses in brainpower, and, of course, a new wave of bigotry against Asian Americans were all likely eventualities.

But would anything in this scenario prompt China to confess its full catalog of bioweapons? We had seen all this saber-rattling and doomsaying before. It had led us into a disastrous war against a country with a fraction of China's economic and military might.

Greene had moved on to questions from the other journalists—many of whom, being daily reporters (as opposed to someone gathering material for a book), were clearly angling for what could perhaps be viewed as a news-breaking nugget. In Greene's case, however, it was hardly unfair to ask whether, because she believed Dr. Fauci should resign for allegedly spreading misinformation, she should quit for the same reason; or whether she felt any responsibility for the deaths of non-obese under-age-sixty-five Americans; or how she could reconcile her own vaccine skepticism with the pride her favorite president took in developing those same vaccines at "warp speed."

My approach had been different, and probably foolishly earnest. I had decided to take her opinions seriously. My questions were searching but in no way barbed. Was her objection to social-media platforms that they had no business banning *anyone*, or that they should simply be consistent in their banning? Did she think it was inadvisable to release the COVID-19 vaccines before they had been approved by the FDA? How did she propose to coerce China into disclosing its state secrets?

The next day, after her Twitter suspension had expired, I noticed that Greene had posted an eighty-second snippet of our China dialogue—editing out my questions so that she sounded tough and determined rather than evasive. It was a savvy move, I had to admit, and I had emerged as the chump.

Less than a month later, Greene would receive a full week's suspension from Twitter, for ludicrously claiming that the COVID vaccines developed during the Trump administration were "failing & do not reduce the spread of the virus & neither do masks." By early January 2022, she would join her favorite president: her personal account would be permanently suspended from Twitter.

It did not matter. Her breakthrough was complete. Pilfering the decorative innovation of Alexandria Ocasio-Cortez that Greene had once mocked as "almost like a high school locker," the wall of her office doorway was now covered with notes from admiring conservatives, many of them from outside Georgia: "We truly admire your grit and fearlessness as you battle against the Radical Left." "We thank God for you & others like you who are willing to stand (and yes, 'fight') for the Constitutional rights of the people!" "Do not despair, we, the common folk, are behind you all the way!" "Wish I could donate more but I am retired—Something has to be done to stop the left, socialists, democrat[s], communists from destroying our Republic."

The letters served as a helpful reminder, to a passerby such as me, that a large constituency existed for Greene's high-volume, factually challenged antics outside the Beltway bubble. This was not a fringe thing. It was not a Georgia thing. Hers was a national following. Millions of Americans believed as she did: their once-great country was under assault from within. It was a truth they could see and feel. As such, the movement of which they and she were a part represented a striking migration from the Tea Party movement just a decade or so earlier. No longer was the government merely intrusive and fiscally reckless. Now it was satanic.

Ten days into her Twitter suspension, Greene would introduce three articles of impeachment against President Biden for his sundry incompetence and "pseudo-dictator" power-grabbing. In this manner, Marjorie Taylor Greene remained in full fighting mode, the proximate warrior to their exiled king—who, because of his permanent ban from Twitter, was now resorting to the carrier-pigeon method of blast emails. With his customary absence of abashment, Trump bragged about his rally sizes and his TV ratings and his continued chokehold on the Republican Party, railing against the fraudulent 2020 election and the continued "witch hunt" against his allies, all while warning the "patriot" recipients of the emails that he was personally reviewing his latest donor list and the patriot recipient had yet to pony up.

But it was now Greene and not Trump who was leading on the Republican message. Following the Georgia freshman, the ex-president was now hedging on his earlier boasts about the vaccines, saying instead that no one should have to take them if they didn't wish to. And, following Greene, it was Trump now taunting Biden's haphazard execution of the troop withdrawal from Afghanistan that Trump had proudly set in motion the previous year.

The apt pupil was now the headmistress of misinformation.

COVID-denialism rally

Chapter Twenty-Four

THE KILLING LIE

For months, American scientists and U.S. government officials knew that the B.1.617.2 strain known as the Delta variant was headed this way, to a population that to a considerable extent took its public health information from ideologues and political performance artists rather than nonpartisan experts.

Its appearance, the fourth new mutation of COVID-19, was first noted in India in December 2020, well before any vaccine had been disseminated. The Alpha strain that had first appeared in the UK had spread 50 percent faster than the original strain, and the Delta variant's spread rate was 50 percent faster than Alpha's.

By late May 2021, when the first Delta variant cases were identified in north Texas, 120 million Americans had been fully vaccinated. A shared jubilation extended across state and political lines as restaurants reopened, retail stores shed their mask mandates, and vaccines became increasingly available to any adult who wanted them. After horrific nationwide daily death tolls that had crested at 5,463 on February 12, daily fatalities had plummeted to 131 by May 30. By the end of June, consumer confidence had risen to pre-pandemic levels. That same month, nonfarm employers added 943,000 new jobs. President Biden's goal of having at least 160 million Americans fully vaccinated by July 4 seemed well within reach.

On July 10, during a CPAC conference in Dallas, Georgia congressman Jody Hice and former *New York Times* reporter Alex Berenson sat on a panel to discuss the lingering effects of COVID-19 on American society.

Throughout the thirty-minute discussion, neither of them made any mention of the 600,000 Americans who had lost their lives to the virus. Instead, Hice said, "I think the most stunning thing to me with this whole pandemic is how easy it has been to lead Americans down a pathway of them willingly surrendering liberties."

Berenson had spent the past year distinguishing himself as an avid COVID "truther" who had dismissed its effects as only "slightly worse than a bad flu year" while hailing Sweden for its anti-lockdown policy—a libertarian approach that would result in a death rate ten times higher than that of its neighbor Norway, which did enforce lockdowns. At CPAC, however, the packed and maskless audience was there to praise Berenson, not bury him. Claiming falsely that school shutdowns and mask-wearing had "done nothing, *nothing*" to protect Americans, he vowed, "I'm not gonna stop. Because the lies that are being told, and the misstatements, are becoming only more consequential."

"And here we go again with the Delta variant," sighed the moderator, Toni Angelini, who worked for something called Job Creators Network. After coming home from CPAC the previous evening, she said, it was the only thing being discussed on TV—"and I had to turn it off." Referring to imminent shutdowns and mask mandates that would likely arise with the spread of the variant, Angelini said, "It's *Groundhog Day* all over again."

But, Berenson observed, Americans were pushing back against the Biden administration. "Clearly, the government was hoping that they could sucker 90 percent of the population into getting vaccinated," he said. "And it isn't happening, right?"

The CPAC audience erupted in applause. They were cheering the refusal of millions of Americans to take the very steps—wearing masks, complying with lockdowns, and taking vaccines—that would limit the transmissibility of the coronavirus and thus diminish its ability to mutate.

That same month, the Delta variant spread throughout America. Its ability to penetrate all groups and environments was startling. Still, far and away its most hospitable host ecosystem was among the unvaccinated and unmasked. This included sparsely populated rural regions that had largely been spared from the coronavirus throughout 2020. And with a viral load one thousand times that of the original coronavirus, Delta's deadly effects fell heaviest on those who were the least protected. Those communities would soon find their hospitals overwhelmed and their death toll skyrocketing.

In Georgia—the state represented by Jody Hice and Marjorie Taylor Greene, the fifth-lowest state in America in terms of the percentage of residents who were fully vaccinated—new cases had soared to peaks not seen since the height of the pandemic. By the end of August, according to a report by the *Atlanta Journal-Constitution*, one-third of all hospital beds in Georgia were now occupied by seriously ill COVID patients. Almost none of them had been fully vaccinated. Instead, many if not most of Georgia's hospitalized COVID patients had been eligible to receive the vaccine but had elected, for reasons of their own, not to do so.

"A pandemic of the unvaccinated" is how President Biden referred to this disheartening new wave of coronavirus cases. The phrase was misleading, insofar as tens of thousands of fully vaccinated Americans were now experiencing "breakthrough" COVID symptoms from the Delta variant. But just as the spread of the variant was aided and abetted by communities of unvaccinated Americans, so, too, were the symptoms deadliest for those who had not been vaccinated. According to the CDC, over 99.99 percent of "breakthrough" cases had not resulted in hospitalization or death. In other words: even as the Delta variant claimed new victims, its near-complete inability to kill the vaccinated proved yet again that there was only one way to defeat the pandemic, and that was to follow the science.

Other countries, including many of America's closest allies, did not seem to fear such a pathway. Canada, Germany, France, Italy, Spain, and the UK each received adequate supplies of the vaccines months later than the United States did. Once their supply caught up, however, each country had surpassed America's vaccination rate of 53 percent by the end of August. Why was the ceiling of willing vaccine recipients lower in the United States? Was it really that those other democratic countries cared little about liberty? Or was it that they were less subjected to a cacophony of misinformation peddled by craven right-wing opportunists?

Children, long thought to be the least susceptible to COVID, were now at significant risk, thanks to the Delta variant. By the end of August, four

Georgia children would be dead due to the mutated virus. Hice and Greene's state would rank third nationally in COVID-related pediatric hospital admissions. Ahead of Georgia in this ignominious category were Florida and Texas. Besides being large and situated in the South, the two states had something else in common: both had Republican governors with presidential ambitions. During the early months of the pandemic, both Ron DeSantis and Greg Abbott had ordered lockdowns and encouraged wearing masks in keeping with the policies of the Trump administration. By early May, however, DeSantis had declared Florida open for business. A month later, Abbott did the same in Texas. Both of them, along with Republican governor (and fellow 2024 hopeful) Kristi Noem of South Dakota, won praise from conservative pundits for keeping businesses open while allowing residents in their states to play Russian roulette with the deadly virus.

By September 1, 2021, all three states ranked in the top half of COVID cases adjusted for population. Florida was the fifth highest, edging out Noem's South Dakota. (Texas was twenty-third.) Faced with the dire upswing in cases, DeSantis assumed full swagger when it came to lockdowns, declaring in late July, "We're not doing that in Florida." Not to be outdone, on July 29 Governor Abbott announced a statewide ban on mask mandates and compulsory vaccinations—an empty gesture of toughness that many state and local institutions proceeded to defy.

Neither Abbott nor DeSantis had stated outright that masks were ineffectual, vaccinations were dangerous, or that the surge in COVID-19 cases was insignificant. They did not voice the lies. They merely provided the atmosphere in which the lies could spread unchallenged—an atmosphere that might also enable them to win, as long as they kept the lies fully oxygenated and did not let science get in the way of victory.

President Biden's pandemic of the unvaccinated was really a pandemic of the untruthful. Where the truth did not matter, the virus spread like an inferno.

Election worker

———

Chapter Twenty-Five

THE BIG LIE, SPREADING

The lies about the COVID pandemic continued to spread throughout America along with the Delta variant. At the same time, the 2020 stolen-election fable had hardly lost its glitter. Far from it: Trump had provided Republicans with a handy new blueprint for blaming one's electoral defeat on imagined fraud. So appealing was the proposition that in one major American city, a Republican office-seeker and his supporters even decided to use it against their fellow Republicans.

On May 1, 2021, the city of Fort Worth, Texas, held its biennial mayoral election. Though the office has historically been nonpartisan, often occupied by establishment grandees and civic do-gooders, the overheated rhetoric of national politics had begun to seep into the discourse of the city's mayoral aspirants.

By far the most nationally pitched of the twenty-four Fort Worth mayoral candidates was an affable local realtor and pastor named Steve Penate. Much like Marjorie Taylor Greene in Georgia, the self-proclaimed "most conservative name on the ballot" feigned little interest in the pothole-fixing labors of municipal officeholding. Instead, Penate cast himself as a crusader for "Christian values" who would guard the sanctity of the Second Amendment while taking on "terrorist groups like Antifa." His campaign slogan reflected what he saw as Fort Worth's state of embattlement against woke ideology: "Protect the Fort."

Penate was an energetic block-walker and door-knocker. He assiduously courted Trump-voting evangelicals and posted videos urging his supporters to vote early. His efforts were not enough, however. On May 1, Steve Penate

came in a distant fourth, with 9.4 percent of the vote. Penate promptly conceded and urged his fans to support the more establishment Republican candidate, who proceeded to beat her Democratic challenger in the runoff on
June 5 by seven points.

Then something bizarre occurred. Twelve days after the runoff, Steve
Penate posted a video on his Facebook page. Penate had seen the turnout fig-
ures for the May 1 general election and the June 5 runoff—which, as with all
Fort Worth mayoral races held in odd-numbered years, were abysmally low,
roughly 10 percent of what they had been during the 2020 presidential cycle.
Still, turnout had dramatically improved over the 2019 cycle.

There should not have been any mystery as to why turnout had spiked. The
longtime incumbent mayor had stepped down, with Penate and twenty-three
other new aspirants flooding Fort Worth with mailers and ads. But there was
an additional reason why Fort Worth residents had been more energized in
2021. It was that the state GOP was determined to make Fort Worth the one
major city in Texas that did not have a Democrat as mayor. In the furtherance
of that goal, the state party had devoted considerable money and energy to turn
out its people. Now it had a big-city Republican mayor to show for its efforts.

But Steve Penate wasn't convinced. With wide eyes and elaborate hand
movements, he told his Facebook viewers, "It's wild! What's interesting is, one
of two things happened. *Either* we as a city woke so many people up to get out
and vote—*and/or* we need a recount to verify that everything we did in our
2021 elections was done in truth and with integrity."

Voter integrity, Penate now claimed, was "one of the concerns I kept hearing over and over" on the campaign trail, though oddly he had never thought
to elevate it as a campaign issue until he was trounced in the general election.
Now, however, the man who came in fourth place declared that he had "asked
the Tarrant County election board to conduct a hand recount and an audit of
our 2021 election."

What had darkened Steve Penate's demeanor about the election's validity
twelve days after its conclusion? The answer had to do with one of the candidate's biggest donors: William P. Fearer III. Fearer ran a lucrative law practice
in Illinois and had donated infrequently to Republicans over the years—until
2020, when he retired, relocated to Fort Worth, and began cutting checks to

Trump's reelection campaign. Believing as he did that the 2020 election was rigged and the American republic hung in the balance, the retiree decided to forgo his dreams of endless golfing. Fearer and a small group of like-minded Fort Worth Republicans filed an open records request with the Tarrant County Elections Office to see if there were signs of fraud locally in 2020.

Busily ferreting through the data, Fearer and his friends found seventy-nine cases where registered voters had used vacant lots and P.O. boxes as their addresses. Then came the 2021 mayoral election, with its inflated turnout that did not inure to the benefit of Fearer's chosen candidate. He shared his view with Steve Penate that something was rotten in Fort Worth.

But what was it, exactly? There existed, as Penate himself had suggested in his Facebook video, an entirely innocuous explanation: more Fort Worth residents, particularly Republicans, were motivated by this distinctly partisan race than they had been in past cycles. There was precedent for this, after all. No Republicans squawked about electoral abnormalities when Trump upset Clinton in 2016. No one in Fearer's group had ever contacted the Tarrant County Elections Office to express concerns about voter fraud prior to November 3, 2020. For that matter, Fearer and Penate had not viewed with suspicion any of the 74.2 million votes cast for Trump in 2020, which had amounted to an all-time high among Republican candidates in American history. Only the 7 million more votes cast for Biden warranted inspection.

Meanwhile, Fearer and Penate did not think to bring their findings to the Tarrant County Elections Office and ask for an investigation. The possibility that several dozen Tarrant County voters had mistakenly registered with an outdated address, or that homeless people might have used a vacant lot as their designated address, or that the elections office was in fact tabulating voter data by their home addresses rather than their P.O. boxes, did not seem to occur to Bill Fearer. Far likelier, apparently, was the prospect that a sinister Texas cabal had interceded to cheat Steve Penate in favor of . . .

Another Republican?

ABOUT A MONTH AFTER PENATE CALLED FOR A RECOUNT OF THE FORT WORTH mayoral election, Bill Fearer and a few other conservative evangelicals hosted a two-hour conference in a Tarrant County recreation center. They were doing so because Fearer's group had mass-mailed a notice to residents throughout the county, asking them to input their voting data on the group's new website, VerifyMyVoting.com, to see whether their vote had actually been tallied by the county elections board. (To help compel a response, the organization had used an image of the common "I Voted" sticker, photoshopping it to say "I Think I Voted.")

Several people had supplied their data—and lo and behold, VerifyMy-Voting.com had informed them that their vote had not been counted. This was suspicious! The same thing happened when the county's elections administrator, Heider Garcia, visited the website. He plugged in the data of ten Tarrant County voters. According to VerifyMyVoting.com, only five of those votes had actually counted. But since Garcia knew that every one of those ten votes had in fact been tabulated, it was obvious to him that there was some kind of flaw in the group's software. (What did not occur to either Garcia or to the VerifyMyVoting.com founders was this: if Tarrant County was somehow failing to count so many votes, then how did the county wind up with such a big bulge in its mayoral turnout?)

These matters aside, a number of Fort Worth residents did not know what to make of the mysterious VerifyMyVoting.com card that had arrived in their mailboxes asking them to type their voting data into a website of unknown origins. Members of the media and local officials raised concerns about the idea of offering up personal information on an anonymous and non-secure website.

Fearer and the others had therefore convened this meeting to allay such suspicions. A few dozen residents were in attendance, including one member of the media, *Fort Worth Star-Telegram* columnist Bud Kennedy. The organizers sent someone over to Kennedy to pray for him.

The meeting began with shadowy overtones. One of the organizers, a Penate donor, West Texas rancher, and former securities broker named Jay Meadows, explained that he and Fearer and three other individuals had gotten together in January, sometime after Joe Biden's electoral victory had been certified on the heels of the Capitol insurrection. "We just saw something that just wasn't right," Meadows explained to the audience. "We weren't clear what was happening. But we were sure that what we were seeing didn't match. It was as if the sun was coming up in the west instead of the east."

Meadows further explained that he had nurtured these unnerving suspicions since Election Night, when he spoke on the phone with another Fort Worth–area resident, Seth Keshel. That night, Keshel told Meadows that he had detected "anomalies" in the voting patterns.

Keshel was a traffic-light software salesman with a background in military intelligence and baseball statistical analysis. But because he was also an ardent Republican who found the possibility of a Trump loss to be suspicious on its face, he was about to become a much-sought-after "election data analyst" in MAGA World. Within days of his phone conversation with Jay Meadows, Seth Keshel would be flying to Washington to assist Trump allies like former Overstock CEO Patrick Byrne, attorney Sidney Powell, and General Michael Flynn in their efforts to reverse the 2020 election results. In the ensuing weeks and months, Seth Keshel would claim that Trump had in fact won *every* contested state—Arizona, Georgia, Wisconsin, Pennsylvania, Michigan, and Nevada—and also threw in Minnesota, which Biden had carried by seven points. It would fall to actual election experts to discredit Keshel's bogus claims.

Meanwhile, his wife, Carissa Keshel, was mining past conspiracy theories that might aid Trump's cause. While volunteering on behalf of Sidney Powell and fellow lawyer Lin Wood's efforts to overturn the election results, she sent out this blast email on December 15, 2020:

PATRIOTS!!!!

We have been asked to start combing through all WIKILEAKS Entire Clinton's emails!! Sidney and Lin said get the most important things first so they can start putting them out!!!! Find all the things that will make people literally freak out! This is what we must do to WAKE PEOPLE UP TO THE TRUTH!!!!!

Jay Meadows then introduced the audience to Seth Keshel. The lanky former military intelligence officer began his talk by insisting, "This is not a conspiracy presentation—this is not a QAnon gathering." Carefully, Keshel asked for a show of hands as to who was a "believer." The audience seemed to understand that the speaker was referring to fraud in the 2020 election. Most of them raised their hands. Keshel then devoted the next half hour to buttressing their suspicions with his usual disproven claims. He did not mention anything about the Fort Worth mayoral race. Keshel's role was simply to show that fraud was rampant, leaving it to the next speaker, Bill Fearer, to connect the dots to their own backyard.

The retired lawyer from Illinois was careful in this public setting not to use alarmist language. He did not say that fraud was manifestly evident in Fort Worth. Rather, he likened his inquiry to that of a doctor's examining a patient "who's exhibiting symptoms." Fearer then displayed a slide featuring the local turnout statistics in the mayoral race, showing a 125 percent increase in voter turnout from 2019 to 2021. Such data, the slide blared, was "just the tip of the iceberg."

Fearer said, "There's a lot of talk around the country about computer intervention in our elections." There was indeed a great deal of talk, spectacularly unsubstantiated, and now Bill Fearer introduced a new wrinkle: "It stood to reason," he said, "that computers played a part" in the mayoral election's increased turnout. To show how reasonable such a scenario was, Fearer then cited the musings of Douglas Frank, the leading "expert" for Sidney Powell's universally defeated legal arguments, who had mounted the stage at Trump rallies to broadcast his foolhardy claims that Bill Fearer now framed as the learned analysis of "an expert out there, a PhD in chemistry, physics, and statistical analysis."

After Fearer was done, Pastor Rafael Cruz—who had once been accused by a (likely Trump-planted) story in the *National Enquirer* of having played a role in JFK's assassination, and whose son, Senator Ted Cruz, had been accused by Trump of stealing various Republican electoral contests from him in 2016—concluded the gathering with a prayer.

A CURIOUS CIRCULARITY WOULD ACCOMPANY THE FORT WORTH MAYORAL episode. Just as it sprang from the Trump-fueled narrative that the MAGA base was being robbed of its electoral voice, so, too, was the saga quickly deployed by conservative media to reinforce suspicions about the left. Paranoia begat paranoia in a fact-free barrage of questions that flooded the zone of reason.

On July 12, Newsmax host John Bachman brought Jay Meadows on the air to discuss what the right-wing TV channel's chyron advertised as THE LEFT'S WAR ON ELECTION INTEGRITY. Meadows was, of course, an odd choice for this segment, because his energies had been focused on supposed *Republican* theft of votes. Teeing up his guest, Bachman asked, "Why do the Democrats seem to be against, you know, getting to the bottom of this stuff?"

The west Texas rancher conveyed a kind of doleful bewilderment. "You know, I can't answer that," he admitted. "I don't know why, if there's nothing to see here, they wouldn't just open the books. We want to find out the integrity of our votes."

Meadows was channeling familiar language. His feigned innocence was steeped in the 2020 Trump campaign's electoral challenges. It echoed the what-are-they-afraid-of arguments made by Paul Gosar and other Arizona conservatives who had whipped up support for the Cyber Ninjas "audit."

These calls for federal scrutiny did, however, clash with the GOP's native opposition to firearms registration and IRS audits of faith-based activists. And in the months to come, as the January 6 committee began issuing subpoenas to Trump allies who might be in a position to shed light on the events of that day, Republicans would suddenly abandon their zeal for transparency while discovering their inner civil libertarian.

What made this yearning for "election integrity" especially specious was that it was an overnight phenomenon. Before 2020, when Donald Trump began forecasting that his defeat could only be made possible by theft, none of these 2020 truthers—not Meadows or Fearer, not Seth Keshel or Sidney Powell or Lin Wood—had joined Democrats in advocating that the nation's electoral infrastructure be secured. To them, the system had looked rock solid, because their candidate had won in 2016. Any insinuation to the contrary— such as the possibility that Russia had influenced the outcome—was simply an outrage.

Yet when Trump lost four years later, it was because a great conspiracy— joining hands overnight, consisting of Republicans and Democrats and possibly foreign entities, with an intricate understanding of localities and a gift for secrecy—had made it so.

ON SEPTEMBER 14, 2021, CALIFORNIANS VOTED ON WHETHER TO RECALL their sitting governor, Democrat Gavin Newsom. Eight days prior to the vote, Newsom's right-wing opponent, conservative talk radio host Larry Elder, posted a website, StopCAFraud.com. The website stated that Elder's team had "detected fraud" in the "results"—an intriguing viewpoint, given that no such results yet existed. Elder also warned that he had an armada of election lawyers in place who would be prepared to file lawsuits "in a timely fashion."

When the results did materialize eight days later, Larry Elder's recall movement did not fare well: over 64 percent of California voters chose not to recall Governor Newsom. The defeated Republican gamely acknowledged that he had "lost the battle," though the longer war continued.

Still: in a blue state like California, it took a nearly two-to-one electoral defeat to convince a Republican to desist from a baseless fraud claim. By contrast, in a red state like Texas, a candidate like Steve Penate could come in fourth place with 9.4 percent of the vote and still attract sympathizers to the claim that the vote had been rigged against him.

The lie was irresistible. After all, it explained so much more than election results. It delineated good from evil—the forces aligned with America and those determined to annihilate it.

Organizers of the Justice for J6 rally

Chapter Twenty-Six

THE PATRIOT WING

Of course, the small group in Fort Worth were hardly the only Texans to express concerns about the 2020 election. As tabulated by George Washington University's Program on Extremism, 71 of the 825 individuals indicted for crimes committed during the January 6 insurrection hailed from Texas—making it the state with the second-most offenders, after Florida.

The Texas rioters came in all forms. They included a Midland jailer, a Houston Police Department officer, two retired marines, a winemaker, a coffee-roasting entrepreneur, a mortgage branch manager, and an *Infowars* host. Among them were several couples, including Mark and Jalise Middleton, both of whom were later detectable in body-cam footage fighting viciously with the police at the lower West Terrace "to get to the Capital [*sic*] to send them bastards a clear message that this won't be tolerated," as Jalise posted on her Facebook account. Two father-son couples made their way inside the Capitol, as did an entire family of six, the Munns from Borger, only one of whom was not indicted, as that child was a minor.

The Munns, like numerous other Texas insurrectionists, tipped off their whereabouts that day by proudly memorializing their place in history on social media. This was also the case with Nick DeCarlo, who wore a shirt that read MURDER THE MEDIA and posed for a photograph with his thumbs up next to a Capitol door with the same message etched into it. While a few participated in the storming of the Capitol as a kind of patriotic frolic—like the two real-estate agents who flew in on a private plane—for others the insurrection constituted a personal apogee. "Proudest day of my life," wrote one rioter. "This was the first time I felt invincible," wrote another. Taking umbrage at claims from some on the right that the riot had been instigated by Antifa, one Texan wrote back, "Nah we stormed it," while another wrote that "every single person who believes that narrative have [sic] been DUPED AGAIN." And though some remained insistent that the episode had been a peaceful one, several other Texans made clear on social media that their intentions were not pacifistic: "men with guns need to shoot there [sic] way in." "Pence better do the right thing, or we're going to MAKE you do the right thing." "It wasn't the building we wanted . . . it was them!" "Assassinate AOC."

In assaulting the police, the Texas rioters used whatever was at their disposal: pepper spray, stolen batons, a skateboard, a crutch, a tabletop. But at least one of the Texans brought guns with him to Washington. Guy Reffitt, from the north Texas town of Wylie, belonged to an extremist militia group called the Texas Freedom Force. On the morning of January 6, Reffitt—having driven twenty hours from Wylie to Washington with a fellow militia member and at least two firearms—had sent out messages about the need to "do the recon and then come back for weapons hot." According to statements he later made to a family member, Reffitt brought plastic wrist restraints as well as a loaded gun with him to the Capitol. Images from news outlets showed Reffitt that afternoon standing by the West Terrace, wearing a black helmet with camera attached as well as other tactical gear, flushing his eyes with water.

Back home in Wylie five days later, Reffitt learned that he had made the news. He told his eighteen-year-old son and sixteen-year-old daughter that he needed to delete the contents of his helmet camera. Warning them not to tell anyone, the two children would recall to the FBI that their father said to them, "Choose a side, or die" and "Traitors get shot." Meanwhile, according to federal prosecutors, Guy Reffitt "bragged to fellow militia members about his involvement in the riot, recruited other rioters into the militia, and ordered bear spray and riot shields to his home to prepare for further violence." He also advised his colleagues that "DC is a futile effort now" and that "MSM and Big Tech need to feel the rathe [sic] of the Republic now." Reffitt promised that he could equip them with sufficient weaponry, since he had set up a security LLC "to circumvent the 2nd Amendment issue."

Reffitt was arrested on January 16, 2021, and subsequently ordered to remain in federal detention at the DC Jail, where he would spend the next fourteen months. On March 7, 2022, Guy Wesley Reffitt, the first Capitol riot defendant to face a federal trial, would be found guilty on five counts.

I LEARNED ABOUT GUY REFFITT WHILE ATTENDING A "JUSTICE FOR J6" RALLY in Washington on September 18, 2021, that had been organized as a show of support for the alleged rioters like Reffitt who were still being detained eight months after the attack on the Capitol. That, at least, was the stated purpose. Neither of the principal organizers—a former Trump campaign staffer and a female boxer turned conservative activist—had any known history of criminal-justice activism prior to January 6. Like so many who had profited during the Trump era, they clung like barnacles to the great rusty MAGA schooner. And though the two hundred or so rally-goers gathering a half mile from the heavily policed Capitol had abided by the request not to show up wearing partisan regalia, their sympathies toward Guy Reffitt and the other J6ers seemed to animate them less than the usual discontents, like the fake news media, the tyrannical COVID mask mandates, and the stolen election.

"So, you're totally happy with the election?" one man demanded of me. He wore an American flag as a cape and had brought his electric guitar and a portable amplifier, along with a song list of FM classics like "The Boys Are Back in Town" and "Born to Be Wild" that he had repurposed as January 6 anthems.

When I replied that I wasn't sure what he meant by "happy," the guitarist cackled and said, "You guys are always going to be on the side of the establishment and the Uni-party." He clarified the latter term at my request: "Like McCain, Lindsey Graham, Bush, Pelosi, Romney. They're all the same. Bluebloods. They're all the same to us. We're populist. They inside-trade. You guys never blow the whistle on them."

I gravitated away from the caped guitarist and toward a young man who had been parading about with an oversized flag that bore a quote from the Declaration of Independence. I asked him what brought him out to this unshaded grassy acreage on a muggy Saturday afternoon.

"The fact that people are still locked up from January 6," he replied. He added that there were about six hundred such individuals. I said that the precise number of those in pre-trial detention was seventy-eight, and that the others had already been released pending trial.

"The ones who weren't violent who are still locked up—that's who I'm here for," the young man then said.

"Yeah, those guys aren't locked up," I said.

Grinning defensively, he said, "OK, great. Well then, we're all just wasting our time. Have a good day," and the young man scurried away from me.

An elderly fellow wearing a nonpartisan bright yellow CHINA JOE BIDEN T-shirt was holding aloft a sign protesting the "excessive bail" that the January 6 detainees were faced with. "Sir," I asked carefully, "are you sure that those in prison are there because they couldn't make bail?"

"No, I don't think so," he quickly acknowledged. By "bail," he said, he really just meant "They shouldn't be in jail at all."

Then I noticed the message on the other side of his sign: BLM RIOTERS NOT EVEN PROSECUTED. "You do know that a lot of Black Lives Matter protesters *were* prosecuted last year, right?" I said.

"Well, the majority was not," the elderly fellow maintained. "The vice president was collecting money and urging people to bail them out. Sweet Kamala. That incompetent witch. She got selected by Biden because she was a woman and Black. Talk about racism!"

"So," I said, "have you been following the cases of any of the particular January 6 guys who are behind bars?"

"No," he said. "Just generally, the concept of *any* of them being in jail. If anybody should be in jail, it should be the guard that shot Ashli Babbitt!"

Noticing that the afternoon's first speaker had taken the stage, I thanked the man in the yellow T-shirt, who replied, "So you can see, we're not all wackos out here."

The rally co-organizer, boxer Cara Castronuova, had some distressing news to share. She informed the audience that one of the scheduled speakers, Guy Reffitt's wife, Nicole, had been met at the Washington airport by FBI agents, who then detained her at her hotel room. They had seized her laptop and informed her that she was now on a no-fly list.

Castronuova read from a lengthy text sent by Nicole Reffitt. She described her husband as "a political prisoner" who "was arrested for rhetoric and charged with a thought crime." She decried "the false narrative of January 6 being an insurrection." It was merely an act of peaceful protest that was being "criminalized by the current administration." But, Guy Reffitt's wife continued, "We the people will not be afraid—whether it is 1776 or 1/6/21."

Of the Reffitts' predicament, Cara Castronuova intoned, "You can't make this stuff up, guys."

In fact, such things *could* be made up. On Monday, two days after the rally, I checked with federal law enforcement sources to see if Nicole Reffitt had been detained by the FBI and placed on a no-fly list. She had not. I called her husband's attorney to see what he knew of this egregious violation of an innocent woman's civil rights.

"The first I'm hearing of it is you telling me about it now," the attorney said pleasantly.

I left several messages on Nicole Reffitt's cell phone. She did not call back. The matter of Reffitt's wife's being detained by federal authorities and placed on a no-fly list did not come up in any subsequent court filings or at Reffitt's trial, where such claims would have been subject to perjury charges.

WHILE INCARCERATED, THE TEXAS MILITIA MEMBER WHO HAD THREATENED to kill his children and vowed to commit acts of violence against tech executives and journalists had now assumed the beatific guise of a political prisoner. Of January 6, Guy Reffitt piously reflected in a letter that was obtained by Pro-Publica, "I hope that was the day in American history we would without doubt, feel the need to notify our government, they have transgressed much too far."

Reffitt was locked up in the DC Jail's protective custody wing with thirty-six other accused rioters. Reffitt and the others referred to it as the "Patriot Wing." They recited the Pledge of Allegiance and furtively passed paper notes known as "kites" from one cell to the next. Given that they were nearly all white male inmates of right-wing ideology, prison officials had deemed it unwise to comingle them among the general population of predominantly Black and Latino men. This meant, however, long hours of isolation in the grim bowels of America's criminal justice system.

I had done a fair amount of research about the DC Jail for an earlier book project. I had also visited at least two dozen penitentiaries in my thirty-five years as a magazine journalist. In more ways than one, the "horror stories" from the Patriot Wing were laughable in comparison to the medieval Texas lockups I knew from the early 1990s. To "do the time," it was tacitly understood back then, meant to run a daily gauntlet of gang violence, sexual assault, and unchecked harassment by sociopathic corrections officers. This was the lot in life for inmates, nearly all of them Black or Brown, whose offenses were not that they had assaulted a police officer or attempted to overthrow a presidential election—but instead, often enough, that they had sold a few ounces of marijuana to an undercover cop and were too poor to afford a lawyer who could stay awake during trial.

The federal judge had deemed Guy Reffitt—who had tried to cover the tracks of his alleged crimes while also allegedly planning future mayhem—as both a flight risk and a danger to his community. Detaining Reffitt without bail was not a terribly hard call. Still, as a *Washington Post* analysis would note, only about 13 percent of the accused insurrectionists were being held without bond, while the number of defendants in the overall federal prison population being detained until trial was nearly six times that amount. There was indeed a "two-tiered prison system," as the J6ers liked to say. But it skewed heavily in their favor—unless, of course, one truly believed (as 78 percent of all Republicans did, according to a CNN poll taken in September 2021) that the *true* insurrection had occurred on November 3, 2020, necessitating a second "1776" on January 6, 2021.

None of this made Reffitt and the others in protective custody at the DC Jail any more deserving of inhumane treatment, however. Cockroach-infested cells, black mold on the walls, dinner consisting of white bread and tartar sauce, casual threats levied by prison guards, indiscriminate denial of showering privileges—no human deserved such conditions.

But in their state of isolation from the general population, the inhabitants of the Patriot Wing could cling to the same fiction that had ultimately landed them here. It was the fiction I had heard randomly voiced throughout the Justice for J6 rally. The fiction was that they, Trump's Deplorables, were exclusively the persecuted ones. Everyone else had it luckier, even in prison. The fake news media and the "Uni-party" establishment had seen to that. Blacks and anarchists could loot and burn with impunity.

You can't make this stuff up, guys.

THE RALLY, ESPECIALLY BY TRUMPIAN STANDARDS, WAS SOMETHING OF A
flop. That was not entirely unexpected, given that Trump himself had predicted that the event would be a "setup," a pretext for Biden's deep-state agents
to round up another herd of innocent patriots. The Capitol grounds had been
fenced off; hundreds of law enforcement officials combed the perimeter, on
the lookout for the violent militia groups who, according to intelligence reports, had planned to descend on the area. It was difficult to envision the
Justice for J6 event offering any outcome other than the riotous bloodbath
many feared or the desultory nothingburger it turned out to be. And so nearly
everyone stayed away.

Still, the dismal showing was notable, given the grandiose display of solidarity toward the J6ers offered up by certain usual suspects of the Republican
Party. On July 27, Marjorie Taylor Greene, Paul Gosar, Matt Gaetz, and
Louie Gohmert held a press conference outside the U.S. Department of Justice headquarters after they had been denied an audience with Attorney General Merrick Garland. Bellowed Gohmert as he faced the TV cameras, "We
still need to know, do we have political prisoners here in America, or not?"

When Gaetz's turn came to protest the treatment of the insurrectionists,
someone in the audience yelled out to the Florida congressman being investigated for sex trafficking: *We know why YOU'RE concerned about jail conditions!"* The press event was otherwise plagued by a protester's incessant
blowing of a whistle—leading Greene's communications director, Nick Dyer,
to step in after about fifteen minutes and say firmly, "The left is interrupting
this press conference. We need to end it."

The tell that the event might have been driven less by sincerity than by political opportunism was that it took place while the January 6 select committee
was holding its first hearing, a feat of counterprogramming that Greene openly
acknowledged during her remarks. Two days later, on July 29, Greene, Gohmert, and Gaetz showed up at the DC Jail—unannounced, though accompanied by several members of the right-wing press. In an eerie reenactment of
then-citizen Greene's provocations on Capitol Hill just two years earlier, the
Georgia freshman rapped loudly on the glass door of the facility's lobby, de-

manding an audience. When the guards saw the publicity stunt for what it was, Greene declared to the cameras, "Oh, now they've got their backs turned. Unbelievable."

Given their newly acquired interest in criminal injustice, it was therefore notable that none of the four Republican House members showed up to speak at the Justice for J6 rally. For that matter, when I asked Joseph D. McBride III, the most publicly visible attorney for the alleged rioters, about what level of support he had received from Greene and the others, he replied flatly, "None of those members has reached out to me, and neither has any other member of Congress."

I caught up with McBride on a Thursday afternoon in late September, just after he had concluded a three-hour visit at the DC Jail with one of his clients, Ryan Nichols. It was Nichols, from Longview, Texas, who had hollered into a bullhorn on the West Terrace, "If you have a weapon, you need to get your weapon! . . . This is not a peaceful protest!" More than two weeks before January 6, Nichols had forecast his intentions on social media: "Pence better do the right thing, or we're going to MAKE you do the right thing." Body-cam footage had captured images of the former marine using pepper spray on law enforcement officers. Now he was held without bond, a detainee in the federal jail's "Patriot Wing."

Like many of the Capitol rioters who had been indicted for more serious offenses, Nichols was reluctant to entertain any plea deals stemming in part from the recognition that accepting felony status would mean forfeiting one's firearms. "That's a big sticking point for all these guys," McBride told me. "For them, the Second Amendment is as important as the First Amendment."

His client was therefore likely to continue to languish in the DC Jail until his trial date sometime the following spring. Because Nichols had refused the COVID vaccine, he was in turn prohibited from getting his hair cut or shaving. "He looks like the Tom Hanks character in Castaway," McBride said, while acknowledging that his client had it better than most of the others on the "Patriot Wing," because the guards seemed to respect Nichols's military background.

The environment that Ryan Nichols had described to his lawyer, if accurate (and DC Jail officials would not confirm or deny the details), suggested a kind of inverse to the quotidian cruelties meted out to largely darker-skinned inmate populations by white correctional officers. In the DC Jail's restrictive housing area, the Capitol rioters were almost entirely white, the guards mainly Black. Nichols had told McBride that the only periodical available for reading on the Patriot Unit was *The Final Call,* published by the Nation of Islam, its articles replete with denunciations of the white race.

"It's psychological warfare," McBride maintained. The cruelty was the point, he asserted. But, the attorney claimed, the experience had in fact lifted the scales from their eyes regarding America's criminal justice system. Mc-Bride, a native New Yorker who began his career representing indigent Black and Latino clients, had talked to his four clients about his experiences. And while locking up so many individuals pre-trial flew in the face of the 1984 Bail Reform Act, and while McBride rejected the idea that his clients in any way resembled privileged individuals, it was still the case that the clients he once represented "have had it very, very hard. And I told them this. I said, 'This should be a wake-up call for you.' And to a man, they were 100 percent in agreement that they'd been wrong on this issue. And that should they get into a position when they get out to speak on the issue, they will be the most vocif-erous advocates for people who are being treated unfairly."

With skepticism, I told McBride that I'd been hearing that a lot lately— from the Justice for J6 organizers and from Republicans like Marjorie Taylor Greene and Paul Gosar. After again acknowledging that none of the GOP members had reached out to him to express concern for his clients, the lawyer smirked. "I'm a street guy, OK?" he said. "I can see a snake oil salesman a mile away."

But McBride and his clients reserved their greatest disappointment for the man they had all voted for in 2020, the man for whom the patriots now in custody had flocked to Washington on January 6. "Despite the fact that he's connected to every rich person in the freaking world," the New York attorney said bitterly of Trump, "not one of them has stepped up and contributed to any of these defenses. For me, and for these guys, that's a major fucking problem. That's a major problem." Instead, Trump's rich friends were donating to the ex-president's legal fund.

Yes, Joe McBride acknowledged, the MAGA masses—"the people on the outside"—still believed that Donald J. Trump was their champion. But, he said, "the guys *inside* don't fucking feel that way."

Representative Marjorie Taylor Greene heckling abortion-rights Democrats

================

Chapter Twenty-Seven

AT THE FAIRGROUNDS

W e call her Dingell-berry," snickered one of Marjorie Taylor Greene's top advisers, referring to Congresswoman Debbie Dingell, who a few hours ago had become the latest Democrat to bring a knife to a MTG bazooka fight.

The confrontation had taken place on an early Friday afternoon in late September 2021, when a group of Democrats were speaking to members of the press on the steps of the Capitol about the party-line passage of an abortion-rights bill that would essentially codify *Roe v. Wade* in the wake of a new Texas law that all but eliminated abortion rights in that state. Having just exited the House chamber to encounter this spectacle, the Georgia freshman proceeded to heckle the Democrats, yelling, "You should all be ashamed."

Then Dingell—the latest of that name, after her deceased husband and his father before him, to hold a Michigan congressional seat for nearly ninety years running—hollered back from the steps: "You should be ashamed for your lack of civility!"

But of course, Greene had no interest in being civil.

"Killing a baby up until birth is a lack of civility—it's called murder!" Greene yelled back. When Dingell angrily responded that the freshman should show a little respect, "the basic thing you're taught in church," Greene guffawed, "Taught in church? Are you kidding me? Try being a Christian and supporting life!"

The encounter had left Debbie Dingell, a member of the Problem Solvers Caucus who counted many Republicans as friends, feeling somewhat debased.

But it was another day in the Thunderdome for Marjorie Taylor Greene, whose two advisers sat with me that evening at a suburban steakhouse, chortling about their boss's latest Democratic victim while fielding my questions with genial wariness. Just as I had spent the past several months trying to understand exactly who Greene was, her team had been pondering the same thing about me. They sought clues from my social media feeds. They took stock of my engagement to a CNN political analyst (Kirsten Powers). Of course, the default option for most Republican House members—particularly of the Freedom Caucus variety—was to treat interview requests from the mainstream media as one would a windshield flyer solicitation from a gutter salesman. At no point had I assumed Greene would make an exception with me.

But nine months into her career as an elected official, Greene didn't want to limit herself to someone else's template. Hers was a "movement," her advisers said. Already, they pointed out, the freshman had been the leader in calling for Biden's impeachment, for forcing roll-call votes, for hauling in millions in small-dollar donations. Why stop there? Why constrain the movement to whatever the Freedom Caucus's agenda was?

It had also occurred to Greene and her team that building a movement required developing relationships beyond the usual right-wing suspects. At a certain point, the advisers told me, one needed to quit picking fights with everyone in sight. "You don't want to be a clown," one of them said. The departure of Greene's combative chief of staff, Patrick Parsons—announced by his boss over Twitter during our dinner—afforded an opportunity to find someone who possessed diplomatic skills that the rest of her staff lacked.

It still wasn't quite clear to me how a politician who was too conservative for most Georgians could amass anything approximating a national movement. By now, Marjorie Taylor Greene's "policy agenda" was clear. She wanted to impeach President Biden. She wanted to expel AOC and other members of the Squad from Congress for being communists. She wanted to label Black Lives Matter a terrorist group. She wanted to ban all abortions. She wanted to end all mask mandates, starting within the halls of Congress. She wanted to finish building Trump's wall and keep immigrants of any kind out of America for the foreseeable future. She wanted to discard rights for transgendered people. She wanted to start a trade war with China and expel their students from the United States. She wanted to eliminate any and all regulations that were intended to address climate change, because, in her view, "The climate has always changed, and no amount of taxes and no government can do anything to stop climate change." She wanted to unravel gun-control laws. She wanted prayer back in schools.

If there was a mass constituency for such a movement—and perhaps there was—I had yet to see any evidence of Greene's mobilizing them, apart from soliciting their money. Still, she was just getting started. As one of the advisers challenged me: "Who do you think are the top five Republicans in the House, other than the ones in leadership?"

Figuring he was talking about who had the most stature within the GOP Conference, I conceded that their boss already had enough sway to be on the list. I also named Jim Jordan, Jim Banks of the Republican Study Committee, Liz Cheney, and Tom Cole, the ranking member of the Rules Committee and vice-ranking member of the Appropriations Committee.

"I don't even know who Tom Cole is," the adviser said impatiently. He was stunned that I had named Cheney, whom he termed a "useful idiot who's auditioning for a job at CNN every time she's on TV."

The adviser then clarified himself: "I'm not talking about who K Street wants. I'm talking about, if you had five House Republicans on a national ballot, who would the public vote for?"

"That's an interesting exercise," I conceded. It was also a revealing one. Former Republican House majority leader Tom Delay had once told me that there were three career paths for any member of Congress: to be in leadership, to be a committee stalwart, or to be a tireless advocate of one's district. Marjorie Taylor Greene had chosen a fourth path. Her ambition was to be a national figure.

I then recalled the previous week, when I sat in the House press gallery while votes were being tallied for the National Defense Authorization Act. Among the 424 who had voted while I was there, Greene was the only one not wearing a pandemic mask—ensuring that she would yet again be fined $2,500 for her act of defiance. Her masklessness happened to coincide with skyrocketing COVID-related hospitalizations and deaths in her own district's medical centers. The mayor of Dalton, the second-biggest city in her district, had declared a state of emergency because of the virus. Greene had not been in touch with Mayor Pennington or with the three major hospitals in the Fourteenth Congressional District. She had offered no public sympathies for the many COVID casualties that now included children—unless one categorized "we can't live forever" as sympathy.

Instead, the maskless congresswoman sat on the House floor, vigorously tweeting about how the Democrats' Green New Deal would enslave the United States to China—apparently unaware of the fact that one of her district's biggest employers, the solar panel production company Hanwha Q Cells, had been pushing for tax incentives that would enable the supply chain of solar panel production to shift *away* from China and toward the United States. Greene had not offered to support tax credits for one of her district's most important job creators. She had not even visited Hanwha Q Cells.

At one point, I asked her two advisers why Greene hadn't attended the Justice for J6 rally. The answer one of them gave me was more honest than I had expected. Greene had already done her own press events at the Department of Justice and the DC Jail, he said. She was much in demand. Everyone wanted Marjorie Taylor Greene to speak at their event.

Given all that, the adviser said to me, "What does it get her? It doesn't get her more support. It doesn't get her more fundraising dollars."

A TRUMP EVENT, BY CONTRAST, WOULD GET MARJORIE TAYLOR GREENE BOTH of those things—which was why they and I were both in Georgia that weekend.

The Trump rally was held on Saturday, September 25, at the Georgia National Fairgrounds in Perry, Georgia. I had attended many MAGA rallies in the past, but none since Trump's campaign event in Des Moines, Iowa, on January 30, 2020. That rally seemed a world removed from the present. Back then, President Trump was on the cusp of being acquitted in his first impeachment trial. The coronavirus merited little attention. The economy was in full gallop. The Democrats' slate of presidential candidates had yet to produce a worthy adversary, and Trump's reelection seemed probable if not quite assured.

Trump's defeat nine months later had changed the tenor of his rallies, but not in the way I had anticipated. The mood at the fairgrounds on this warm autumn afternoon was not one of baleful nostalgia or even bitterness. Instead, what charged the atmosphere was the supreme confidence that Trump had in fact won in 2020—that the proof of this was mostly in, with more evidence to come—and that all would be made right in due course.

Wandering through the uniformly maskless crowd for a couple of hours before the speeches commenced, I took note of the familiar slogans emblazoned on MAGA regalia: JESUS IS MY SAVIOR, TRUMP IS MY PRESIDENT. I'M STILL TRUMP'S GIRL. There were QAnon shirts and gun-loving shirts. There were anti-Biden and anti-vaccination and anti-media shirts.

But what predominated was a sea of red shirts bearing a simple declaration: TRUMP WON.

It was like staring at a thousand people who were all reading newspapers that were held upside down. No new evidence had surfaced demonstrating that Trump had in fact carried Georgia—or Pennsylvania, or Wisconsin, or Michigan, or New Mexico, or Nevada. Instead, just a day earlier in Arizona, the Cyber Ninjas' partisan "auditors" had produced their much-anticipated report. It concluded that Biden had, alas, carried the state. Even while cataloguing "critical" and "high" concerns—each of which Arizona election officials quickly dismantled in public statements—the Ninja tally actually awarded Biden 99 *more* votes and Trump 261 *fewer* votes than the official tabulation. It seemed that only a mad genius could spin this eventuality as proof that *Trump Won.*

But lo and behold, there was Trump, insisting in a statement that the Cyber Ninjas' report "shows incomprehensible fraud at an election-changing level." No other words were necessary. No call for honest debate would be required. The list of confederates in this *X-Files*-worthy grand conspiracy—Democrats and Republicans, high-ranking officials and voting machine CEOs and lowly poll workers and perhaps a few hundred enforcers in a fleet of unmarked white vans, all apparently sworn to secrecy by Joe Biden or his Chinese puppet master—need not be produced; their myriad communications need not be documented. The case was so prima facie that to believe otherwise was to announce yourself as a liar or a fool. As a red T-shirt worn by one of the rally attendees summed it up: TRUMP WON. THEY KNOW IT. YOU KNOW IT. I KNOW IT.

Perched behind the riser in the press pen, I thought about what the freshman Republican Peter Meijer had observed three weeks after the Capitol riot. His party, Meijer said to me, was afflicted with "a psychosis of denial." Eight months later, that same psychosis was no longer merely reactive. The stolen election was now as central to MAGA theology as the crucifixion of Jesus was to Christianity. In affirming the presence of evil, it brought clarity—and with it, a strange frisson of revelation. The lie brought joy.

Inevitably, it also brought profit. The alternative-facts ecosystem now had its own media megaphone. Two announcers for the 24/7 MAGA livestream channel Right Side Broadcasting Network stood on a riser, describing the pageantry at the fairgrounds in the breathless cadence of red-carpet commentators at the Academy Awards. In turn, the rally-goers swarmed below the riser, waving appreciatively at the RSBN crew.

Seated behind the riser in the shade next to me was John Fredericks, a former journeyman reporter who was Trump's Virginia campaign chairman in both 2016 and 2020. Fredericks now had his own conservative radio station, which he labeled, somewhat ambiguously, "America's Godzilla of Truth." A couple of days earlier, the talk-show host had scored an exclusive interview with Trump, in which the ex-president asserted, without the slightest evidence or the remotest pushback from Fredericks, that the state of Virginia—which Biden had carried by 10 points—had been stolen from him. At the rally, Fredericks was spending his downtime scrolling listlessly through his Twitter feed. Checking my laptop, I noticed that the day before, "America's Godzilla of Truth" had tweeted no fewer than six bogus claims about fraud in Arizona.

The psychosis was no longer exclusively one of denial. It was also a psychosis of professional ambition.

Both Fredericks and I looked up in response to the roar from the crowd. Marjorie Taylor Greene had entered the press pen and was strolling its perimeter to connect with the MAGA crowd, while her security team walked on either side of her. Greene wore an immense grin and a bright red dress. She hoisted a sign that said IMPEACH BIDEN.

"We love you, Marjorie!" they chorused. Others added, *"Kick their asses!"* and *"Fuck AOC!"* Greene submitted to selfies and fist-bumps for several minutes. Then her team escorted her toward the VIP tent backstage.

The Georgia freshman was among the first speakers. Onstage, Greene held aloft her sign while the crowd chanted, "Impeach Biden!" She peppered her ten-minute oration with customary schoolyard taunts. Democrats, she declared, were "Communists." Biden was "a real piece of—" and she nodded happily as the crowd hollered, *"SHIT!!!"* The current president, Greene went on, "has got dementia." She lamented, "Eight months ago, we had a president in the White House that loved America. But we don't have that anymore."

Still, Greene began her speech with the night's theme: "There's something *all* of us know in Georgia: *Trump won Georgia.* And that's why I'm calling for an audit in Georgia. No more excuses!"

Every speaker before and after her cited the need for "election integrity." They demanded audits as a kind of ritual purging. One of the speakers, a candidate for lieutenant governor named Burt Jones, received his greatest applause when he declared, "If I have anything to do with it, we're gonna get rid of those voting machines! Because people don't trust 'em—it's just that simple!"

At 6:30, the undercard portion of the rally had concluded. For the next hour, as the daylight ebbed and the Georgia sky took on a wispy apricot hue, the rally-goers rose to their feet under the gauzy spotlight of dusk. The women swayed to Elton John and the Village People while the men waved their MAGA caps through the air. With the sunlight all but extinguished, a voice boomed: *Ladies and gentlemen. Please welcome the forty-fifth president of the United States, Donald J. Trump."*

He glided onstage, waved, clenched his fist, pulsing in the heat bath of their adoration. Donald J. Trump in his baggy blue suit and elongated red tie, the masses screaming his name and wearing his name, Lee Greenwood's "God Bless the USA" blaring from the heavens—it was a ritual practiced to perfection, unlike anything seen in the nearly 250-year history of American politics.

But it was a bit different that night. For a man so given to fulmination, Trump seemed almost blissed-out, and not because he had lost a bit of weight and no longer had any governing responsibilities. The love he basked in was no different from that at any other Trump rally over the past six years. What had changed were his fortunes. In defeat, Donald Trump could claim a greater glory. The Republican Party was still with him—overwhelmingly so, against all precedent and reason. Far more than that, however: Trump now controlled the party's version of reality. The lies he had told, over and over, without the slightest shame, and with the able assistance of Marjorie Taylor Greene and other foot soldiers in his movement of incandescent narcissism, were now accepted as God's truth by the vast majority of Republican voters. Because the voters and what they believed were now in Trump's hands, the party was faced with a choice. They could speak out against him and risk forfeiting everything but their integrity. Or they could hold their tongues, risk becoming pariahs of the truth-based world, and keep their jobs.

Trump knew all along which choice they would make.

"We're going to take back our country from these lunatics!" he roared to the acres and acres of Georgians. The ex-president had so much to say about how the great heights to which he had brought America had sunk so dismally low during his successor's eight months. That was minor sport, however. Trump reserved the lion's share of his ninety minutes for baring the lush promiscuity of his electoral lies.

Trump described his defeat the previous November as "the most corrupt election in the history of our country," only to amend himself: "the most corrupt election *in the history of most countries.*" The crowd listened, deferring to their president's expertise in world history as Trump merrily denigrated the Marxists and radicals now dedicating themselves to the task of destroying America. But, he said, returning to the original sin: "This is what happens when you have a dishonest election. This is all about a rigged election. None of these disasters ever should have been allowed to happen."

With a kind of mordant glee, he trotted out the sundry outrages that never in fact took place at the Georgia and Arizona ballot boxes. Ballots smuggled under the table. Some 43,000 absentee ballots that violated the chain-of-custody rule. Over 4,000 unregistered votes, another 18,000 from vacant lots, tally sheets gone mysteriously missing, drop-box votes illegally trafficked, overvotes and votes from the dead and ghost votes . . .

The point of this horrific fraud, Trump reminded his followers, was: "In truth, they're not after me. They're after *you*. I just happened to be in the way." Of all his lies, this one—that he was merely a secondary target of his enemies, that it was not all about him—was the one lie that Trump could not possibly subscribe to. Did he believe the rest? Listening to him, it seemed at least somewhat plausible to me that he believed in the hate of his enemies at least as much as he believed in the love engulfing him in Perry, Georgia.

"They want to go after me because they think I have a big mouth," he snickered innocently to the crowd. Shrugging, he continued, "I don't have a big mouth. You know what I have?"

Said Trump: "I have a mouth that tells the truth."

The roar of approval was a great oceanic crest. Truth was what Trump said it was. Everyone knew it.

PART SIX

THE PARTY OF RETRIBUTION

Representative Paul Gosar

Chapter Twenty-Eight

"THE MOST DANGEROUS MAN

IN CONGRESS"

F our months after the Trump rally in Marjorie Taylor Greene's home
state of Georgia, the ex-president traveled to the Arizona congressional district of Paul Gosar.

It was January 15, 2022—a new year, an election year, a year of opportunity for Republicans. They had survived twelve months under President
Biden, at times consoling themselves with a new taunt, *Let's Go, Brandon!*,
which served as code for *Fuck Joe Biden!* Many of the rally-goers wore T-shirts
with the chant inscribed. A woman led the crowd in the Pledge of Allegiance—
and then concluded by grinning and hollering out, "Let's go, Brandon!"

A little more than a year had passed since tens of thousands of Trump
supporters had gathered around the Capitol, convinced that the republic hung
in the balance, and braced as well for civil war against Antifa. That day, and
in the days to follow, battalions of anarchists had yet to materialize in the
streets of the United States. The American flag still flew above the White
House and the Capitol. Easter, Thanksgiving, and Christmas had been celebrated as before.

Still, Trump's Republican followers could point to signs of what they
maintained were proof of left-wing totalitarianism where a great country once
stood. Liberal cities enforced COVID mask and vaccination mandates. Schoolchildren were at risk of being indoctrinated with something called "critical
race theory," which conservatives depicted as anti-American and itself racist.

And as Greene and Gosar had been among the first to bemoan, patriotic Americans were being jailed simply for showing up at the Capitol on January 6, 2021, to exercise their Constitutional rights.

Yesteryear's fear of creeping Sharia law and of Latino gangs like MS-13 raping and murdering their way through the American heartland had given way to an even more paralyzing strain of xenophobia. A new delusion had taken hold: Communist China now controlled the U.S. government.

Such a scenario relieved the GOP from the burden of casting Biden—a ubiquity in American politics for the past half century—as a figure suddenly to be feared. Instead, the seventy-nine-year-old president could properly be viewed a witless tool for the communists. And indeed, just before Trump would take the stage that evening in Florence, Arizona, the ex-president's recorded voice boomed out of the loudspeakers: "Ladies and gentlemen, our country is in trouble. And in many respects, our country is dying."

Then came recorded stammerings of the current president, followed by a newscaster's intoning that "roughly half the country thinks Joe Biden is unstable." And then images on the giant screens of an addled Biden rubbing his face, followed by a montage of skyrocketing gas prices, the chaotic withdrawal from Afghanistan, and other signs of a country in a state of rapid disintegration— all accompanied by a soundtrack of minor organ chords, tolling church bells, and the demented old man in the White House groaning and stuttering his way through the American apocalypse.

In the norm-shattering Trump era, this kind of over-the-top, quasi-Malthusian slapstick was now to be expected. It was easy to forget a time when a former president did not describe his successor as senile and did not characterize those who voted for that successor as unpatriotic. For that matter, it strained the memory to recall that once upon a time, thousands upon thousands of conservative Americans typically did *not* go to a political rally all wearing the same man's likeness on their shirts; or, at that man's direction, begin lustily screaming at the media; or, at the mere mention of the man's opponent, descend into a profane singsong.

Marjorie Taylor Greene had said it, just shy of a year ago: "The party is his. It doesn't belong to anyone else." It was this abiding fealty to the twice-impeached Trump, one year after his incitement of the riot at the Capitol, that staggered the senses. That evening in Florence, the eleven warm-up acts—all Republican officeholders or office-seekers—enthusiastically recited the only three things that mattered to the man who would follow them. They extolled the greatness of the former president. They mocked the current president. They proclaimed the 2020 election stolen.

Somewhere in the middle of the lineup, the emcee called out for a "Paul Goser," rhyming the last name with "poser." The Arizona congressman took the stage, grinning and waving as his hair flapped boyishly about. As he spoke, Gosar's head wobbled from side to side. He slurred his words. He fumbled with the prepared text. On a day replete with assertions that the sitting president was falling to pieces before the nation's eyes, it was unsettling to witness the advancing state of Gosar's unspecified neurological condition—a condition that he still had yet to discuss with anyone on his staff.

Never anyone's idea of a master orator, Gosar struggled badly that late afternoon. Even while checking the requisite boxes—the 2020 election was "absolutely" stolen from Trump, the Democratic majority was imposing "Marxist fascist rule," and "Boy, do I miss Donald Trump!"—his logic often seemed to go adrift. At one point, he tried to ad lib "Let's go, Brandon!" but the phrase collapsed into gibberish. At another, while calling for the unnamed perpetrators of election fraud to face punishment, he blurted out, "If you're gonna do the crime, you gotta pay the time." And in a transparent play for the hearts of the many Arizonans in the crowd who continued to brandish QAnon regalia, Gosar invoked "the storm building"—repeatedly but waywardly, suggesting uncertainty as to what the metaphor was supposed to signify.

Still, Gosar had something unique to offer this event. After reminding the audience that they were gathering in his district, the dentist added, "I'm also the member of Congress that Democrats fear the most. I'm considered the most dangerous man in Congress. And they came after me like they're gonna come after you."

He was referring to a dubious distinction he now shared with his designated mentee Marjorie Taylor Greene: Congress had voted to strip Paul Gosar of his two committee assignments. But in Gosar's case, the Democratically controlled House had gone a step further: they had also censured him, making the Arizona congressman the first to face such a rebuke since New York

Representative Charlie Rangel was censured by his fellow Democrats for ethics violations in 2010.

The offending conduct in question was an animated video that had been posted on Gosar's official Twitter and Instagram accounts on November 9, 2021. In the video, a protagonist from a popular anime series with Gosar's face photoshopped onto it was shown flying through the air and stabbing a second villainous "titan"—one with the photoshopped face of Alexandria Ocasio-Cortez—in the back of her head with a sword. The same anime displayed the Gosar character flying at President Biden with two swords.

Tellingly, it was an intern in Gosar's office who had designed the anime and posted it to the congressman's account without feeling the need to show it to anyone first. Subsequently, Gosar's son told his father that he thought the anime was great. Gosar agreed. ("The creativity of my team is off the hook," he enthused on Twitter.) His staff concurred. They were unanimous in their view that the video amounted to harmless fun. No one in his orbit seemed to think there was anything objectionable about a cartoon image of Gosar's attempting to murder a Democratic congresswoman and a sitting president. Those characters, the Gosarites uniformly believed, were simply representations of Biden's supposed "open borders" policy that a heroic Republican congressman intended to slay. It therefore surprised them when Twitter flagged the post the evening it was posted, saying that it violated rules regarding "hateful conduct."

That wrist-slap struck House Democrats as insufficient. Since Trump's departure, the party's most prominent members of Congress—including AOC, Speaker Pelosi, and members of the January 6 committee—continued to receive an unprecedented volume of death threats. To them, it was disingenuous for Gosar to pretend that a federal officeholder's casual depiction of Democrats' being killed bore no connection to the rising tide of violent animus in American politics.

But that posture of innocence is exactly what Gosar's office maintained. "Everyone needs to relax," said his digital director, Jessica Lycos, in a statement issued late in the evening after the anime began to attract notice. "The left doesn't get meme culture. They have no joy. They are not the future. It's a cartoon. Gosar can't fly and he does not own any lightsabers."

Yet again, it fell to House Republican leader Kevin McCarthy to place a call to House Majority Leader Steny Hoyer. McCarthy told Hoyer that he had summoned Gosar to his office. The Republican leader had not disciplined or even reprimanded Gosar. He had simply asked for the Arizona congressman's version of events.

"It was a staffer who did it," McCarthy told Hoyer. At McCarthy's direction, Gosar had taken down the video.

Hoyer had just returned from a trip to Israel and had not yet taken the temperature of the Democratic caucus. Once he did so, the majority leader notified McCarthy that Gosar's conduct would not go unpunished.

"Would it make a difference if I got him to stand in the well and apologize?" McCarthy asked. In fact, the minority leader was speaking out of school. Gosar had not expressed the slightest remorse for the violent anime. Quite the contrary: it had received 3 million views, a bonanza for a backbencher. In a letter to his constituents, Gosar had defended his actions, saying, "I am entitled to speak to the people and to do so in a way that is engaging."

"Kevin," said Hoyer, "the problem is that this isn't the first time with him."

THAT WAS, INDEED, THE PROBLEM—AND NOT JUST FOR DEMOCRATS. AS ONE veteran House Republican would say with a sigh, "Is this really the most egregious thing Paul Gosar has done?" The question answered itself but also prompted a second question: *If Gosar was allowed to go unpunished for worse offenses in the past, then why punish him now?*

Among many House Republicans, it was understood that Gosar, not for the first time, had taken things too far. Still, the anime's sentiment—that Republicans were doing battle with an evil ideology—was widely shared among conservatives. Gosar made this very point to his Republican colleagues during a conference on November 16. The anime was merely "symbolic," he explained. It was leftist policies, not leftists themselves, that Paul Gosar was doing battle with. In no way did he condone violence. He left for his colleagues to surmise the abiding conservative refrain: *Violence is what the other side does.*

On November 17, the day of the vote to censure Paul Gosar and strip him of his committee assignments, Kevin McCarthy happened to bump into a senior Democratic staffer. While brushing past the staffer, the Republican leader declared icily, "You guys are going to regret this next year."

The debate on the House floor was lengthy and often heated. Democrats, including Ocasio-Cortez herself, argued that words had meaning and that in no other workplace would an intimation of violence against a colleague be tolerated. Republicans, led by McCarthy, maintained that Pelosi's Democrats were more interested in punishing Republicans than in helping the American people. Throughout it all, Gosar sat alone, appearing placid but attentive.

When the vote came, all Democrats and two Republicans—Liz Cheney and Adam Kinzinger—voted to censure Paul Gosar and to strip him of his committee assignments. Marjorie Taylor Greene, maskless as always, sidled up behind Gosar and patted him on the back.

Speaker Pelosi then called for the Arizona congressman to present himself in the well of the chamber for censure. He strolled up toward the rostrum and removed his mask, staring straight ahead. A small crowd formed directly behind him. They were his fellow members in the House Freedom Caucus. Several of them laid their palms on his back in a gesture of commiseration as the Speaker solemnly proclaimed "that Representative Paul Gosar be censured with the public reading of this resolution by the Speaker; and that Representative Paul Gosar be removed from the Committee on Natural Resources and the Committee on Oversight and Government Reform."

An awkward silence followed. Then, from the Democratic side of the aisle, rang out a single voice: "Bye!"

As Gosar and his fellow conservatives turned to go, one of them faced the Speaker.

"What about Eric Swalwell?" demanded Marjorie Taylor Greene. "How about that one? Sleeping with a Chinese spy."

Gosar, for his part, shook a few hands and accepted a couple of hugs. Then he shuffled out through the west side of the chamber. In the days to follow, Gosar did not convene a press conference as Greene had done. He did, however, boast to constituents in his weekly newsletter that Trump had called him after the censure, thanking him for his dogged promotion of the ex-president's America First Agenda. Gosar also told others that it had been pointless anyway to serve on the committees under Democratic control. Far from reprimanding Gosar, McCarthy had evinced sympathy—and even intended to reward him. When the Republicans regained the majority and Kevin McCarthy was the new Speaker of the House, he pledged to Gosar, "You'll be getting *better* committees."

"But you know what?" Gosar told the crowd at the Arizona rally. "They liberated me." His next words—"Not only do I have two committees, I have *every* committee!"—seemed to be Paul Gosar's garbled way of saying that he was now free to work across the spectrum of congressional duties, in tireless service of Arizona's Fourth District. Indeed, one month after he received his punishment, Gosar's office released a press statement: "Gosar Announces Federal Grant Award to City of Kingman to Combat the Spread of COVID."

"I am pleased to announce that the City of Kingman will receive this critical funding," the statement quoted the congressman as saying, referring to a $32,000 grant to help sanitize Kingman's airport. The statement included words of gratitude from Kingman's mayor "for Congressman Gosar's continued support."

The statement from Gosar's office omitted one significant detail: The grant was funded by the American Rescue Plan Act of 2021. Paul Gosar had voted against the bill after saying on Twitter, presumably not as an innocent joke, "This bill is not about COVID relief. It's about funding Democrat's [*sic*] pet projects. The American people should be furious."

Of course, in the very literal sense of things, Gosar himself had not cast the vote against the bill he would later take credit for. Instead, he had voted against it by proxy—because that was the day, in late February 2021, that Gosar had cited his inability to attend the roll-call vote "due to the ongoing public health emergency," when in fact he was in Orlando, Florida, preparing to tell an audience of white-nationalist Groypers the next morning that "Republicans won't win by accepting the framework of the left."

Paul Gosar would proceed to show them exactly how a stalwart Republican went about rejecting the left's framework. First, do it loudly. Then, do it by proxy, a tactic made possible by lying. And in the end, when praise came due, all one needed to do was to step up and behave as if the left's "pet project" was really his pet project all along.

Perhaps some might view this as hypocritical behavior—or at minimum, behavior that fell well short of what one had a right to expect from the self-described "most dangerous member of Congress." If so, then Team Gosar had a ready rebuttal for his detractors, one they had used already:

"Everyone needs to relax. . . . It's a cartoon."

General Mike Flynn

Chapter Twenty-Nine

FAKE AUDITS

I ran twice, and I won twice, and we did better the second time," proclaimed Trump, loudly and falsely, at the beginning of his Arizona rally speech—adding later, "we really did on November 3, we trounced them."

As Republican leaders cast their hopeful eyes on the 2022 midterm election, the party's undisputed leader enjoined his base to remain locked in on yesteryear—specifically, on that one dark night of stolen victory. "The insurrection took place on November 3, Election Day! January 6 was the protest!" was now Trump's stated formulation of recent history. And because of this fictitious electoral theft, "our country is being destroyed" by the simultaneously devious and incompetent Democrats.

To Trump, all roads led backward, to him and to his presidency interrupted. According to his moral instruction, what should most offend Americans, more than Biden's sheer awfulness, was that the awfulness had arrived by theft, snatching away from a stricken country the greatness that Trump had bestowed upon it.

This compulsive, singular focus on the Republican Party's defeated president was inevitable. It was exactly what one might expect from a party that had decided not to write an official platform for the 2020 election—because, by that point, fidelity to whatever it was President Trump wanted at any given time was the GOP's official position.

But the Trump-centricity was problematic all the same. For by early 2022, there was significant reason for Republicans to feel that a corner could be turned. President Biden's Gallup approval rating had plummeted to a dismal

40 percent. By early February 2022, the Morning Consult survey of public sentiment regarding the country's overall direction captured a historical right track/wrong track nadir of 38/62. Surging gas prices, a nationwide increase in violent crime, and the persistence of the coronavirus all combined to exacerbate the historical headwinds Biden already faced as a first-term president. In these and other ways, bad news for America amounted to good tidings for the Republican Party, so long as the subject remained Biden.

Trump would not permit this, unfortunately. His self-interested focus on 2020 had taken a surprisingly literalistic turn. The delusion that the election had been stolen ignited a nationwide flurry of so-called full forensic audits in search of a steal that did not exist.

This trend had begun, of course, in Arizona, home of what its Republican chairwoman Kelli Ward termed "America's Audit." Seven months and $5.7 million later, the Cyber Ninjas had failed to uncover a fraud conspiracy. Unsurprisingly, the dark recesses of the internet seethed with suggestions that Ward, or Cyber Ninjas CEO Doug Logan, or certain Arizona state senators, had squelched the truth for financial gain.

But the truth remained out there.

TWO DAYS AFTER PAUL GOSAR WAS CENSURED AND STRIPPED OF HIS COMMITtee assignments, I flew to Manchester, New Hampshire, a state that Joe Biden had won by seven points. Trump had held a campaign rally in Manchester just nine days before the 2020 election—bragging, as always, about his crowd size, basking in their chants of *"We love you, we love you"* and venturing to suggest that even the great Reagan had not met with such adoration. How could he possibly lose New Hampshire?

How could it have happened?

The "New Hampshire Election Security Seminar" I had shown up to attend in Manchester purported to answer that question. The hosts were a group of concerned local Republicans who had been up in arms about the 2020 results—all the more so when it was discovered that there was a significant numerical discrepancy in the New Hampshire town of Windham between the machine-tabulated vote totals and a subsequent recount by hand.

The disclosure of this occurrence in Windham was first met with outrage, followed by a burst of giddiness. Could this Granite State burg of 15,817 hold the key to unlocking the great 2020 vote-rigging conspiracy?

An audit was demanded and performed. In July 2021, the professional auditing team produced a 121-page report. Their conclusion was that the voting machines had misread several of the absentee ballots that had been folded. Otherwise, concluded the report, "our audit found the Windham election to have been well run under challenging circumstances." No fraud was uncovered.

None of the attendees filling this conference hall in Manchester appeared to be the least bit mollified by the Windham audit results. The atmosphere was one of bitterness edged with deep suspicion. One of the hosts speculated aloud that the senior auditor had "committed treason" and would soon be arrested. (Neither turned out to be true.) A Republican state representative, Mark Alliegro, suggested to the audience that New Hampshire's long-running secretary of state had in fact overseen decades of election fraud, adding, "If you're a communist and you want to shift the powers, all you have to do is to shift it a teeny tiny bit to affect the balance of power, especially in a state like New Hampshire." (The "communist" in question, Secretary of State Bill Gardner, had presided over victories by Reagan and both Bushes.) The stakes in this matter were hardly confined to a single election and a single state, argued a Republican congressional candidate named Julian Acciard: "It took Mao, Stalin, Lenin, and Hitler all about five years to consolidate their power. The left is poised to be able to do it in about three."

Midway through the four-hour event, Seth Keshel took the stage. The Texas-based former army intelligence officer, baseball statistician, and traffic-light software salesman who had recently fed suspicions that the Fort Worth mayoral race had been rigged was now in New Hampshire to fan conspiratorial flames. Trump, Keshel assured the audience, had won New Hampshire. For the next half hour, the lanky, flannel-shirted, cowboy-booted man rattled off election data he archly termed "interesting," "confusing," "curious," "a little bit off," and "head-scratchers." The audience gasped and groaned loudly with each factoid.

Sitting in the back and taking notes, I found myself struck both by what Seth Keshel said and what he did not say. The litany of supposed anomalies

Keshel cited that distinguished the 2020 election from previous ones was missing the most glaring irregularity of them all: Donald J. Trump. Everything about the candidate and the president had pulverized historical norms. Trump had said so himself, repeatedly. That he'd made all the experts look like idiots throughout the course of his maiden campaign in politics was perhaps his proudest achievement.

That millions of voters might take a chance on the wild card Trump in 2016, only to be repelled by his blustering and often disinterested performance as president four years later, was a possibility that Keshel seemed unable to grasp. Yet it was there to be seen in his own data, including the suburban communities of New Hampshire whose shifting electoral patterns he had cited. Just as left-leaning pundits had failed to appreciate the electorate's welling contempt for Hillary Clinton in 2016, Keshel and others on the right failed to recognize that Trump's historic unpopularity was not some confection ginned up by the fake news media. It was real. It was dispositive. It, rather than a vast election-rigging conspiracy, was why Joe Biden had won.

So why was it, I wondered, that an intelligent person like Keshel would possess so gaping a blind spot? Keshel happened to be a conservative evangelical whose animus toward Democrats and "RINOs" ("Republicans in name only") grew exponentially during COVID lockdowns. The lockdowns, he'd told a podcaster, had hurt his business, infringed on his civil liberties, and otherwise constrained him to the point where, he said, "My energy's about to explode." Those resentments were peppered throughout Keshel's ostensibly dry, data-driven presentation in Manchester. He casually referred to the mainstream media as "the enemy," to establishment Republicans as "the enemy inside the wire," and to the prospects of a healthy thirty-seven-year-old man such as him living to be ninety-five as something "you don't want to, in a country that's going this way."

Keshel also warned the audience, "We cannot turn our backs from pursuing the truth from 2020." This, of course, was Trump's backward-facing argument. It occurred to me that many Trump supporters were embracing their perceived sense of highly personal and unjust forfeiture almost as one would a religion. It had become a lifestyle, a way of processing the world.

For some, it also presented financial opportunity. The "election integrity seminar" in New Hampshire was one of many such talks Seth Keshel would give around the country in 2021. Frequently joining him on the 2020 Forever traveling roadshow was the Manchester event's next speaker, David Clements.

Clements was a licensed attorney and business professor at New Mexico State University who had taught a class on business law until a month earlier, when he was fired for refusing to wear a COVID mask or receive vaccinations. His qualifications to speak on election fraud were even thinner than those of Keshel. But the former assistant district attorney and failed U.S. Senate candidate possessed a flair for the theatrical. He opened with a prayer for the patriots who had gathered in Manchester "because of the travesty, because of the crime that was committed." Rumpled and unshaven, Clements allowed that he could use some sleep—but then vowed in a rising voice, "I will not get rest. I will burn my soul out into the ground until we win. Because it's that bad. The Republic is in trouble."

The professor then issued a series of startling claims. He said that "the entire judiciary's corrupt." He said that the propagandists of Nazi Germany "would blush" at the lies to which the globalists were now subjecting Americans. He said that in addition to Nazi propagandizing, "we've got a Marxist culture"— one apparently with a Maoist twist, because, said Clements, Hollywood producers "actually submit our scripts to communist Chinese script doctors and they go through that and they tell us what gets to be put in our stories."

As for the 2020 election: "the entire deep state was in on it," Clements declared, without elaboration. Likening a fraudulent ballot to a murdered child, and the fight to reverse the 2020 election totals to a battle of good versus evil, the former assistant DA then said, "You know what's going to fix the rigged election in 2022 and 2024? Someone being arrested, prosecuted, and shot for treason."

"Yeah!" members of the audience yelled as they applauded.

QUIXOTIC THOUGH THE EFFORTS OF DAVID CLEMENTS AND SETH KESHEL might have seemed, the movement to audit Trump's way back into the White House had gathered a certain momentum. A petition circulated by a conspiracy-mongering Arizona state senator named Wendy Rogers called for 2020 election audits in all fifty states. It attracted signatures from 204 Republican legislators representing thirty-eight states—including Trump strongholds like Wyoming, West Virginia, Alabama, Mississippi, and Oklahoma where even unfounded allegations of fraud simply did not exist. In Wisconsin, the nonpartisan Legislative Audit Board failed to uncover fraud in the contested state, prompting Republican legislators to fund an "election crimes" bureau headed by a conservative former judge who was already on record declaring that Biden had stolen the 2020 election.

And a few hours before the November 19, 2021, New Hampshire event I attended, the Republican-controlled state senate of another critical swing state, Pennsylvania, announced that it had awarded a contract to a vendor to conduct what it termed an "impartial" audit of the past election. The recipient of the no-bid $270,000 contract was an Iowa-based firm named Envoy Sage with two employees and no election auditing experience. The contract did not require that the public would ever see the audit's results.

Two months later, in January 2022, a hearing was conducted in Alamogordo, New Mexico, to determine whether the results of the 2020 election in Otero County should be subjected to an audit. At first blush, the proposition seemed outlandish. Trump had carried the solidly Republican county by 25 points. There had been no reports of fraud in Otero County—not in 2020, or in 2016, or anytime in recent memory.

What made the county audit-hungry was not evidence of suspicious voting activity but the fact that one of its county commissioners, Couy Griffin, was convinced that Trump's victory had been stolen from him. Griffin, a former pastor and barbecue purveyor, was the head of a group called Cowboys for Trump. In 2019, he had paraded on horseback through Washington, DC, a stunt that earned Griffin a visit to the Oval Office. Griffin returned to the capital city on January 6, 2021, and was subsequently indicted for disorderly conduct during the Capitol riot. Thereafter, he referred to himself as a "political prisoner," even as a free man pending his federal trial. (On March 22, Griffin was found guilty of misdemeanor trespassing on restricted grounds.)

Commissioner Griffin had been to Montana in September 2021 to participate in an "election integrity" event. Seth Keshel was among the speakers.

So was Professor David Clements. Intrigued by all the talk of audits, Griffin returned home to Alamogordo and proposed that Clements be brought in to preside over a "full forensic audit" of Otero County's 23,000 or so votes.

The county clerk, Robyn Holmes, had held her position since 1985. Her staff was well trained, and the 2020 tabulations had been executed without incident. Furthermore, as a matter of state and local tradition, the tallies had already been audited multiple times, revealing not so much as a hint of fraud. Still, Holmes had been hearing from other county clerks in New Mexico that David Clements had been roaming his home state, demanding that local government workers drop what they were doing and accommodate a host of document requests.

On January 13, 2022, David Clements and his wife, Erin, showed up to a meeting of the Otero County commissioners. The professor delivered a long-winded presentation in which he alleged rampant voting fraud throughout New Mexico and the United States without providing the slightest evidence that so much as a single vote in Otero County had gone awry. What Clements did insist was that the county's voting machines, produced by the much-demonized firm Dominion, were hooked up to the internet and therefore highly susceptible to hacking.

That wasn't true, protested Holmes. The Dominion machines used by Otero County were only tabulators. They lacked internet capacity. It was like the difference between an adding machine and a computer.

"That is not true," Erin Clements interrupted her. And as the veteran county clerk suggested that she perhaps knew what equipment Otero County had used since 2006 better than the couple from San Cruces did, the professor angrily yelled out his trump card:

"WHAT ARE YOU WORRIED ABOUT?"

At the conclusion of the meeting, Couy Griffin and the other two county commissioners awarded a $49,750 no-bid audit contract to EchoMail, the software firm used in the Cyber Ninjas audit in Arizona. David and Erin Clements would direct the audit.

"This is going to put us on the map," the professor was overheard rejoicing. "We're going to be famous for this."

Evangelical Trump supporters

Chapter Thirty

DEATH CULT

L*ET'S GO, BRANDON! LET'S GO, BRANDON! LET'S GO, BRANDON! . . .*

The chant, now ubiquitous in the early days of 2022, rose up spontaneously in the cavernous sanctuary of Dream City Church in north Phoenix—soon to be followed by chanted slogans of yesteryear, such as *BUILD THE WALL!* and *DRAIN THE SWAMP!* That an evangelical megachurch would host a Trump-friendly event had, of course, long ceased to be newsworthy. In fact, the man onstage during all the chanting was none other than the ex-president's son, Eric Trump. For that matter, the president himself had blessed Dream City Church with a personal appearance eighteen months earlier on June 23, 2020, during the height of the pandemic, in which he bragged about his TV ratings while sternly warning that the "Democrats are trying to rig this election."

Still, the casual acceptability of chanting pseudo-obscenities about a sitting president in a tax-exempt place of worship struck me as a new development in contemporary American life. The churchgoers at Dream City were paying attendees, as was I. Nearly all of them were white. Other than the occasional LET'S GO, BRANDON! T-shirt, they were respectfully attired. Many of them had brought their teenage children. When not chanting pseudo-obscenities, they sat attentively to the day's procession of speakers with expressions that ranged from somber to disquieted to elated, as one might at a tent revival, albeit a tent revival that charged $225 a head.

The megachurch was hosting something called the ReAwaken America

Tour, a traveling road show that wasn't precisely Trump-centric, and certainly was not an official Republican Party function. But it featured three tightly intertwined elements that now defined the Trump-era GOP. One was the apocalyptic loathing with which religious conservatives viewed their fellow Americans on the left. Another was the fervent promotion of truth as lies and lies as truth. The third element, joined at the hip alongside the first two, was a desire to make a tidy living off all this false prophecy.

The organizer of ReAwaken America, a hyperkinetic self-help author named Clay Clark, informed me that Dream City Church's capacity was 3,500 and that this January event was due to exceed that figure. If that kind of draw was typical of Clark's gatherings—which he would stage fourteen times over the course of a year, in sites across the United States that invariably turned out to be megachurches—then ReAwaken America was pulling in annual gross receipts on the order of $11 million.

That unholy wealth was spread among several dozen freedom-loving vendors who displayed their wares on tables throughout the corridors of the megachurch like the canonical money-changers at the Jerusalem temple. LET'S GO, BRANDON! T-shirts were readily available. One booth was well stocked with the products of MyPillow CEO Mike Lindell. Another booth, tended to by the niece of Michael Flynn, hawked T-shirts bearing the likeness of the general. Nearby, an artist named Michael Marrone offered prints for sale of Trump, Flynn, and others doing battle in Revolutionary War garb. Another urged viewers to watch *The Trump I Know,* a documentary of all-female testimonials from women who were either on Trump's payroll or romantically involved with his sons. Yet another booth sold picture books by a Myrtle Beach fellow named Gene Ho, who proclaimed himself to be Trump's "official campaign photographer," a designation that might have surprised those who had actually worked on Trump's two presidential campaigns.

But most of the display items tilted away from MAGA celebrities and toward an encompassing existential anxiety. They warned of end times brought on by the "new world order." They offered pills and elixirs to help the human immune system brave the onslaught of globalist viruses. They marketed "cures" for homosexuality. They provided, in paperback form, meticulous evidence of devil worshippers' running the country.

Still, the commercial bustle in the hallways of the megachurch was a welcome respite from the doom-speak inside the sanctuary. I took a seat in time to hear Dr. Vladimir Zelenko—whose website claimed that he was "nominated for the Presidential Medal of Freedom," though no such nominating process exists for that accolade—describe COVID vaccines as "the poison death shot" and claim falsely that the vaccines had already killed 100 times more people than the virus itself had.

Zelenko, once a beloved physician in the New York village of Kiryas Joel, had been ostracized from his Hasidic community for promoting untested cures for the coronavirus. Now he was a circuit-rider (until his death from lung cancer five months later), as was the next speaker: Dr. Sherri Tenpenny, whose website described her as "a doctor and a voice of reason about vaccines and current events." The Ohio-based physician proceeded to describe COVID vaccines as part of a "transhumanism movement" for which their proponents "should be charged with murder."

"This is right out of the Bible, folks," Tenpenny proclaimed. "It's much bigger than just a shot. This is spiritual warfare."

NO ONE INSIDE THE SANCTUARY OF DREAM CITY CHURCH WAS WEARING A mask. To wear one was to signify that you were a willing dupe, unreachable by the "experts" at ReAwaken America. Still, as the Delta variant of the coronavirus became surmounted by a new and more transmissible mutation, Omicron, hospitalization and death rates skyrocketed once again. On this day, January 14, 2022, 3,980 Americans would die of the virus. It now seemed inevitable that the death toll, for a virus that President Trump had predicted would quickly disappear "like a miracle," would exceed 1 million. And though it would prove impossible to delineate COVID casualties by partisan affiliation, it had become increasingly clear in the second half of 2021 that Trump counties had significantly more deaths than counties won by Biden.

What made the death rate lower in the Biden counties was that their residents were far likelier to be vaccinated. According to the Centers for Disease Control, the chances of death among those who did not receive the vaccine and booster were 53.2 times greater than for those who had received both shots. Those most resistant to the idea of being vaccinated were Republicans, according to a study conducted by the nonpartisan Kaiser Family Foundation. Their reservations, said the Kaiser study, correlated to misinformation they received from their trusted messengers at Fox News, Newsmax, and One America News. Many of them had come to believe that the government was concealing vaccine deaths, or that the vaccines themselves caused COVID, or that they contained a microchip, or that they altered one's DNA.

During the middle of January 2022, just as the ReAwaken America Tour convened in the Phoenix megachurch, the Pew Research Center conducted a survey to determine public attitudes about the coronavirus. Asked whether the virus was being made a bigger deal of than it really was, 38 percent of Americans responded affirmatively. Aggregated by partisan affiliation, the number of Democrats who believed COVID was being hyped was 16 percent. Among Republicans, it was 64 percent.

By my estimate, the percentage of COVID eye-rollers at Dream City Church hovered somewhere between 99 and 100.

TWO YOUNG WOMEN SEATED NEXT TO ME WERE TAKING PHOTOS OF DR. TEN-penny's slides showing how the vaccines would enable satan-worshipping globalists to track the movements of every human 24/7. I excused myself and eased my way out of the crowded sanctuary. Stepping into the corridor, I saw a familiar lanky figure in a leather vest and cowboy boots sipping on a cup of coffee while studying the Michael Flynn paraphernalia on display. It was Seth Keshel. I hadn't known that he was on the speaking agenda, and the self-spun election-data expert seemed out of place in an event that, at least thus far, was obsessively fixated on COVID vaccines as a sign of the apocalypse.

But as the day wore on and a more sweeping narrative began to reveal it-self, I came to understand how cozily Keshel fit into it. There was Mike Lin-dell the pillow czar, sputtering onstage about how he had been "de-banked" by Minnesota Bank & Trust, just as Fox News had stopped airing his election conspiracy theories after Dominion Voting Systems slapped the media com-pany with a $1.6 billion lawsuit. There was Tulsa pastor and U.S. Senate can-didate Jackson Lahmeyer, decrying Christian meekness: "Faced with evil, you can't purr like kittens—you must roar like lions!" And there was a self-proclaimed independent journalist calling herself Mel K, who termed the United Nations "the Fourth Reich," controlled by "the most evil man alive," George Soros.

At the root of each and every fevered monologue was fraud: election fraud, medical fraud, monetary fraud, media fraud, religious fraud, institutional fraud. Everything was a lie. Everything required audit after audit, until a more palatable truth emerged. Until then, the ReAwaken America Tour offered its dazzling constellation of alternative pastors, journalists, and medical experts to guide its ticket-paying patriots through the darkness.

But it also offered, among its thirty-eight speakers on day one, six politicians, all of them Republicans—from Arizona, Nevada, Oklahoma, and the Trump family. For all the scattered denunciations of the Bushes and RINO enablers of godless socialism, there was only one home in American politics for this wandering tribe of fraud purveyors. The tribe constituted a critical stratum of the GOP base. There were enough of them to choke off a Republican's political prospects at the primary level.

The final speaker that night at the Phoenix megachurch was Michael Flynn. Among the MAGA circuit-riders, only Trump commanded a greater following than the three-star general. The former Defense Intelligence Agency director and national security adviser was now a full-time 2020 election denier, anti-vaxxer, endorser of right-wing political aspirants, and, some speculated, 2024 Republican presidential candidate. He spoke with the authority of an acclaimed patriot who had been done in by the deep state. (This narrative was somewhat inconvenienced by Flynn's having pleaded guilty to lying to the FBI and having been a cooperating federal witness for an entire year.)

Tonight, "America's General" explained to the crowd, truth was not what was in one's mind. Truth was instead sensorial. "Whenever I didn't follow my gut-feel," the veteran intelligence officer said, "I made a mistake and I was listening to my mind." After all, Flynn then observed, "It's not gut-feel. It's God-feel."

As the crowd murmured in wonderment at the revelation, it seemed to me that all the distinctions between the day's speakers had gone ablur in the Phoenix megachurch. Preachers, politicians, and doctors alike were conveying, in the same spiritual overtones, the same sense of delusion, of upended reality—one in which Mike Flynn could casually claim, without the slightest need for proof, that "we've had fraudulent elections for over a hundred years," just as other speakers could postulate that COVID was a phony pretext for gene editing and mind control. The more hyperbolic and impossible to believe their assertions were, the greater the distance separating themselves from the elites they mocked as confirmed professional liars.

America had been lied to; now cometh the ReAwakeners on a crimson stampede of counter-lies. It was a wave that rode Donald Trump to victory in 2016. It was one that delivered Marjorie Taylor Greene from CrossFit to QAnon to Congress, and Paul Gosar from utter obscurity to minor celebrity.

There was, in short, an audience for losing one's mind and espousing lies as "God-feel." Doing so, and deluding audiences en masse, was a fateful proposition, however. It was not a traffic lane one could swerve in and out of on a whim. As when Caesar and his army crossed the Rubicon to commit treason against the Roman Empire, there could be no turning back.

This was now true of another former warrior, Michael Flynn, who had cast his lot with the apostles of fraud. "I don't know that he could get a job today," Clay Clark told me. "So I view it as an honor to pay him to speak at our events."

Representative Lauren Boebert

Chapter Thirty-One

STATE OF THE UNION

I t was a committee workday on Capitol Hill, which meant a free day for Marjorie Taylor Greene.

I arrived in Rome, Georgia, a half hour before noon on a sunny Wednesday in mid-February. It's a small and somnolent city (population 37,713) with gracious lawns, pleasant walking paths along the Coosa River, and a disproportion of gray-haired, elderly white residents. The city's name had, according to the local museum, literally been drawn from a hat in 1834. Otherwise, and notwithstanding the faux-Roman aqueduct installed outside the city limits, Rome proudly maintains its roots as a Confederate cotton town. At the outbreak of the Civil War, more than one-third of Rome's population consisted of enslaved Black people; their value as "property" well exceeded the rest of Rome's assessed property combined.

In 1963, nearly a century after Sherman's Union troops had torched the town, Rome's professed image as a racially harmonious city was jostled when several dozen Black students attempted to eat at white-only lunch counters. Waitresses poured water mixed with ammonium on the demonstrators, egged on by several jeering white Romans who referred to the students as monkeys. A young NAACP lawyer and Atlanta native named Vernon Jordan—who would one day achieve distinction as a powerful DC lobbyist and President Bill Clinton's consigliere—represented the sixty-two defendants, all but five of whom were found guilty and jailed for up to ten days. (The five who were set free were all fourteen years of age.)

Shortly after noon, an ebony SUV with tinted windows rolled up to the curb beside John Henry's Grill in downtown Rome. A linebacker-sized Black man in locs, wearing sunglasses and a necktie, opened the passenger door. Out stepped the local congresswoman. Greene expressed approval that I was wearing jeans like her, shook my hand, and asked me what had brought me to Rome.

"You," I said.

"Oh!" she exclaimed, clearly taken aback at the idea that I had come all this way solely to speak to her. Her two aides hovered nearby. One of them had warned me in advance that the interview would need to be off the record, at least at the outset. (Nearly everything she and I spoke about would ultimately be confirmed in subsequent on-the-record conversations.) To the boss, he said, I was still "the *New York Times* reporter," a species she casually demonized.

"Fine," I said, realizing my options were few. Being viewed warily, if not with outright contempt, by the right was par for the course for journalists in the Trump era. Until this point Greene had never submitted to a one-on-one interview with a national mainstream publication. That day's lunch was originally supposed to be dinner—but that had been changed the day beforehand, on her orders. Apparently, she wished to avoid the cognitively dissonant spectacle of Marjorie Taylor Greene's having an evening glass of wine with "the *New York Times* reporter."

Still, I had three things going for me. First, I had made the effort to show up on her turf, which seemed to pique her curiosity. Just as much, my having done so amounted to an implicit challenge: was Trump's favorite warrior-goddess really going to shy away from a reporter's polite inquiries?

But what likely worked most in my favor was Greene's hunger for attention. Six weeks earlier, her personal account had been permanently suspended from Twitter for continuing to post lies about the COVID vaccine. Her response to the ban was almost identical to her reaction to having been stripped of her committee assignments. First, she complained that it was unfair to be punished for the same misconduct that she insisted others on the left had committed. Next, Greene voiced displeasure on behalf of her constituents, because, after all, it was really their voice that Twitter had silenced. At the same time, she feigned indifference: none of her true followers were on Twitter, anyway. Meanwhile, behind the scenes, Greene schemed to find a way to reclaim her Twitter platform—including urging Kevin McCarthy to speak to his donor, Twitter shareholder Paul Singer, about the matter.

In the interim, however, the Georgia freshman was perhaps less of a mind to turn down a media request after having been deplatformed. We filed inside the restaurant, with Greene's bodyguard closely behind her.

A few of the locals waved to their congresswoman, who grinned and drawled out a few pleasantries. We moved to a booth in the back. Greene sat directly across from me, with the two aides sitting nearby, mostly silent throughout, and the bodyguard hovering somewhere behind us. I delivered a preamble about me and the book I was writing. Greene did not let on at the time that she, too, was working on a book, though she had yet to find a publisher for it.

For the next ninety minutes, Marjorie Taylor Greene was unwaveringly cordial, direct, and self-assured. Listening to her, I felt an odd sensation of déjà vu. Following the two years I had spent doing interviews inside the White House of George W. Bush, the question I most often fielded from others was: *Is he as dumb as he seems?* And now I anticipated a similar question about Greene: *Is she as dumb AND crazy as she seems?*

In both cases, the answer was a qualified no. In one-on-one conversations, Bush often surprised me with his incisive ability to dismantle intellectually shaky assertions. What hamstrung him and ultimately his presidency was not stupidity but incuriosity. Bush knew only what he was comfortable knowing. He refused to confront his own biases, to challenge his own gut impulses, to solicit contrary viewpoints. This aversion, combined with his gift for mangling the English language, caused him to act in a manner that could seemingly only be explained as the behavior of a dunce.

Greene presented a somewhat different case. A week earlier, she had committed a malaprop that would have done Bush proud: she decried Speaker Nancy Pelosi's supposed "gazpacho police spying on members of Congress"— presumably meaning "Gestapo" rather than the famed Spanish soup. (Greene insisted to me that she found her rhetorical bumble to be "hilarious.") That slip aside, Greene tended to speak fluently, in paragraphs, and nearly always without the benefit of notes, in a way that Bush never did. She was not a dummy.

Still, Greene's unfamiliarity with experiences much different from her own could make her appear to be less intelligent than she was. She had never lived anywhere other than Georgia. Her situational awareness of the world was palpably limited to the talking points supplied by right-wing media. She was unfamiliar with hardship. By the time of our get-together, roughly $150,000 in fines for not wearing a COVID mask in the House chamber had been automatically deducted from Greene's congressional salary—or would have been deducted, except that Greene had forfeited her paycheck altogether while pursuing a lawsuit against Pelosi. This voluntary deprivation did not seem to have put the slightest dent in her lifestyle.

And now here she was, tooling through Rome in a chauffeur-driven SUV. Though she claimed that she subscribed to both the *Times* and the *Wall Street Journal,* her only awareness of the place where I worked seemed to be that in her view, the *Times* had promoted the "Russia collusion hoax" and therefore owed America an apology. ("Just kidding," she then said.)

Early in our conversation, I'd asked Greene if she had read *Hillbilly Elegy,* the bestselling memoir by J. D. Vance, who was now running for the U.S. Senate in Ohio. She replied that she had not. Unsaid was that Greene hadn't needed to: GOP candidate Vance had actively sought out her endorsement, and not for her literary acumen. Vance's primary opponent, Josh Mandel, also coveted Greene's seal of approval. Ultimately, she judged Vance to be the more ideologically sincere of the two. "Honored to have Marjorie's endorsement," the author proclaimed on Twitter on the morning of January 25, moments after Greene tendered her verdict.

Greene and her aides told me that they were being besieged by endorsement requests—a reality that was confirmed by media reports, and one that would have been unthinkable a year ago. The Georgia freshman intended to bestow them judiciously. She was looking for candidates who were decent people, who cared about America, and who understood the mechanics behind a winning campaign. Greene was not about to waste her energy on someone who was likely to lose—naming, by way of example, one Republican House candidate who had bombed the previous cycle, but not before raising millions in small-dollar donations, which struck her as grifting. Trump, Greene said, admired that she had managed to win without his endorsement, though of course she had aggressively sought it.

Greene also believed Trump appreciated her disinterest in being among the gadflies buzzing around Mar-a-Lago, angling for a selfie with the ex-president that would stand as proof that they had the boss's ear. She didn't need any of that. Trump's affection for her was there for everyone to see. Privately, he had floated the possibility of her being his running-mate in 2024. Greene didn't seem to be counting on this occurring. "We talked about it eyes wide open," she later told me. "The last person the RNC or the national party wants is me as his running mate. So I don't have any expectations for that. Because they don't have the guts to do it. Here's what would happen. If you put me in that role, I'm a very strong figure. The Republican Party would finally do what they claim they're about. And they don't want to do what they claim they're about. They never want to do it." Besides, from her perch here in Rome, Georgia, the House freshman commanded more influence than anyone else in her conference. Her imprimatur meant more than any other save for Trump's.

Marjorie Taylor Greene knew that she had the upper hand, and so did the GOP House's titular leader, Kevin McCarthy. The more unctuously he wooed her, the more turned off she became by his desperate quest for power. Sitting with her that day, it was evident to me that McCarthy did not have her vote to be Speaker. It also seemed to be the case that she didn't have an alternative candidate in mind (which, of course, was McCarthy's ace in the hole). Greene didn't put forth the name of anyone in the House Freedom Caucus. Though she took a back seat to no one when it came to performative reflex, I could tell that she saw some merit to the dim view that many held of the Freedom Caucus as a rump society of crimson-jowled preeners who never got much of anything done.

As she talked while picking at her salad and then her salmon, it became obvious to me that Marjorie Taylor Greene's dislike of her chosen political party had only deepened during her first full year in office. She used the term "Uni-party" to describe the Democrats and Republicans in tandem, seeing no meaningful distinction between Pelosi and that of the RINOs with whom she often feuded, like Dan Crenshaw of Houston, who to this day continued to insist that Joe Biden was legitimately elected.

When I asked Greene if that meant she was open to the idea of starting a third party, her answer was an emphatic no. That would be tantamount to handing every election over to the Democrats. Instead, her goal was to move the

GOP toward where Greene was—"to the right," she said, but then waved off her own words, because they implied that her views were outside the mainstream.

"There's a civil war taking place in the Republican Party," Greene said factually. "And I'm all in for it. I'll go toe-to-toe with Dan Crenshaw all day long."

YES, BUT WAS SHE CRAZY?

Without any hesitation, Greene talked about her days as a follower of the QAnon conspiracy theory. *Lots* of people she knew had been drawn to Q. Many of them were well educated and highly successful. All the same, that belief system hardly captured the sum total of who she had been in 2017 and 2018. And in any event, by the end of 2018, she had come to the conclusion that she had been misled by Q.

Greene's account of her days as a believer seemed far more credible and less defensive than the blame-it-on-CNN monologue she had offered a year earlier. QAnon was its own community, a tribe of digital warriors for whom each Q drop of a riddle prompted an endorphin rush of discovery. Exploring them was a dark thrill, but never a gratuitous one. Everyone along for the ride, they were incessantly reminded, was a patriot. Every Anon was enlisted in the battle to help President Trump save America.

It was the flipside of the QAnon proposition—that there existed a demon-culture of baby-eaters, most of them Democrats, several of whom were household names—that exposed the sad and deluded fabric of Greene and other believers. And this she had not let go. In Marjorie Taylor Greene's universe, RINOs like Dan Crenshaw might be cowards and phonies, but Democrats were evil. Perhaps today she might concede that they weren't (all) pedophiles. But their radical worldview conjured up a Hieronymus Bosch–like hellscape of open borders, anarchy, atheism, loss of liberty, and socialist indoctrination in which every child might as well be cast into the pyre.

Near the end of our conversation, I had asked Greene about how her many attempts to visit the DC Jail had finally paid off: on November 4, 2021, she, her Republican colleague Louie Gohmert, and five of her staffers were granted a tour. In violation of federal prison policy, one of her accompanying staffers had recorded the tour, from which they later produced a highly detailed twenty-eight-page report.

It was evident from Greene's report that she had found the conditions of the jail appalling. If the congresswoman ever wished to work with Democrats on an issue, criminal justice reform struck me as the lowest-hanging fruit imaginable. So I asked Greene: had she reached out to any of the opposition party following her visit to the jail?

"Well, I sent out the report to every member," she said. No one had replied to her. So that was that.

Because I had read the report, I had a pretty good idea why no Democrat apparently regarded it as a sincere gesture of concern about the conditions of the DC Jail. That was because of the attention that the report lavished on the forty or so inhabitants of "the Patriot Wing." After welcoming her and Gohmert with tears and chants of *"USA! USA! USA!"*—a reception far more effusive than what they had gotten in the cell blocks she had visited earlier—the detainees trotted out the gruesome details of their experience. Their food was horrible and sometimes contained pubic hairs. They did not have regular access to the internet. The unvaccinated among them—which were many—were not permitted to receive haircuts. They said that they were mocked and at times abused by their jailers.

Concluded Greene's report: "The congressional visit to the D.C. jail on November 4 unquestionably proved that there is a two-track justice system in the United States. This two-tiered system is not based on race, violence, or conviction of crime, but politics." Her basis for this conclusion was that she and Gohmert had also visited two wings reserved for the prison's soon-to-be released model inmates—who, in accordance with their youth and their exemplary conduct, were rewarded with access to televisions, iPads, and reading materials.

But the vast majority of the DC Jail's inmates—overwhelmingly Black and Latino—were warehoused in maximum-security cell blocks. Greene and Gohmert had visited one of these blocks as well. But because of the intense reek and unbearable noise, they moved on after ten minutes, in contrast to the sixty-five minutes they spent hearing the testimonials on the Patriot Wing.

It happened that Greene, Gohmert, and their entourage were accompanied by members of the DC City Council for the first hour of their visit. One of them, Christina Henderson, later discussed the tour with me. Of the congresswoman's report, Henderson said wryly, "Well, congratulations, Representative Greene, if this is the first experience you've had of the criminal justice system in the U.S. But if this is a space you'd like to work in, I'd like to see you prove your sincerity. Saying there's a two-tiered system of justice and not in any way acknowledging the role race plays, unless it's for the January 6 defendants . . ."

Henderson sighed as she contemplated Marjorie Taylor Greene's jailhouse experience. Then the councilwoman added wearily, "OK, girlfriend."

"WE'D LOVE TO GET TO KNOW HER MUCH BETTER, AND I THINK THIS IS GOING to be the beginning of something great," the young white-nationalist leader Nick Fuentes enthused as he welcomed the Georgia freshman to the stage at the Orlando World Center Marriott on Friday evening, February 25, 2022.

Marjorie Taylor Greene basked in the applause of the 1,500 or so youthful white male Groypers. Her designated mentor, Paul Gosar, had spoken to this group the year before (and was there again, albeit via video): the unapologetically racist right-wing America First PAC (AFPAC) gathering down the road from the more conventional, MAGA-centric annual CPAC convention. Already in town for CPAC, Greene had weighed AFPAC's standing offer before deciding to accept it about five hours before she took the stage.

"We knew there'd be blowback," one of her staffers told me later. "Some short-term pain." The reward, however, transcended a single speaking gig. Like Gosar in 2021, Greene and her aides viewed the twenty-three-year-old Fuentes as immature but also savvy. He possessed something Greene and Gosar both wanted: an energetic base of young right-wing Christians who craved a patriarch. Trump had been that in 2016. That election cycle, the mainstream media had been largely unaware of the wildly proliferating MAGA memes and trolling energy on Reddit, 4chan, and other subterranean outlets of the online community. Now here were the makings of a new movement, lacking only a proper leader. Greene's staffers found themselves nodding along to a tweet written by liberal MSNBC show host Chris Hayes: "Something struck me about Trump at CPAC, which is that he's somewhat a victim of his own political success. Because the entire GOP now sounds like Trump, Trump in turn now sounds like a generic Republican. So much of his success in 2016 was sounding *different* and standing out."

Much like the white male Capitol rioters detained in the DC Jail, Greene would later describe the audience she encountered in Orlando in the most maternalistic of terms: "a lost generation of young people who are desperate for love and leadership." Or, as she later put it to me: "I was like, 'Those are like the age of my kids!' Sure—why wouldn't I go talk to them?" But there was certainly another way to view them when, seconds before Greene took the stage, they chanted *"Pu-tin! Pu-tin! Pu-tin!"* in exaltation of the Russian autocrat whose troops had just invaded Ukraine.

By Greene's standards, the speech she gave that evening was standard fare. Her white male allies in the audience were "canceled Americans." Her foes on the other side of the aisle were "the Communist Party of the United States of America." And she, Marjorie Taylor Greene, was "a forgiven sinner, washed in the blood of our savior, Jesus Christ."

The following morning, a Saturday, Greene found herself swarmed by the media as she attempted to enter the VIP area behind the stage at CPAC, following a panel. The congresswoman and her staff huddled furtively backstage. In the twelve-hour period between Greene's speech at AFPAC and her appearance at CPAC, her team had belatedly familiarized themselves with Nick Fuentes and his boy-crush on Hitler. Though she had a plane to catch, they agreed that distancing herself from an avowed Nazi sympathizer while projecting empathy for his following was probably the smart way to go.

Greene and her staff returned to the waiting media. "I do not know Nick Fuentes," she insisted as her aides and her bodyguard hovered nearby. "I've never heard him speak. I've never watched a video. I do not know what his views are." Greene had accepted the invitation, she told the press, because she felt the need to address the "generation I'm extremely concerned about."

"It's a white-nationalist group," CBS reporter Robert Costa informed her.

"Excuse me—excuse me a minute," she said, jabbing a finger toward Costa. "I'll tell you exactly why I went." Greene reiterated that she wanted to have an America-first policy discussion with the Groypers—that this was about saving Americans from their weak president.

Then she flew to Atlanta. That evening, the staff of Georgia GOP U.S. Senate candidate and former football star Herschel Walker contacted Greene's staff. Walker was due to attend a Second Amendment rally the congresswoman was hosting in her district the following weekend. Greene's brief alliance with a white nationalist had now made that appearance undesirable for Walker, who seemed to believe that he could seize the Black vote from Democratic incumbent Raphael Warnock.

Greene's staff requested that they not leak Walker's new intentions until the two had a chance to talk. The following morning, Walker called Greene. The Senate candidate wanted to hear her side of what had transpired in Orlando. Walker listened, then assured her, "You didn't do anything wrong."

An hour after the call, the *Atlanta Journal-Constitution* received word that Herschel Walker would not be attending the pro-gun event hosted by Marjorie Taylor Greene. Steve Bannon subsequently was a no-show at a public event in Georgia in February that he was expected to attend with Greene. "He was upset over the AFPAC thing," she told me three months later. Though she had been a frequent guest on Bannon's popular *War Room: Pandemic* podcast, "We have not really talked" since her speech at the event held by Nick Fuentes, with whom Bannon had a running feud. Whatever Bannon's problems with Fuentes, it made little sense to Greene that he would no longer have her on his show: "If he cares about the things he says he cares about, then why wouldn't he?"

Of her momentary association with Fuentes and his racist conference, Marjorie Taylor Greene said, "It was like a flippant decision that lit the world on fire." Still, she now realized, her presence at the conference, as an elected federal officeholder, had conferred legitimacy on the event. "I did learn that," she acknowledged. "That was a lesson that I learned. I'm learning on the fly—under a microscope."

GIVEN THE VERY FACT OF GREENE'S DECISION TO SPEAK AT A WHITE-nationalist conference, whatever her motives for doing so might have been, an additional point she had made during her two-minute press conference at CPAC failed to receive any attention.

"Now in regards to Russia," she had said, bringing up the subject herself. "Putin is a murderer and he should have never invaded Ukraine. What he's doing is completely wrong. I stand with our NATO member allies. And I'm completely against this war."

The declarative statements contrasted markedly with her tangled messaging just three days earlier. On February 23, Greene dismissed "rumors of war" as the media's convenient "lie to use as a reason for our shattered economy and out-of-control inflation." Then, after Russian troops invaded Ukraine the very next day, Greene shamelessly observed, "It's no surprise to anyone that Putin invaded Ukraine. Biden gave him the green light by saying that the U.S. is not going to war with Russia"—which, she then appeared to suggest, was in fact a good thing, because "Americans don't want to be dragged into more never-ending foreign wars."

But now, with her condemnation of Putin and expressed solidarity with Ukraine, Marjorie Taylor Greene was, for a moment in time, squarely in the center of mainstream American sentiment. The valor displayed by the besieged Ukrainians and their president, Volodymyr Zelensky—who, less than three years earlier, had to beg for U.S. missiles from President Trump, while the latter demanded dirt on Biden in exchange for them—had all the makings of a flash point, a starburst of clarity in which all the ginned-up divisions in America now seemed embarrassingly trivial. Overnight, the world seemed to have changed. President Biden's speechwriters shredded his prepared State of the Union address. The emphasis of the speech would now be on Ukraine, and what its people were reminding the world about courage and the meaning of democracy.

The seventy-nine-year-old president took the rostrum in the House chamber shortly after nine in the evening Eastern time on the first day of March. The place felt oddly desultory: a few House Republicans had elected not to attend, three House Democrats had also stayed away after testing positive for COVID, and only a few members were permitted to bring guests. Biden's delivery was halting in places and he stepped on several of his applause lines. But the conservative trolls who had predicted on social media that Biden would collapse mid-speech out of sheer decrepitude were disappointed. There was only one embarrassment that evening, and it occurred near the end of his speech, as the president spoke mournfully of the American soldiers who after their deployments suffered from trauma and other ailments that would put some of them "in flag-draped coffins."

"You put them there!" yelled a woman from somewhere in the chamber. "Thirteen of them!"

A chorus of boos and disapproving grumbles silenced her, and Biden then continued to talk about his son Beau, a veteran who had died from cancer. The offending party turned out to be the newly selected communications director of the House Freedom Caucus, Lauren Boebert. But at the time, it was widely assumed that Marjorie Taylor Greene, sitting two chairs away from Boebert, was the culprit. Just a few minutes earlier, when Biden mentioned the need to secure America's southern border, Greene and Boebert had proceeded to clap and chant loudly, "Build that wall! Build that wall!"

The freeze-frame of the two conservative congresswomen hooting at the president during his State of the Union address like beer-swilling hockey fans elicited exactly the bifurcated reaction one had come to expect. Overtly, Republicans recoiled. Across the Beltway, the assumption was that the Georgia freshman was sure to face ridicule from her party. Already, Kevin McCarthy's office had assured the press that the House minority leader had scolded Greene for her association with Nick Fuentes, which McCarthy publicly termed "appalling." Along the same lines, the *Atlanta Journal-Constitution* observed that Herschel Walker's decision not to be seen with the Georgia freshman at the gun rally "is just the latest sign that Republicans in Georgia and across the nation are distancing themselves from Greene."

Behind these public-facing reproaches, however, Greene was having her way. McCarthy had extracted nothing in the way of remorse from her. She already had his number. The titular leader had invited her to high-level conferences in his office, making a show of sitting next to her and soliciting her opinions. In doing so, McCarthy had showed his weak hand. Having already calculated that his party could not win without Trump, McCarthy correctly viewed Marjorie Taylor Greene as the ex-president's proxy, one whose platform dwarfed that of the House minority leader.

Just after Biden's address on the evening of March 1, a designated Republican, Iowa governor Kim Reynolds, delivered the GOP's customary response.

But then after Reynolds had finished, Marjorie Taylor Greene stepped behind a podium in a conference room rented by Women for America First, a pro-Trump group. Addressing the camera furnished by Right Side Broadcasting Network, she offered up her own rebuttal.

During her twenty-eight-minute speech, Greene said nothing about standing behind Ukraine or about Putin's evil act of aggression, except to cite it as a ghoulish diversion from the grim realities facing ordinary Americans. She made no common cause with the Democrats, or even with her own party. Instead, she spoke of authoritarianism right here at home, in the form of pandemic shutdowns and mask mandates. She linked creeping globalism with a rise in not only joblessness but "sexual perversion" and "moral decay." In both tone and substance, her speech bore little difference from the QAnon rants she had written five years earlier.

Biden's speech, Greene declared, could be summarized as "China First, America Last." She referred to the president and vice president of the United States as "traitors within" who were "flying illegal aliens in the dark of night across America, maybe to a suburb near you, and you're paying for it." She accused Biden of being "totally compromised, because every world leader has the contents of Hunter Biden's laptop." She said that climate change was a hoax and that Biden's plan to combat it would throw every American into poverty and make them all "slaves to China."

Speaking of the January 6 defendants she had visited in the DC Jail, Greene spoke of "the hopelessness in their eyes" and then asked, "In America, aren't we considered innocent until proven guilty in a court of law? Not if you're a Trump supporter."

And, of course, she reminded Americans that "stolen elections have consequences. It's imperative that every single American trust our elections, and no matter what Nancy Pelosi, Liz Cheney, and the propagandists in the fake news media try to make you believe, no one trusts the results of the 2020 election."

Kevin McCarthy said nothing to Marjorie Taylor Greene about her rogue and radically off-message speech. What could he say? That the Republican Party could not control her was, in a sense, the speech's underlying message. As she had told me in Rome, the GOP's civil war was here, and she was all in for it.

The U.S. Capitol, fenced in

Chapter Thirty-Two

THE UNWINDING

On a drizzly Wednesday morning in early March, I paid a visit to see Paul Gosar's chief of staff, Tom Van Flein.

A few weeks earlier, I had checked into a hotel near Phoenix's airport with the expectation of interviewing Gosar there the following morning. His communications director had asked for my questions in advance. This had become standard procedure for GOP members, and it said more about them than about us in the mainstream media. Gosar had served in office for over a decade. During that period, he had offered his thoughts for the record countless times, but almost always to sympathetic ears on the right: Daily Caller, Breitbart, Gateway Pundit, Daily Wire, Newsmax, *National Pulse*, Real America's Voice, Right Side Broadcasting. On the extremely rare occasion when Gosar subjected himself to an interviewer who might evince skepticism or point out a contradiction, things did not go well.

Still, after summarizing the topics I wanted to discuss, Gosar's scheduler had confirmed a time and place for our interview, at the Phoenix hotel near the airport. Fully two weeks after that, I was getting ready to go to bed the evening before my flight to Phoenix when I noticed an email from the press aide in my inbox. Noting that the January 6 committee now regarded Gosar as "a person of interest for their sham investigation," the aide said that the congressman would not be available for an interview.

The non sequitur was jarring, particularly at that late hour. I responded with the offer to refrain from asking Gosar anything January 6–related and with the reminder that, as he could see from what I had sent over earlier, we had plenty of other things to talk about.

The following morning, while checking into the hotel where Gosar and I were scheduled to meet the next day, the press aide replied to my offer. "We will need to take a pass" was his answer in full.

"There are a lot of dipshits in your profession," Tom Van Flein informed me as we sat in his office on March 9. People, he went on to say, who might look dazzling on TV but were vapid and dishonest at their core. Van Flein invoked the 1987 movie *Broadcast News*. In this cultural reference, my apparent analog was the old-school and decidedly anti-telegenic Albert Brooks character, soon to be made extinct by a generation of handsome if empty-suited William Hurts.

That day happened to be one of the few on Capitol Hill when members on both sides of the aisle largely put aside their own customary dyspepsia in the service of a greater cause. As I sat in Van Flein's office, a bill was before the House that would ban imports of Russian oil, following Putin's invasion of Ukraine. Nothing about the legislative initiative suggested a desire to create a wedge issue that would cause political discomfort. Despite Trump's continuing tendency to compliment the Russian leader while expressing no admiration for the heroism of Ukraine's president Volodymyr Zelensky, Republicans as a group did not wish to side with a murderous dictator. Only Madison Cawthorn saw the war as a chance to make a play for white-nationalist Putinistas in the GOP base, telling one North Carolina crowd, "Remember that Zelensky is a thug. Remember that the Ukrainian government is incredibly corrupt and is incredibly evil and has been pushing woke ideologies."

Van Flein interrupted our conversation to say that the Russian oil bill was nearing a vote and Gosar's staff needed to huddle about it. From what I could pick up in their conference call, Gosar preferred to be a "yes" on the ban. American sentiment was squarely behind the Ukrainians. Both the Democratic and Republican leaders supported the bill. During the floor debate, the two House managers of the legislation, Democrat Jim McGovern and Republican Tom Cole, referred to each other with collegial sentiments while lobbing occasional criticisms. Biden had not done enough to keep gasoline prices down. Republicans under Trump had been too soft on Putin. And so on.

The problem for Gosar, when it came to the pending vote, was that he was boxed in. Not by his staff, or by the needs of his district, or by the Democrats, or by the dipshits in my profession. Rather, a few of the more performative members on the right—the TV-friendly William Hurt characters, one could say—had seized upon an appealing talking point. That argument was that President Biden, in his determination to appease Green New Deal socialists by throttling oil and gas production at home, was now desperately seeking potential energy supplies in Iran and Venezuela, among other countries. As Matt Gaetz would put it in an op-ed for the *National Pulse* that morning, "Biden hates American energy so much he would open energy production in Venezuela and Iran before Colorado and North Dakota. America Last, for sure."

Any opportunity to cast Biden and his fellow Democrats as haters of America was simply too good to pass up. Gosar ultimately adopted Gaetz's irresistible line of reasoning. "This bill is a case in point on how Americans are the last priority and the Democrats will bend over to help anyone but the voters here" read the statement he and his staff put together. Gosar joined Gaetz, Cawthorn, Marjorie Taylor Greene, Lauren Boebert, Louie Gohmert, and nine other stalwarts of the right—along with two strange bedfellows from the left, Cori Bush and Ilhan Omar—in voting against the Russia oil ban, which an overwhelming 414-member majority supported.

Yet again, Paul Gosar had found himself on the margins of U.S. policymaking—just as he had been one week earlier, on the losing side of a 426–3 vote stating America's support for Ukraine. (That resolution, Gosar had insisted in a statement, "threatens to get the United States into another dangerous, expensive, and lengthy war and there is no reason to be there.")

I considered Gosar's combative posture as his chief of staff proceeded to describe to me the Arizona congressman's ongoing lofty ambitions: bringing more water to his state through a desalination plant; designating the production of rare-earth minerals a national security priority; and converting the entire U.S. power grid to one that would be driven by a combination of nuclear, solar, wind, and hydropower.

Such legislative feats would require sweeping and sturdy alliances with other lawmakers. Unlike his younger Republican colleagues in the House, Paul Gosar seemed determined to have something more to show for all his years in office than a file stuffed with fawning articles in Breitbart. Unlike them, Gosar had worked with Democrats in the past. But when I asked Tom Van Flein whose support his boss was lining up for these grand initiatives, the answer was: a few state representatives. A few fellow conservatives in the Western Caucus. A pro-nuclear environmentalist whose climate skepticism had been savaged by scientists.

When I had seen Van Flein a few months earlier, I had mentioned to him that Democrats were largely unwilling to work with someone like Gosar who continued to suggest that Biden was not legitimately elected. Back then, the chief of staff's reply was that Gosar was waiting for the results of the "Cyber Ninjas election audit" in Arizona. If the effort validated Biden's victory there, then Gosar would acknowledge as much.

It did—and he didn't. Instead, the conclusion by the Republican-controlled state senate—that the Cyber Ninjas' final hand count "matches Maricopa County's official machine count"—was greeted by Gosar with abject silence. Like others in the MAGA universe, Van Flein insisted to me that the audit contained a great deal of damning evidence about the 2020 election. Unfortunately, he sighed, "the report appeared to be written by an engineer. It was so technical and obtuse."

But, Gosar's chief of staff added, it didn't matter. There wasn't any point looking backward. "Where we are today," he said, "is seeking to avert any avenues for fraud in 2022 and beyond."

Was that really where Paul Gosar was today? It wasn't where he was a few weeks earlier, when I heard him declare at the Trump rally in Arizona: *Was there fraud? Yes! Absolutely! Was there enough to overturn the election? Absolutely! And it has to continue—somebody has to pay the price! If you're gonna do the crime, you gotta pay the time!*

I left Tom Van Flein's office thinking about the anime that had gotten his boss censured and stripped of committee assignments a few months earlier. "We still scoff and laugh about it," he had told me. "It was so over-the-top to censure him for something so innocuous—and to push this lie in the media: 'Gosar Threatens to Kill AOC!'"

What stuck with me was that Gosar had given his seal of approval to a representation of himself as an anime character. Ostensibly, he had done so as a show of good humor and as a means of appealing to a younger audience. Still, it was hard to shake the notion that Paul Gosar now viewed the world in similarly hyper-animated terms. He was the ultimate warrior in the fight to save America from the ultimate evildoers on the left. At the same time, he was Super Legislator, cutting monumental deals with the otherworldly acumen of that other superhero, Donald J. Trump. Though Gosar's signature tag still ended with "D.D.S.," I found it all but impossible to imagine him returning to his prior life, that of a mild-mannered Clark Kent in white scrubs, blandly engaged in a forever war with the questionable dental hygiene of strangers.

Today, the dental scrubs might as well be puddled on a closet floor back in Flagstaff. The cartoon had become a way of life. In that sense, the cartoon was reality.

OF COURSE, THE CARTOON WASN'T LIFE. EVEN WITH A REPUBLICAN MAJORITY, and even with the "better committees" Kevin McCarthy had promised him, Paul Gosar with his outlier's portfolio was unlikely to bring any of his legacy projects to fruition. Even without his unspecified neurological condition encroaching on the boundaries of his mental acuity, time worked against him.

The cartoon also wasn't sustainable for a few other fellow Arizona conservatives who, along with Gosar, had immersed themselves in the quasi-apocalyptic "Stop the Steal" hallucination. One of them, Jacob Chansley—the so-called "Q Shaman" who famously paraded through the Capitol on January 6 wearing horns and carrying a spear—was now serving forty-one months in a federal prison for obstructing a proceeding of Congress. A former law student named Staci Burk who helped lead the charge that ballots in Arizona had been stolen, forged, invalidated, or otherwise destroyed thereafter watched as her life crumbled, and the truth with it. In texts and phone conversations, Burk now told me that people with sleazy motives had "gaslighted" her. She remained afraid for her welfare and suspicious of everyone. After being fed shadowy tales of voting ballots' being secretly harvested by Trump's Pentagon on behalf of Biden—conspiracies involving South Korea, the United Arab Emirates, and individuals at the highest levels of the U.S. government—Staci Burk had lost all sense of discernment. Life, for her, meant doubting everything.

Shortly before I went to visit Gosar's chief of staff, I called another Arizonan, Ryan Hartwig. It was Hartwig, the self-proclaimed "citizen-journalist" and Trump supporter, who had joined Tom Van Flein four days after the election at a Phoenix airstrip to eyeball the mysterious Korean Air chartered jet ostensibly crammed with illegal ballots.

I wanted to get a few more details about the incident from Hartwig—who, after writing a book about his time at Facebook and then trying his hand at journalism, now ran something called the Hartwig Foundation for Free Speech, which seemed to serve as an advocacy group for individuals like Hartwig himself who had been banned from Twitter for spreading misinformation. Most of all, I wanted to know whether he still believed there was anything to the conspiracy theory, because I had just finished discussing the matter with Staci Burk, who had been prominent in its promotion.

Well, Hartwig acknowledged, "I honestly think Staci's sources were more legitimate than the one tip I got." He was referring to the rumor he had heard—that a flight attendant had seen the illegal ballots on the airplane—versus the supposed whistleblower with whom Burk had been in contact: a Federal Express employee who purported to see ballots being transported from a Seattle airstrip as well.

"I've spoken to Staci," I told Hartwig. The FedEx employee now disavowed her earlier claim. She had been spun up by rumor-mongering, just as Burk had.

"Someone may have gotten to that source," Hartwig speculated.

He was still intrigued by the Korean Air angle (though the airline had released a statement denying that any of their aircraft had been used to ferry election ballots, legal or otherwise). "Geopolitically speaking," he said, "South Korea's new president isn't as much of a U.S. ally as they've been in the past fifty years. So, is China using South Korea as a proxy?"

Then again, Hartwig reasoned, the fact that no fishy ballots were discovered could itself be significant. "I mean, if you're the opposition, and let's say there *was* a coordinated attempt at election fraud—which I still believe—then this whole thing could've been a coordinated psy-op."

"So, Ryan," I said, "who would have been involved in this conspiracy?" In his scenario, Hartwig was implicating two foreign countries. Also Biden and his team. Also Georgia's Republican secretary of state, Brad Raffensperger, as well as Arizona's Republican-dominated Maricopa County Board of Supervisors. And, presumably, a clandestine infrastructure of county clerks and poll workers.

"Yeah, that's a good question," he admitted. He did not have an answer, or even a theory, even as he spent the last few minutes of our conversation thinking out loud. He had only a core belief.

A few hours later, Ryan Hartwig emailed me a prepared statement summarizing his views of the 2020 election and the Korean Air episode. "The movement of ballots could very easily have been facilitated using the same methods used to transport drugs," he wrote. Fraud occurred all the time—Hartwig had seen this firsthand when he worked as a content moderator for Facebook. Furthermore, he said, "when stories do go public, it becomes easier for sources to be coerced or pressured into recanting or modifying their story. This may have been the case for some of the sources that Staci Burk contacted, and for other potential witnesses."

Said Ryan Hartwig flatly, "The 2020 election was stolen." Again, he failed to answer the question of who the players were in this vast and nefarious election-stealing conspiracy. Instead, what seemed to eat at him most was the reaction he had received by local police officers at the Phoenix airstrip on the night of November 7, 2020, when Hartwig told them that there might be illegal election ballots on the Korean chartered jet.

"Law enforcement," he wrote, "should be deeply concerned about any allegations of election fraud, and should be investigating them thoroughly, instead of laughing at an accusation of a crime."

Ryan Hartwig was right, I concluded. The accusation that a mysterious cabal had conspired to steal the 2020 presidential election was many things. Funny was not one of them.

Representative Peter Meijer

Chapter Thirty-Three

THE WAY OF THE IMPEACHERS

The plan proposed to save Liz Cheney from losing her congressional seat was certainly a novel one.

"This can be accomplished with a two-step process" went the argument in the February 4, 2022, op-ed in the *Washington Post*. "First, Cheney runs for reelection, not in the primary to become the official Republican nominee but as a principled independent in the general election who retains her personal Republican allegiance. Second, Wyoming Democrats do not support a candidate to oppose her."

It was a challenge to both Cheney and the Democratic Party. She could prevail, so went the argument, by formally turning away from the party that had already turned away from her, and by the opposition party that had showered her with so much praise of late finally putting its money where its mouth was.

What made the column particularly unusual, however, was its author: Barney Frank, the retired liberal congressman from Massachusetts and the first openly gay member of the House. Frank, who retired from office in 2013, had never met Liz Cheney and did not contact anyone in her orbit before publishing the piece. Throughout his thirty-two years in the House, he was a frequent antagonist of Cheney's father, who served with Frank in Congress before becoming George H. W. Bush's secretary of defense, and later the younger Bush's vice president. The two men butted heads on nearly every issue of significance, from both Iraq wars to financial reform. In his memoir, Frank meticulously described how Dick Cheney had lied in *his* memoir about Frank's voting record.

For all their disagreements, however, both men belonged to a political era in which the search for common ground was considered part of a legislator's job description rather than evidence of apostasy. As secretary of defense, Cheney had testified to Frank in a House Budget Committee hearing that the notion of gay military members' being a security risk was "an old chestnut." Barney Frank would recall that moment as a critical step toward repealing the Don't Ask, Don't Tell military service policy toward gay enlistees.

Frank also remembered what happened in the runup to the 2010 midterm election, when some of his Democratic colleagues thought they had caught a lucky break by facing a rabble of Tea Party candidates. But, as Frank would recall, "The reductio ad absurdum argument didn't work then, because the voters embraced the absurd. And that was my worry about Liz Cheney's primary. The strategy of Democrats just standing back and letting the vicious elements of Trumpism take over the Republican Party was a risky strategy and was likely to empower extremists."

A couple of days after the *Washington Post* published his column, Barney Frank received a call from his old friend Steny Hoyer. "I think this is a good idea," the House Democratic majority leader said of Frank's recommendation that their party not field an opponent against Cheney. Hoyer then asked his staff to see what additional role the Democrats could play in assisting Cheney's efforts.

At the end of March, three of Hoyer's senior staffers submitted a memo to the majority leader. Knowing how eager their boss was for encouraging news, what his subordinates had to offer was "a small possibility that Democratic and unaffiliated voters can affect the outcome" of Cheney's race. Though there were "currently no Democrats filed to run" against Cheney, that could easily change if some random aspirant—including "someone put up to it by Rs"—ponied up the $750 fee before the May 27 deadline.

Even if the Democrats did succeed in clearing the field on their end, the memo writers struggled to imagine a pro-Cheney insurgency in the heart of Trump country. After all, a mere 74,000 of the 278,503 Wyomingites who had voted in the historically high-turnout November 2020 election had done so for Biden. "Getting half of those General Election voters to show up to vote for Cheney in a primary would be very tough," the memo said.

Overall, Hoyer's staffers concluded, Frank's proposed strategy amounted to "a huge uphill climb."

OF COURSE, THE VIEW OF THE UPHILL CLIMB WAS NOT SIMPLY AN APPRAISAL of the climber but also of the hill itself.

Throughout the early months of 2022, wishful thinkers residing in the Beltway seized upon every available data point suggesting that the hill—Trump's grip on the Republican Party—was fast eroding. Attendance at the ex-president's rallies appeared to have tapered off. A few of his high-profile endorsements had already fizzled out. The new Virginia governor, Glenn Youngkin, had triumphed while assiduously maintaining a distance from Trump. As for the GOP office-seekers who continued to pose as heirs to the MAGA throne, their mimicry was hardly proof of Trumpism's resiliency. After all, these candidates tended to be acting on the paid advice of former Trump aides who were all too aware that the good times would end by 2024, when the big man would decide not to run and thereby take the play away from all his grifting minions. Or so went the wishful thinking.

On March 14, 2022, over two hundred wealthy Republicans gathered at a fundraiser for Liz Cheney in McLean, Virginia. The host, GOP political adviser Bobbie Kilberg—who had served with Dick Cheney in the Nixon White House and had babysat his three-year-old daughter Liz—was obliged to relocate the event from her house in McLean to the nearby Hilton to accommodate the swelling RSVP list.

Many of the attendees at the Hilton were avowed foes of Trump, such as the event's special guest, Senator Mitt Romney, as well as Joe McCain, brother of the late Arizona senator John McCain. In his brief speech, Romney told the other donors that he kept a chart on his office wall that traced the history of democracy across human civilization. What the timeline revealed, said the Utah senator, was how fleeting democratic governments tended to be. Defending them against authoritarianism was the duty of every citizen, as exemplified by Liz Cheney.

But most of the attendees were simply keepers of the conservative faith who had been around long enough to know what a Republican was and wasn't. One of them, Jay Timmons, the president and CEO of the National Association of Manufacturers, had once praised Trump as "a true champion for our industry." By the late afternoon of January 6, 2021, Timmons was calling for the invocation of the Twenty-Fifth Amendment to remove President Trump from office. At the Cheney fundraiser, Timmons urged his fellow titans in the private sector to assert their clout. "It's time for businesses to step up," he said.

Implicit in Timmons's remark was the acknowledgment that their timidity had come at a cost. Six weeks earlier, the Republican National Committee had voted to censure both Cheney and her fellow January 6 committee member Adam Kinzinger. According to the RNC chairwoman, Ronna McDaniel—who happened to be Mitt Romney's niece but who, out of apparent deference to her party leader, no longer went by his surname—Cheney and Kinzinger had "crossed a line. They chose to join Nancy Pelosi in a Democrat-led persecution of ordinary political citizens who engaged in legitimate political discourse that had nothing to do with violence at the Capitol."

McDaniel later explained to a Republican associate that she had endeavored to make the best of a dismal situation. A longtime Trump sidekick, David Bossie, had designs on taking over the RNC, she said. Bossie had been pushing a resolution that would expel Cheney and Kinzinger from the GOP altogether. Ronna McDaniel had come up with the compromise gesture of a censure "to keep everything from going off the rails," she told the associate—though to the latter, it sounded more like *to keep Trump from being angry with me.*

Among those who were astonished by the committee's vote was Marc Racicot, the former governor of Montana, who had served as the RNC's chair two decades earlier. Racicot promptly sent a letter to McDaniel, urging the committee to withdraw its decision to censure Cheney and Kinzinger. A week went by without a reply. Racicot thereupon sent his letter to the *Billings Gazette* to be published in full.

"It's been overwhelmingly positive, from all over the country," Racicot told me when I asked about the response to his open letter. "My theory is that there's this Great Middle of America. I'm absolutely convinced of it."

The former RNC chairman went on to say that, somewhat against his better judgment, he had begun speaking before Republican groups in Montana. His musings about the rise of Trump, the spread of misinformation, the incentivizing of conflict by the internet, and the quiet yearning for unity were met with surprising warmth. "There hasn't been a Republican yet, to this day, who has pushed back on what I've had to say," he told me.

It was evident to me that, fully two decades removed from elective office though he was, the politician's determined optimism had not left Marc Racicot. In a state that Trump had carried by 16 percentage points in 2020, there did in fact remain a few old-time Republicans who were happy to invite a popular former governor to reflect on a less divisive yesteryear. Still, the sample size buttressing Racicot's Great Middle of America theory fell even further below the threshold of scientific validation than did Trump's super-sized rallies.

Instead, it seemed more akin to the line of reasoning Bobbie Kilberg had shared with me after the Cheney fundraiser, which had raised $532,000 for her friend's Wyoming campaign. In maintaining to me that Trump's influence was on the wane, Kilberg cited the annual Gridiron Dinner in April, the very quintessence of Beltway insiderism. At the off-the-record-but-always-leaked dinner, New Hampshire's Republican governor, Chris Sununu, skewered the ex-president for several minutes, calling him "fucking crazy."

"Do you really think Chris Sununu would say what he said if Trump still had so much influence?" Kilberg asked me.

FOR THOSE TEN HOUSE REPUBLICANS WHO HAD VOTED TO IMPEACH TRUMP, Kilberg's question was not rhetorical.

The first of them to go was Anthony Gonzalez, announcing his decision not to seek reelection eight months after casting his fateful vote against the ex-president. The Ohio congressman and former professional football player was only thirty-six, not even midway into his second two-year term. But Gonzalez had a well-financed primary opponent, former Trump aide Max Miller. More to the point, according to the statement he released on September 16, 2021, "the toxic dynamics inside our own party" had become a forbidding proposition for the young congressman. Strangers had called his house, threatening to pay a visit. His wife and children had to be escorted by security through airports. This was not what Anthony Gonzalez had signed up for.

"Good riddance to Anthony, he can now get a job at ratings-dead CNN or MSDNC!" crowed Trump in a statement following Gonzalez's announcement. Six weeks later, the man Trump labeled "Cryin' Adam Kinzinger" (for his emotional reaction to the January 6 committee testimony of the police officers who defended the Capitol) also announced his retirement. The Democrats who controlled the Illinois state legislature had evaporated Kinzinger's district. The same fate also seemed likely in New York for Republican John Katko, who decided in January not to stick around and wait for the new maps. Katko insisted that the MAGA target on his back did not factor into his decision, which hardly prevented Trump from boasting, "Another one bites the dust!"

Finally, in early April, the veteran Michigan lawmaker Fred Upton consulted his unfavorably redrawn district and the prevailing MAGA headwinds and announced on the House floor that he, too, would be retiring. "As a former Boy Scout," said Upton, who at sixty-nine still looked the part, "I believe in leaving the campground better than when you found it." He spoke of bipartisan achievements, of his career-long "push for civility," of lasting friendships on both sides of the aisle.

A few minutes later, Marjorie Taylor Greene stepped up to the dais Fred Upton had just vacated and introduced legislation that would fund an investigation into all the unfortunate thousands of people she believed may have been killed by the COVID vaccine.

"FOUR DOWN AND SIX TO GO," THE BLOODLUSTY EX-PRESIDENT DECLARED after Upton's retirement speech. "Others losing badly, who's next?"

Kevin McCarthy had succeeded in dissuading Trump from supporting a challenger to David Valadao, the impeacher whose California district neighbored McCarthy's, and who the minority leader believed was the only Republican capable of holding down that swing district. Otherwise, McCarthy sat by while Trump went after five members of the House Republican Conference: Liz Cheney, Jaime Herrera Beutler, Tom Rice, Dan Newhouse, and Peter Meijer.

In particular, Trump's decision to endorse a challenger to the freshman Meijer stood as telling proof that vengeance meant more to him than the greater good of the Republican Party. Meijer had carried his Michigan district by six points in 2020. Thanks to redistricting, however, his seat was now rated a toss-up. It seemed highly unlikely that Trump's preferred candidate—John Gibbs, a former aide to Trump's secretary of Housing and Urban Development, Ben Carson—could prevail in a general election. Gibbs's campaign website included the schoolyard refrain *Let's go, Brandon!* His past tweets suggested that Democrats were devil worshippers. Gibbs was, in short, an ideal fit for a district like Marjorie Taylor Greene's and a disaster anywhere else.

Those who made this point to Trump found it falling on deaf ears. "He would rather have a Democrat in the seat," Peter Meijer acknowledged, "than a Republican like me. Someone who doesn't pledge their fealty."

Meanwhile, in an apparent effort to win over conservative primary voters, Meijer had begun to affect a kind of caustic demeanor that seemed an awkward fit with his Problem Solvers Caucus portfolio. On social media, the freshman snarkily applauded President Biden for being punctual to his State of the Union Address. He labeled the administration's COVID policy "beyond absurd" and the president's handling of the Ukraine crisis an "absolute clown show."

That temperamental spasm lasted only a few weeks, however. Late on the evening of April 24, Peter Meijer sent out a series of tweets that resembled a Dear Colleague letter: "If you think you can harness an angry crowd with a clever message + willingness to betray principles (assuming you hold any), you might be successful. But mobs are fickle; it won't be long until your moment passes and you wind up a has-been like the rest. Better to stay true to who you are. Have a north star; point your political compass in that direction.

"If you lose," the thirty-four-year-old congressman concluded, "you lose with honor intact. Fleeting fame is never worth being able to look yourself in the mirror. You won't gain the world, but your soul will be yours."

———————

ON THE MORNING OF APRIL 27, 2022, THE HOUSE REPUBLICANS CONFERRED to hear their leader, Kevin McCarthy, explain himself after *New York Times* reporters Jonathan Martin and Alexander Burns released audio tapes of conversations involving McCarthy that took place just after January 6, 2021. On the tapes, McCarthy could be heard telling colleagues that Trump was likely to be impeached and that he intended to recommend to the president that he resign. In the audio snippet, the minority leader also fretted over incendiary tweets being sent by Matt Gaetz, Lauren Boebert, and others, saying, "Can't they take away their Twitter accounts too?"

To his conference, McCarthy assured them that he had just been speculating and gaming out scenarios. He said that the *Times* was doing all it could to make trouble for the Republicans and distract from Joe Biden's disastrous presidency. After he was finished, the House Republicans in the conference room stood and applauded.

Liz Cheney was not there to witness McCarthy's breezy prevarications. Hearing about the conference later that day, she found herself laughing. It was classic Kevin: orchestrating a standing ovation that would find its way into the press, followed by another leak saying that he had raised $1.8 million in small donations. Despite the performance, Cheney doubted that McCarthy would be the next Speaker. Two of the loudest voices on the right, Steve Bannon and Tucker Carlson, ripped the minority leader to shreds on their shows.

By this point, the mutual disdain between Cheney and McCarthy was there for all to see. On *60 Minutes,* the Wyoming congresswoman said of the minority leader's enabling of Trump, "I don't know how you explain that to your children." That remark had infuriated McCarthy. He declared his support for Cheney's opponent Harriet Hageman, explaining to CNN reporter Melanie Zanona, "This is a very special case." McCarthy also began calling Cheney a "Pelosi Republican," which was true only in the sense that Cheney had spoken more frequently to the Democratic leader in the past year than she had to McCarthy.

A few hours after that Wednesday conference, Liz Cheney sat alone in a hideaway office in the basement of the Capitol, immersed in committee work and preparing to make a few donor calls while awaiting a dozen roll-call votes that were scheduled to take place on the House floor later in the afternoon. Two plainclothes Capitol police officers sat in an adjacent room. The security detail was stationed there because of continued threats on Cheney's life. The additional office space came after she joined the January 6 committee. Both were given to her courtesy of Speaker Pelosi.

Cheney marveled at her current predicament. As a child surrounded by Republicans, she had strained to imagine what it would be like to attend a Democratic convention. *It's like a different planet,* she would think.

But what planet was she on now? Referring to the audio tapes released by the *Times* reporters, Cheney said, "Listening to the tapes was a reminder that there was a moment when the Republican Party hadn't lost its mind. You listen to the leaders on the call reacting to a situation and you're like, 'Those people are adults. They're rational.'"

Cheney believed that it would take more than one cycle for the GOP to regain its sense of reason. If Trump was to become the nominee in 2024, she felt certain that the party would suffer a fracture that could not be mended. And if the GOP continued to embrace the lie that Trump's victory had been stolen from him, then in her view the party was beyond salvation.

Until then, Liz Cheney maintained a posture of optimism about her own electoral chances. She was outraising Hageman ten to one. Wyoming voters would not take kindly to any outsider—even one named Donald Trump—telling them who to vote for. The MAGA loudmouths in the state party who had formally renounced her were not representative of the average Wyoming Republican.

Stiff-upper-lipped though she was, the exiled congresswoman conducted what could well be her final year in office with monomaniacal intentionality. The January 6 committee was now her legacy project. The vice chairwoman spent much of her business hours interviewing witnesses, poring over the charging documents issued by the Department of Justice, and discussing potential subpoenas with her fellow committee members. She received regular updates from the committee's various investigative teams: the green team, looking into money trails; the red team, focusing on the January 6 rally planners; the gold team, investigating Trump's inner circle; the blue team, probing the police and national guard response to the riot; and the purple team, related to the violent groups at the Capitol that day.

Along with January 6 committee chairman Bennie Thompson and the DOJ, Cheney now found herself overseeing what, she soon realized, was the largest criminal investigation in U.S. history—one that was inextricably linked to her political party. Its key actors, beginning with President Trump, had conducted a highly sophisticated, multistep plan to overturn the 2020 election. All of them were Republicans. So, for the most part, were the thousands of individuals who had stormed the Capitol, addled by the lies fed to them by the GOP's loudest messengers. By their own testimony, they had flocked to Washington at the behest of the Republican leader. Some were explicit in their commitment to use violence to overturn the election results on January 6. One of them, a thirty-four-year-old Alabama resident and Oath Keeper named Joshua James, had acknowledged his group's intention to "use any means necessary, up to and including the use of force, to stop the lawful transfer of presidential power."

It chagrined the vice chairwoman to see how numb the nation had quickly become to the insurrection perpetrated by James and other rioters. But this reality, like the sad shape of her party and her own precarious standing in it, were matters largely out of her control. As she said that afternoon in her hideaway while awaiting House votes, "Since January sixth, there have been moments where I've had to make decisions. And the only thing that you can be guided by, because we're in this circus hall-of-mirrors moment, is just to do the next right thing."

That next right thing for Liz Cheney was to carry on with the sprawling investigation, racing the clock to unearth the truth about January 6 before her party shuttered the committee after likely regaining power in November. This was her duty, to sit alone at a wooden table in an office that had been given to her by a Democrat, reading criminal filings inside a thick and slightly weathered leather binder that had been given to her by a Republican who once used the same binder as Wyoming's elected representative in the House four decades earlier, back in the day when a Cheney could serve both the party and the country at the very same time.

Mob on the west side of the Capitol

Chapter Thirty-Four

ONE DAY IN GEORGIA

I n the old railroad depot town of Rockmart, Georgia, an oversized white van and a black SUV pulled up to Linda's Place just before seven in the morning. The van disgorged ten members of the press: local and national, print and television and digital. They slouched by the doorstep of the diner, insufficiently caffeinated, their cameras trained on the passenger door of the SUV.

Marjorie Taylor Greene stepped out and awarded Rockmart a broad smile. Among the first to greet her inside were two senior citizens wearing matching LET'S GO, BRANDON! T-shirts. One of them carried Trump's coffee-table book, *Our Journey Together,* for the congresswoman to autograph. Most of the diner's seventy or so customers either held Greene campaign posters or wore shirts bearing her name, or both. The locals appraised the camera- and notepad-toting strangers with curious disfavor, as one might a crew of inmates bagging up litter along a highway.

It was May 2, 2022, the first day of early voting before the Georgia primary three weeks hence. Greene's preceding ten days had been fittingly episodic. She began it on a witness stand in an Atlanta courthouse, as a defendant in a lawsuit brought by a liberal group claiming that the congresswoman had spurred on the insurrection at the Capitol and should therefore be disqualified from office. Publicly, Greene's response was one of indignation. She mocked the group on social media as "Communists." As a hostile witness, she treated the plaintiff's attorney to a defiant litany of "I don't recall" and "I don't know." Meanwhile, Greene's online donation requests affected a more alarmist tone: "The Deep State is trying to kick me off the ballot . . . I'm not going to lie: the D.C. Cabal and their minions have got me over a barrel . . . It's not looking good." (The lawsuit would soon be dismissed.)

Three days later, Greene was in Eagle Pass, Texas. Standing in front of Kevin McCarthy—who was only too glad to retreat from Washington following the disclosure of tapes of his denouncing President Trump's conduct on January 6—Greene warned of "so much human suffering if Title 42 is repealed." There was no irony in her voice as the ardent foe of COVID restrictions was now demanding that President Biden extend Title 42, a public health emergency order intended to halt the spread of the pandemic, as a pretext for expelling migrants who might otherwise be seeking asylum. "Imagine what they could do to your kids," Greene said.

That was Monday. Late that evening and into the following morning, Greene turned her attention to Elon Musk's imminent acquisition of Twitter. "Bring back the canceled nation," she declared on her official Twitter account, referring to the suspended personal Twitter accounts of her, Trump, Alex Jones, and other not-exactly-canceled leaders of the right.

On Wednesday, Greene trained her Howitzer on leaders of the Catholic Church who had demanded an apology for her recent claim that the Church's bishops were "controlled by satan." The president of the Catholic League for Religious and Civil Rights, Bill Donohue, sputtered that he would be contacting Kevin McCarthy about the "loose cannon on his hands." Greene responded with an open letter that fell somewhat shy of contrition. Claiming to have left the Church years ago "to protect my children from pedophiles," she offered Donahue some unsolicited advice: "I know they've made you rich, Bill, but before you meet Almighty God, you might want to consider new clients."

After two more days in Washington spent picking fights with the Biden administration and CNN, Greene flew to Ohio with her friend Matt Gaetz to campaign with Senate candidate J. D. Vance. At the time of her endorsement of Vance three months earlier, establishment Republicans wondered if the candidate had taken leave of his senses. But Greene had pressed Trump to join her in supporting Vance; he had done so, and now the *Hillbilly Elegy* author who once imagined Trump as "America's Hitler" was two days away from being the Republican nominee for the U.S. Senate.

Greene's own ascendancy was unmistakable. That a press bus was now following her through northwest Georgia was the most visually obvious manifestation of this reality, but far from the most meaningful example. The House Republicans had wholly embraced Marjorie Taylor Greene's appetite for vendetta. Six months before the midterm election, there could be little doubt that a new GOP House majority would mean that Democrats like Eric Swalwell, Maxine Waters, Rashida Tlaib, and Ilhan Omar would swiftly be stripped of their committee assignments as Greene had been of hers. Investigations into Hunter Biden and Dr. Anthony Fauci were inevitable. Perhaps the House would even do what Greene had been advocating since Biden's inauguration and impeach him before, as she told an interviewer, "America ends up in a nuclear war or something worse."

Would her colleagues resist? Could they? The fate of the ten impeachers could well extend to others deemed by Greene unhelpful to the cause. One such member with a target on her back was Nancy Mace, who had been at odds with her fellow freshman since the insurrection, often publicly. Trump knew very little about Mace. Greene sought to change this. As she told me, "I have expressed to him exactly how I feel about her. And it has not been positive." On March 17, 2022, the ex-president released a statement denouncing the "terrible Nancy Mace" and offering his "Complete and Total Endorsement" to Mace's GOP primary challenger.

But these gestures of payback also failed to fully capture the growing influence of Marjorie Taylor Greene. Her most outlandish rhetoric had become GOP talking points. At the confirmation hearing of Supreme Court justice nominee Ketanji Brown Jackson in March, Republicans on the Senate Judiciary Committee all but accused the twice-confirmed federal judge and mother of two daughters of being, as Greene herself pithily put it, "pro-pedophile." The senators' pointed questions—how did the judge define "woman," did she think babies were born racists, did she believe sexual predators were given a bad rap—could have been scripted by the Georgia freshman. The White House team prepping Jackson had anticipated low blows and shrill posturing. But one of them later told me, "We didn't think they'd make the full pivot to QAnon-signaling." (Later, House GOP conference chair Elise Stefanik would also mimic Greene when she labeled the Democrats "pedo grifters.")

As further testament to Greene's power, establishment Republicans who once scoffed at her were now donating hundreds of thousands of dollars to the campaign of a rival GOP congressional candidate: Georgia businesswoman and political neophyte Jennifer Strahan. As Strahan herself stated during a debate with Greene and four other aspirants, the out-of-state donors "aren't supporting me because they know me. They're supporting me because they know Representative Greene."

The incumbent's swing through northwest Georgia on May 2 constituted a counteroffensive. Each of the eight locales Greene visited was festooned with campaign literature in which the freshman improbably boasted of being "the most effective GOP member of the conference this session." Her campaign signs, ubiquitous throughout the Fourteenth District, exhorted voters to SAVE AMERICA STOP COMMUNISM. ("We've moved the needle," one of Greene's staffers explained, referring to her maiden campaign slogan, SAVE AMERICA STOP SOCIALISM. When I speculated aloud that 2024's slogan might pledge to stop the apocalypse, a second staffer jokingly replied, "Or satanism.")

Back in Washington, I had seen a great deal of Marjorie Taylor Greene yukking it up with her Freedom Caucus buddies and throwing beanballs at the press. But this was my first experience witnessing her interact with her most adoring constituents. "Hearing your feedback," she told the gathering in the Rockmart diner that morning, "just fills me back up and supports everything I think and say." This was a literal truth. In this conservative echo chamber of rural Georgia, they and their congresswoman drank deeply from the same information pool. To no great surprise, then, when Greene exclaimed, "Do you think Hunter Biden ought to be investigated?" the reply was, "Yes! He should be in jail!" Or: "What about Dr. Fauci—do you think he still should have his job?" "No! Lock him up!"

But Greene was also hearing what she wished to hear. At a campaign stop in LaFayette, she commiserated with the local police officers about the alarming spike in fentanyl overdoses. Her number one takeaway from their dialogue was "Secure the border." As the officers well knew, however, much of the fentanyl in LaFayette was being produced in local labs, or was being shipped in from China. Sealing off the Mexico–U.S. border would not address the deeper malaise afflicting northwest Georgia.

Similarly, when a construction-company owner lamented how no one had shown up to a recent job fair in Rome, Georgia, the freshman nodded knowingly and repeated one of her standard refrains: "We're paying people to stay home." When I later asked the owner if he believed welfare and COVID relief checks explained why no one had attended the local job fair, he shook his head.

"I just think people don't want to work anymore," he said.

BRINGING ALONG THE PRESS, GREENE FREELY ADMITTED TO US, HAD NOT been her idea. As to whether the idea was a good one, the jury was still out. At the end of one stop, a reporter with the local CBS affiliate proceeded to ask her, with the cameras rolling, about her past social media posts relating to QAnon and Jewish space lasers. Greene lit into him, calling him a liar, while several of her supporters standing a few feet away booed the reporter. "That right there is why we don't trust the media!" spat one of them later—adding, "I'm pissed off!"

If Greene shared their anger, she was determined not to let it show. She made a point of riding on the press bus between two of the stops, breezily answering whatever was asked, always with her Sunday-best half-moon of a smile. At lunch in Rome, she motioned for me to sit next to her. By now, Greene and her staff had come to know me better than they did the others on the bus, and she endeavored to elicit from me a few more biographical details while maintaining a palpable wariness when I attempted to do the same from her.

On a certain level, Greene was MTG, an assiduously crafted figment of comic-book politics. On a different level, she was a forty-seven-year-old Southern white woman trying to hold it together while both of her daughters were marrying, her son was graduating from high school, and her young career was beset by legal action and death threats. Presumably the media, being well acquainted with the MTG persona, had been assembled here in the Fourteenth District to discover the human version of Marjorie Taylor Greene.

But that proposition worked both ways. Sitting beside her, I imagined in Greene a kind of psychic seesawing as she small-talked with all these well-behaved individuals—some with kids, some with accents like hers, none emitting sulfur fumes. *What was real?* Was this all a ruse, perpetrated by trained practitioners of deceit? Or could she trust her own eyes and ears to consider the possibility that the journalists she routinely vilified as craven liars and enemies of America were just trying to do the best they could?

"Robert, I don't believe anything until I see it," she said in a depleted voice. "I'm pretty smart. I've been around people. People take me for granted a lot. I've been around the block one too many times to be handed a load of shit, so to speak."

The two of us were seated in the back of her black SUV, headed toward the town of Ringgold, where Greene would be addressing one last worshipful crowd before finally calling it a thirteen-hour workday. I was asking her about Kevin McCarthy's vow to her, which the minority leader had also made to Paul Gosar: she would not only be reinstated after the Democrats had stripped her of their committee assignments, she would in fact be assigned to "better committees." Greene did not take McCarthy's promise to heart. Neither did she have any idea what he viewed as "better committees." She had her own view. She wasn't going to tell McCarthy just yet. Both knew who held the stronger hand.

Then again, I reminded her of her own words: *There's a civil war taking place in the Republican Party. And I'm all in for it.* Could Greene really say that she was winning the war on all fronts? After all, here it was, fully six months before the election, and already McCarthy had the speakership sewn up.

"Or is it sewn up?" she replied.

"It's sewn up if no one runs against him," I said.

She nodded. "Someone has to run against him." Then she added, "We aren't there yet."

Greene's greater preoccupation was what the Republican Party would accomplish once they regained power. "I've said it to them at conference," she said. "I've said it over and over. 'The whole reason I ran for Congress was, you basically shit the bed when you had your chance. You didn't fund and build the wall. You didn't repeal Obamacare—you didn't do *anything* about it. You call yourselves pro-life, and you guys funded Planned Parenthood. You can't fail any worse than that!' So, no: I literally ran for Congress because they failed so badly that Nancy Pelosi became Speaker again."

Already, she noted with distaste, McCarthy intended for a Republican-controlled House to model its border-security initiative after a bill sponsored by John Katko, the soon-to-be retired New York congressman who had voted to impeach Trump. "One of the biggest moderates, if you can even call him a moderate Republican—I call him a Democrat," she said. "So we're going to go with *his* watered-down bill? I don't think so."

Of course, Greene observed, all this presupposed that the Republicans would in fact win in November. Among the things that stood in the way of that eventuality was the possibility that conservative voters would stay home, having been convinced by Marjorie Taylor Greene and other Republicans that Democrats steal elections. During her debate the previous day, Greene had reiterated her skepticism about election workers, even those in the Fourteenth District: "You know, after everything we've seen in the election in 2020 and our government overall, no, I don't trust our government—period."

Today, however, Greene had made an elaborate show of voting on this, the first day of early voting for the Georgia primary, dutifully casting her ballot on the very Dominion machine she had warned might be susceptible to fraud. Her campaign signs urged northwest Georgians to "flood the polls!" Such encouragement was taking place without once assuring her constituents that the wrongdoers of 2020 had been brought to justice or that new voting restrictions would see to it that such wrongs would never be repeated—or that it was Greene who had been wrong all along. Quite the contrary: when asked during the previous day's debate if she still believed Biden had lost the election, she replied, "Yes, I do think he lost the election."

"If you don't trust the government, then why waste your time voting if it's already preordained?" I asked her.

"Yeah, but I think that's a failure to let people think that way," she said. "They're giving up if they do that. You can't give up. Of *course* you have to vote. And let's be honest: there's probably always been election fraud in all kinds of elections."

"There's also a difference," I suggested, "between fraud that's of a low scale, and an actual conspiracy to steal an election, right? Those are two very, very different things."

"Right," Greene said.

Wait, I thought. *What is she agreeing to here? That the 2020 election was NOT compromised by a vast conspiracy? Or that it was a one-off, never replicated before or hence? That crooks always steal but that law-abiding patriots should go about their civic obligations regardless?* At that moment, Marjorie Taylor Greene was coming close to sounding like every reasonable Republican I had grown up with. Or she was just saying whatever came to mind.

Putting all that aside, I reminded both of us that she had once been regarded by Georgia's GOP professionals as—to use her words—"a three-headed monster." That hardly seemed to be the case anymore. Nowadays, every Republican candidate in the state seemed to be mimicking her. Georgia's Tenth Congressional District, for example, had a field of candidates that included three MTG wannabes. One was a demolition-company owner whose kickoff ad featured the candidate bashing various walls and doors with a hammer while promising to "crush the woke mob and their cancel culture." A second pledged to introduce articles of impeachment against Biden on his first day in office, just as Greene had done. A third had vowed during his announcement speech, "I'll make a great teammate for Congresswoman Marjorie Taylor Greene."

"It's almost cookie-cutter for some of these candidates," Greene acknowledged.

She didn't look or sound especially happy to be the recipient of such flattery. It took me a second before I realized why. "If everybody starts acting like Marjorie Taylor Greene," I said, "then Marjorie Taylor Greene is no different from anyone else. And in the view of some people, this is Trump's problem now."

"Too much Trump?" By the way she asked it, I could tell that the question was one she had already been pondering. Like Trump, Greene was at risk of being a victim of her own success. In victory, her voice might well become drowned out amid the Greek chorus of MAGA supplicants.

Impeach Biden? When she first proposed it in January 2021, eyes rolled heavenward. Now it was all but a given that a GOP House majority would swiftly begin impeachment proceedings.

Radical socialist Democrats were in fact communists? When Greene first said of "many members in the Democrat Party," in answer to my question at the border-security press conference in June 2021, that "you could call them communists," few elected Republicans echoed her sentiments. Now far-right fundraising solicitations routinely warned of creeping communism. Her message was winning. But would the messenger be forgotten along the way? As William Butler Yeats wrote, "How can we know the dancer from the dance?"

Said Greene in a reflective voice, "Part of my problem is, I've been too early."

BY COINCIDENCE, FRED UPTON, WHOSE THIRTY-FIVE-YEAR CAREER SERVING his Michigan constituents in Congress would soon be expiring, also was in Georgia that day. He was there to celebrate the ninety-eighth birthday of his father, who served under General George Patton during World War II and fought in the Battle of the Bulge. Though the elderly Upton was wheelchair-bound and physically frail, he remained lucid enough to detect a change since his son had announced his retirement a month earlier. "Fred, you look a lot more relaxed now," the father declared.

Upton had not told any colleague of his intentions until the early morning of his announcement. At that time, he called his close friend and fellow Michigander Debbie Dingell, a Democrat. Dingell saw that it was Upton on the line, had a good idea about what he had to tell her, and was too grief-stricken to answer. Her late husband, the dean of the House, John Dingell, had been Upton's mentor; the latter had spoken at the former's funeral in the National Cathedral three years earlier. Upton and Debbie Dingell routinely sat together on the House floor. The Democrat and Republican even held joint fundraisers together: *Bring two checks!* Their reflexive bipartisanship now resembled a soon-to-be-extinct language, with only a few tribal elders left to speak it.

"I've never spoken to MTG in my life, by design," Upton said with a laugh. "I avoid her. I'm actually one of the eleven that voted to strip her of her committees. She put out my office phone number after that. We didn't dare answer the phone for a week."

Nonetheless, the eighteen-term Michigander and the Georgia freshman had something in common: both were being sued in connection with the 2020 election. In Upton's case, a Utah Republican had filed a federal complaint against every member of Congress, Democratic and Republican, who had voted to certify the 2020 election results. The Utah man's complaint accused Upton and the other defendants of treason for their refusal to investigate "a rigged and fraudulent Presidential Election."

"Billy Graham Jr. called us all Judases," Upton said. "We've had death threats. Now today I get this citation and have to respond in federal court in Utah in a week. Oh my goodness, when is this stuff going to end?"

He had not foreseen the GOP's current state of madness. After all, Upton had managed to abide the Tea Party class of 2010 while serving as chairman of the Energy and Commerce Committee. One of those renegades, Jeff Duncan of South Carolina, now served on the committee with Upton. "He's pretty intense," Upton said of Duncan. "But he does his homework—the witnesses better know their stuff. The Tea Party guys who are my colleagues, they're committed, driven, but honest and decent people. Jeff has a conscience. He cares, he works hard, he's not going to be embarrassed.

"Some of this new crowd," Upton went on, "they're just off-the-wall. They say some incredibly stupid things. And they don't care."

Upton had been working alone in his office in the Rayburn Building when the insurrection occurred. From his office balcony, he had a clear view, through the leafless trees, of the Mall on the west side of the Capitol. What he saw compelled him to lock the doors. He could clearly make out the discordant spectacle of the hangman's noose outside the Capitol and just as clearly hear the chant "*Hang Mike Pence!*" The distinct whiff of tear gas and the disordered cacophony of the rioters punctuated by flash-bang grenades, combined with the images flashing across the two TV screens in his office, were "petrifying," Upton recalled. "I was talking on the phone to my colleagues who had been inside the chamber. If the rioters had breached the House floor as they did the Senate, those people would have been gone. They would've been killed. I'm convinced of that."

When Upton returned to the Capitol later that evening to proceed with the certification vote, he first stopped in the Rotunda. He stooped to pick up a few shards of broken glass on the marble floor. Several officers in riot gear were splayed out on the floor, next to the statues of Presidents Ford and

Reagan. Fred Upton had been present for the unveiling of both statues a decade earlier. Now he was witnessing history of a different kind.

The morning after Upton voted to impeach former President Trump, he had breakfast with an old friend, the bestselling author Arthur Brooks. "You know, Fred," Brooks said, seeking to console the congressman who was now experiencing an avalanche of threats on his life, "former presidents tend to fade away." A few of them invested their energies in charitable work or made the speaking rounds, the author said. Still, they faded from the public consciousness. "It's going to happen with Trump too."

Upton managed a smile as he shook his head. "No, it's not," he said. "Not with this guy. I still think he's going to be our next nominee."

And if Trump lost to Biden again, he later thought, Trump would still loom over his party, perhaps even physically. Upton could imagine Matt Gaetz's wish coming true: Trump becoming his party's choice for Speaker of the House and sitting directly behind the president during his State of the Union Address, theatrically ripping up Biden's speech as Pelosi had done to Trump's address in 2020.

No, it would instead be Fred Upton, and other Republicans like him, who would fade away. Upton wasn't bitter. He had three grandchildren and a wonderful wife to spend his days with. There were other things to be thankful for too. For example: he had planned to wander around outside of the Capitol on the afternoon of January 6, 2021. But, Upton noticed when he arrived at work that morning, it was bitterly cold outside, and he had not brought a suitable overcoat.

So he had watched it all from a distance, with the doors locked, thankful for his safety, if not his country's.

EPILOGUE

I'm going to blow the place up," Kevin McCarthy angrily vowed to Steny Hoyer on the afternoon of May 12, 2022, upon receiving a subpoena demanding that he appear before the January 6 committee.

The House minority leader's threat to the House majority leader was telling. Though McCarthy had made an elaborate show of establishing policy-focused "task forces" as an on-ramp to being the likely governing party in Congress after this November's elections, several of those groups had never even bothered to convene since their formation a year earlier. The Republican party's energy was instead focused on bloodlust, and the expected next speaker, Kevin McCarthy, would be egging them on.

In the weeks to come, political observers would view the 2022 primaries through the same dubiously Trump-centric lens, choosing the results that served their narrative while ignoring the factually inconvenient ones. Congressman Tom Rice, the South Carolinian who had voted to impeach the ex-president, had been demolished in his primary. But in the same state, Nancy Mace had weathered Trump's attacks and prevailed. In Georgia, the two state elected officials who had incurred Trump's wrath in refusing to overturn the 2020 election results, Governor Brian Kemp and Secretary of State Brad Raffensperger, handily beat back their primary challengers. But so did Trump's favorite member of Congress, Marjorie Taylor Greene, against a GOP opponent favored by the party establishment.

The question of Trump's influence was the wrong one. The more salient question of the 2022 political season was whether it would augur the return of sanity to the Republican party.

In North Carolina, after a succession of scandals—multiple speeding-related driving infractions, twice attempting to carry a firearm through an airport, an allegation of insider trading, and the suggestion that he had carried on an inappropriate relationship with a twenty-three-year-old male staffer—Madison Cawthorn was defeated in his primary. Was Kevin McCarthy's refusal to defend Cawthorn a principled stand against the North Carolinian's serial misconduct? Or could it be that he had taken to heart the warning given to McCarthy by one of his senior advisers—namely, that Cawthorn's absurd claims of Republican cocaine-fueled orgies could prompt a federal prosecutor to launch a very public investigation into the matter?

In its quest with McCarthy to regain the House majority, the National Republican Congressional Committee was relying on golden-oldies messaging, in which they vilified Nancy Pelosi and her "radical left agenda." But by May, the NRCC's fundraising solicitations included a new line of attack, a reprise of the baseless Trumpian mantra that had led to violence at the Capitol eighteen months earlier: "Democrats across the country are trying to RIG elections."

In Alamogordo, New Mexico, the "audit" of Otero County's 2020 election results ran aground in early May, with no finding that fraud had occurred. Undeterred, the instigator of the effort, Professor David Clements, insisted that the state's June 7 primary results were corrupted from the use of voting machines and therefore should not be certified, even in red counties like Otero where conservatives had won. On June 17, as officials in one county ignored Clements's demands and certified the results anyway, audience members shouted out, "Shame on you!" and "Traitors!"

A day later in Houston, Texas, state Republican delegates gathered to ratify their official 2022 platform. "We reject the certified results of the 2020 Presidential election," read the final version, "and we hold that acting President Joseph Robinette Biden Jr. was not legitimately elected by the people of the United States." The platform urged Republicans to show up in force this November to "overwhelm any possible fraud."

In Nevada, Republican voters chose for secretary of state an unsuccessful 2020 congressional candidate named Jim Marchant, who claimed on his campaign website that he had been "a victim of election fraud" and who suggested to Ed Pilkington of *The Guardian* that his defeat two years ago had been the handiwork of "a global thing." Pressed by Pilkington to offer evidence of such claims, Marchant insisted, "It is out there. Shoot, you can find it." If elected secretary of state in November, Jim Marchant pledged to do exactly that.

In Pennsylvania, the winner of the GOP gubernatorial primary was state senator Doug Mastriano, who had worked aggressively to overturn the 2020 election results in his state and had been on the lawn of the U.S. Capitol on the afternoon of January 6. Just before winning the primary, Mastriano attended a large gathering in Gettysburg hosted by QAnon devotees who screened a video at the event claiming that Hitler had "faked his death," that the ensuing "Nazi succession" included the Queen of England and George H. W. Bush, that "ritual child sacrifice" was taking place in the "Satanic city" of the nation's capital, and, of course, that "Trump won in a landslide." At the event, Mastriano contributed to the apocalyptic rhetoric, saying of the January 6 investigation, "Last year was a dark year. I could not believe my country had become such a dark, evil place, with the power being used, the FBI being used, the Department of Justice, to oppress innocent civilians."

And in Arizona, Congressman Paul Gosar responded to the horrific massacre of nineteen schoolchildren and two adults in Uvalde, Texas, on May 24 after first consulting the musings on a far-right 4chan message board. The shooter, Gosar concluded that day on Twitter, was "a transsexual leftist illegal alien named Salvatore Ramos." Everything in that claim, other than the shooter's last name, was false. But Gosar, for the second time in his career, had opted to abandon his congressional district and run in a more politically favorable one—in this case, the newly created Ninth District—where he was unlikely to be penalized for outrageous, fact-free behavior.

He was, instead, far more likely to be rewarded for it.

"SO, DO YOU REALLY THINK JAMIE RASKIN IS A COMMUNIST?" I ASKED MARJORIE Taylor Greene, referring to a recent comment she had made about the Maryland Democratic congressman.

"Yes!" she exclaimed. "Have you read about his father?"

Of course, even if Marcus Raskin had been an actual member of the Communist party, rather than the longtime progressive government staffer he happened instead to be, Jamie Raskin was no more culpable than Greene was for her father's belief that the laws of gravity controlled the stock market. But such logic was beside the point. The hyperbole was the point. The demonization was the point.

We were meeting at a Washington restaurant on a Monday night. The last time I had seen the Georgia freshman, a month earlier in her district at a restaurant in Rome, she was crying. "They just overturned *Roe v. Wade!*" she said, referring to the stunning news leak of a U.S. Supreme Court ruling that would eliminate a woman's right to have an abortion. Greene's tears were presumably genuine tears of joy—though I did wonder at the time why she felt the need to walk over and exhibit them to me and *Time* reporter Molly Ball as the two of us sat several tables away from where the congresswoman gathered with her entourage. (Among the latter was the newest member on her campaign payroll: Milo Yiannopoulos, a right-wing provocateur who had once achieved infamy as the self-styled "world's most fabulous supervillain," now claiming himself to be a celibate "ex-gay" who had recommitted to Christ and who now regretted his previous statements defending pedophilia.)

During our dinner together, Greene repeatedly assured me that she wanted to make a positive difference in a Republican House majority. But now, positioned at the cusp of power, she seemed just as distrustful of it as she was of the party itself. McCarthy was hinting at a leadership position for her. Was it a meaningful offer, or simply an attempt to co-opt her? Would she work with Democrats? Absolutely—though it seemed unlikely that she would receive an audience with Pelosi, whom Greene had accused of treason, or even with the more moderate Hoyer, who, she said, "hates me." Would she meet with the families of school-shooting victims? Absolutely—though Greene had already passed on the offer to meet with one victim's father, Fred Guttenberg, citing a scheduling conflict. The real reason for not making herself available to Guttenberg, she told me, was that her friend, Breitbart senior editor and right-wing influencer Joel Pollak, had advised against doing so.

By this point, Marjorie Taylor Greene had been made aware by her aides that my book's cover would feature her image with the word "delusion" in the title. I was surprised that she didn't bring it up over dinner. So I did. I suggested that it was delusional to claim that a vast conspiracy, yet to be revealed with any credible evidence, had stolen the 2020 presidential election. Adherents to that delusion, I said, had lost their minds, as anyone could plainly see who had been at the Capitol on January 6, 2021, as she and I had.

"You know what? We can have that conversation," Greene said. But what she had in mind was a somewhat different conversation. The FBI, she went on to say, had received reports well in advance of January 6 that violent forces were intending to descend on the Capitol that day. Why hadn't the FBI shared that information with her, so that she could reach out to her hundreds of thousands of conservative followers and beseech them to protest peacefully?

"I might have been able to do something," she lamented. "I might have been able to help stop the violence." Reaching into her purse, Greene pulled out a tissue and dabbed at her eyes.

This emotional concern for stopping the attack might have been put to better use on the day the attack actually happened. But on January 6, even as Greene and her colleagues were being evacuated from the House floor and the Georgia freshman was warning Trump's chief of staff in a text (which, over dinner, she authenticated) that "This isn't the way to solve anything," her ever-blaring Twitter megaphone fell unusually quiet while the mob engulfed the Capitol. The next day, she would hold Trump blameless for the violence while pointing the finger at Antifa agitators. A year later, she would abandon the Antifa defense entirely, instead finding some justification for the violence at the Capitol, telling Steve Bannon on his podcast, "If you think about what our Declaration of Independence says, it says to overthrow tyrants."

The Bible had told Marjorie Taylor Greene that the truth would set her free. Was this God's word? Or was it fake news? For the truth was like democracy, an unholy mess. You could spend your entire life in devotion to it, like a spider to her web. Ask the spider if it had made her free.

Amid the tangled threads of American life, only one strand, straight and true, stood out: evil. It was omnipresent, stable, and oddly stabilizing, a kind of dark lodestar to measure one's worth against. So long as there was evil, there was righteousness. Identify evil, and the details did not matter. Facts did not matter. Lying was justified. Theft was justified. Cruelty was justified. Violence was justified.

In the never-ending war against evil, you could do no wrong. As Marjorie Taylor Greene's former leader had almost done, and as her future leader promised to do, you could "blow the place up."

NOTE ON SOURCES AND ACKNOWLEDGMENTS

Adecade ago, I wrote a book about the Republican Party's "Tea Party" class of 2010. I spent an enormous amount of time with a half dozen members of those freshman House members. Today, I remain on very good terms with nearly all of them.

That said, it has become an increasingly difficult proposition for journalists such as me to gain access to GOP elected officials and their aides. Many if not most of them have embraced Donald Trump's view of the media as "enemies of the American people." From our perspective, many Republicans have gravitated to the safe space of a right-wing media ecosystem in which their views and utterances are rarely challenged.

I bring this up here for two reasons: first, to thank the many Republicans who did agree to assist me with this new endeavor; and second, to recognize why most who did talk feared having their words attributed to them. The same holds true for many of the Democrats I spoke with. As this book amply documents, Trumpism has unleashed violent forces to which elected officials and political reporters were previously unaccustomed. In all, about 150 individuals spoke with me for this book, nearly all of them "on background." I'm deeply grateful for their insights and for the trust they have put in me to tell this story.

It's a story that I've attempted to navigate with honesty. By that, I mean not only conveying the factual truth but also describing my reportorial journey for it—one that literally and fatefully began on the morning of January 6, 2021. Someone else who was there at the Capitol that day was a Canadian-born documentary photographer named Louie Palu. The day after the insurrection, both Louie and I published separate first-person accounts of our experiences on the website of *National Geographic*. I'm honored to have my book include thirty-four original and highly poignant images by this masterful photographer.

As the subtitle of my book suggests, my aim has been to capture a defined (and, I believe, defining) moment in time for the Grand Old Party. That eighteen-month period was a highly episodic one, however. For better or for worse, the narrative choices, writing, and interviews done for this book were of my doing, as was most of the background reporting. Still, I was lent critical assistance from two sources in particular. Sacha Feinman provided a great deal of archival research relating to several of the book's principal characters, as well as lay-of-the-land information ranging from the emergence of the QAnon conspiracy theory to the history of the right wing in Arizona. My thanks to Sacha and to my longtime friend Mark McKinnon for recommending him.

I also owe a debt of gratitude to the local media across the United States, and especially to the journalists in Arizona and Georgia, where much of this book is centered. Facing immense challenges, they have continued to do remarkable work reporting in their respective states on the aftershocks of the 2020 election. My thanks in Georgia to Greg Bluestein and Tia Mitchell of the *Atlanta Journal-Constitution*, Lawton Sack at GeorgiaPol.com, and podcaster Ben Burnett; and in Arizona, to Ronald Hansen and Yvonne Wingett Sanchez of the *Arizona Republic* (Yvonne has recently moved on to *The Washington Post*), Brahm Resnik at NBC's Phoenix affiliate, Justin Lum at the Phoenix affiliate of Fox News, and Jeremy Duda with Axios Phoenix. I also want to thank Bud Kennedy of the *Fort Worth Star-Telegram* as well as the journalists at the *Texas Tribune* and the fabled *Texas Monthly* for their coverage of that vast and complicated state. And for their personal recollections of January 6, I'd like to thank Matt Fuller of *Buzzfeed*, Emily Cochrane of the *New York Times*, Jonathan Tamari of the *Philadelphia Inquirer*, and Robert Johnson of the Capitol Service Center.

This is my sixth serious book-length project overall, and the fifth with my great friend and literary agent Sloan Harris, the copresident of ICM Partners. A titan of the publishing industry, Sloan remains one of the most decent and approachable eminences in the business. For twenty-five years now, I've been lucky to have him in my corner.

I hope to continue a similar run of good fortune with my book editor, Scott Moyers, the publisher of Penguin Press. This is our second book together, and I've never felt in surer and more supportive publishing hands. It was Scott who urged me to pursue the subject of the Republican Party after Trump's presidency (rather than, say, a memoir of wine-drinking in northeast Italy). His wisdom and humaneness are rarities in this trade. Equally rare is the team at Penguin that helped make this book possible. Associate editor Mia Council provided excellent editing advice while deftly keeping the trains running on time. Copyeditor Rachelle Mandik provided a highly discerning additional pair of eyeballs, as did Penguin attorney Yuki Hirose. Gail Brussel is far and away the best publicist I've been privileged to work with at any publishing house. I also want to extend thanks to Penguin Press's Matt Boyd and Danielle Plafsky in marketing for drumming up interest in the bookselling community.

Writing this book, even at a breakneck pace, required the indulgence of the two publications for which I've been fortunate to write over the past several years: the *New York Times Magazine* and *National Geographic Magazine.* At the former, editor Jake Silverstein, deputy editor Jessica Lustig, and politics editor Charles Homans (who now writes full-time for the *Times*) were as patient in my absence as they have been magnificent when working with me. At *Nat Geo*, I want to thank my talented and straight-talking editor John Hoeffel, as well as the recently departed editor in chief Susan Goldberg, a newsroom legend whom I'm proud to call a friend.

Though I have not worked in the office of any publication since I left *Texas Monthly* in 1997, I've always been the beneficiary of a shape-shifting but robust writing community. Their support has always been meaningful to me. Still, nothing has been as essential to my overall well-being as my family. My brother, John, has been my constant and my best friend throughout our decades of togetherness, apartness, shared glories and misadventures, and personal tragedies. He and his wonderful wife, Laura, have been steady and always loving forces in my life.

My wife, Kirsten Powers, is more than the love of my life. She is the most inspiring person I've ever known, not to mention the wisest. Every day with her is full of surprises and joy. And speaking of the latter, I would be remiss not to mention our Shih Tzu, Lucy, who contributed absolutely nothing to this book other than welcome distraction.

I want to mention two other important family members, for different reasons. My niece Delilah Draper, having just now graduated from Kenyon College, is set to embark on the pursuit of her dreams as an actor. I'll continue to be inspired by Delilah's determination to take the hard and solitary path while pledging to be there for the darker moments in her journey. I know that journey well.

While I was reporting and writing this book, my beloved cousin Joe Jaworski was campaigning to be the state attorney general in Texas. As a Democrat in a red state during a midterm year that favored Republicans, Joe knew that his chances of victory were slim—which, indeed, proved to be the case. But I'm proud of his willingness to call out the falsehoods and mean-spiritedness that have become sadly characteristic of that state's GOP. America is better when candidates stand on truth as a baseline.

I prefaced this book with a few words about my late father, to whom I dedicated it. I'll close by thanking my mother, who died on May 24, 2020, two months before my Penguin Press book *To Start a War: How the Bush Administration Took America into Iraq* was released. Before Alzheimer's took away her brilliant mind a few years ago, Claire Jaworski Draper was the single greatest supporter of my writing career. Because of her, I never felt unloved or alone. I miss her and I thank her every day.

INDEX